McDonald's™

COLLECTIBLES

Happy Meal™ Toys and Memorabilia
1970 to 1997

GUESS

Peter Rabbit and Piggsburge Pigs,
Moveables and Muppet Kids,
Frybenders and Funny Fry Friends,
Cosmic Crayola and tops on pens.

Twisting Sports and Tale Spin.
Looney Tunes and Lion King.
Dragonettes and Dinosaurs.
101 Dalmations and lots of paws.

Aristocats and an American Tail.
Berenstain Bears and Beachcomber Happy Pail
Rescuers Down Under and Rocking foods.
Ghostbusters and all those dudes.

Water games and Winter Sports,
Yo Yogi and Young Astronauts.
On the Go and Out for Fun,
Valentine and Your Special One.

ET and Earth Days,
Zoomballs and Zoo Face.
Nature Watch and Nature's helpers.
Kissyfur and Friendly figures.

Intergalactical Adventurer and I Like Bikes.
Hot Wheels and High Flying Kites
Skybusters and Spaceships.
Jungle Book and toys that flip.

Collectors, Yes, you must have guessed...

McDonald's™
COLLECTIBLES:

Happy Meal™ Toys and Memorabilia, 1970 to 1997

CO-AUTHORS

Ray and Ruby Richardson • David and Lesley Irving

Color Photographs by David Irving

Poems by Ruby Richardson

CHARTWELL
BOOKS, INC.

A QUINTET BOOK

Published by Chartwell Books
A Division of Book Sales, Inc.
114 Northfield Avenue
Edison, New Jersey 08837

This edition produced for sale in the U.S.A., its
territories and dependencies only.

ISBN 0-7858-0803-5

This book was designed and produced by
Quintet Publishing Limited
6 Blundell Street
London N7 9BH

Creative Director: Richard Dewing
Art Director: Clare Reynolds
Designer: Peter Laws
Project Editor: Kathy Steer
Editor: Kimberly Chrisman
Photographer: David Irving
Additional photographs: Paul Forrester
Poems: Ruby Richardson

Many thanks to Debbie A. Metz for the loan of her
McDonald's Beanie Babies collection.

Typeset in Great Britain by
Central Southern Typesetters, Eastbourne
Manufactured in Singapore by Bright Arts Pte Ltd
Printed in China by Leefung-Asco Printers Ltd

Authors' Note

McDonald's Collectibles covers different premiums from all over the world
and to the best of our knowledge the information is correct. We have supplied
dates, names, and countries of origin. The countries which issued the premiums
are listed at the head of each page, followed by subsequent releases. Where we
have stated a promotion to be "regional", this relates to certain parts of the
United States only. The reference to "national" means the promotion was run
throughout the States. "International release" means throughout Europe.

CONTENTS

The following companies own trademarks and service marks™ ® SM:

McDONALD'S Corporation, Oak Brook, Illinois, USA

McDonaldland, The Golden Arches, Big Mac, Birdie, Birthdayland, Captain Crook, Earlybird, Flykids, Grimace, Hamburglar, Happy Meal, Happy Pail, McGhost, McJack, McNugget Buddies, McWitch, Ronald McDonald, Professor, McBunny, Fry Girls

WALT DISNEY
Ducktails, Talespin, Pocahontas, Snow White and the Seven Dwarfs, Bambi, Dumbo, 101 Dalmatians

WARNER BROS
Sylvester, Tiny Toon, Bat Duck, Bugs Bunny, Daffy Duck, Animaniacs, Tas-Flash, Road Runner

MATTEL INC.
Barbie, Hot Wheels, Mini-Streex, Attack Pack

JIM HENSON PRODUCTION INC
Muppet Babies, Snoopy, Fraggle Rock, Bonzo, Kermit, Miss Piggy, Muppet Workshop, Doozer

UNIVERSAL CITY STUDIOS
Flintstones, Fievel, Tomy, Dragonoids

JR MAXX CHARLOTTE
Nascar

MATCHBOX INTERNATIONAL
Matchbox

LEGO GROUP
Lego

TRI-STAR PICTURES
Hook, Captain Hook, Peter Pan

PARAMOUNT PICTURES
Kirk, Klingons, McCoy, Spock, Star Trek

NINTENDO OF AMERICA INC
Super Mario Bros, Koopa

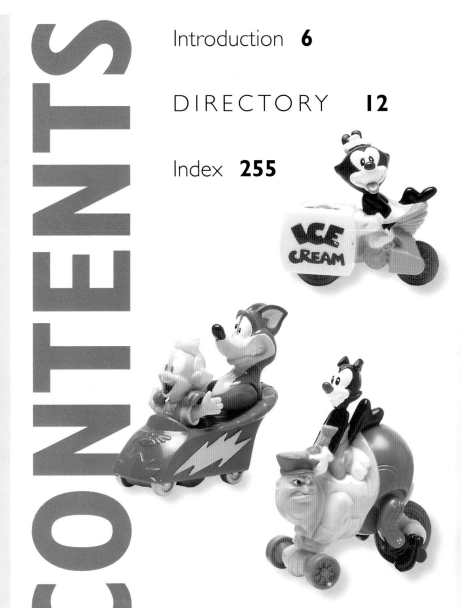

Key to Price Guide

A price guide appears with most premiums and purchases throughout this book:

A Band: $2–6
B Band: $7–13
C Band: $14–20
D Band: $21–30
E Band: $31 + over

In The Beginning

This is an introduction to the history of the McDonald's™ Corporation and their hugely successful Happy Meal™ toy promotions operating worldwide.

In 1932 Americans enjoyed their first carhop drive-in, known today throughout the world as fast-food drive-in restaurants. The very first carhop was opened in Hollywood, California.

By the mid 1930s, large carhops appeared across the USA. Two of the first famous restauranteurs were the Carpenter brothers and Sydney Hoedemaker, who came from California. They introduced an innovative way of eating out. Drivers, with their families, were able to pull into parking bays at restaurants and order through a speaker phone. They would then be served by staff on roller skates, without having to leave their cars. Many

fast-food carhops opened up: Big Boy, Bad Wians, Shoney's, and these famous names are still to be found operating throughout the USA. It was in 1937 when two brothers, Dick and Mac McDonald came on to the fast-food scene. Dick and Mac opened their first carhop drive-in in Pasadena. It was very small compared with all the others, yet the brothers had an edge over their competitors. Service to their customers was based primarily on speed.

The brothers next opened a hamburger store, where customers could sit along the front under a canopy and watch their orders being cooked. No other restaurants allowed customers to watch the preparation of food, but soon others followed the McDonald's example and the McDonald brothers soon became aware of competitive pressure.

It was this competition that provided the impetus to open another innovative restaurant which they named

the "Dimer". The name was chosen because everything to be sold at this new restaurant was to cost just a dime, and when one pulled out a dime to spend, one would think of the "Dimer." The brothers even went as far as giving customers their change in highly polished dimes to emphasize the name.

Despite the successful inauguration of this dimer restaurant, the McDonald brothers still felt the need to improve their drive-ins. Parking lots were getting jammed up, service was getting slower, customers were demanding faster service.

Dick and Mac closed all their carhops for renovation in late 1948. They installed service windows. China cups and plates were replaced with paper wrappings and cardboard plates and cups. The kitchens were completely rearranged for fast-food service with volume production. Service by roller skates stopped. One was now able to drive up to the service window, order, collect, and drive off.

They started to franchise their drive-ins and restaurants, but found that by the mid-1950s franchising was not developing the business as they had hoped. That is until they met Ray A. Kroc, the salesman who held marketing rights to the five spindle mixers being used in the McDonald's outlets and Dimers to make milk shakes.

Kroc was an entrepreneur through and through. He took a great interest in what was happening in the fast-food business and had kept notes on the McDonald brothers' ventures over the previous years. When he heard they were having trouble with franchising, he introduced himself to them. This marked the true beginning of the growth of the McDonald's™ empire, which within three decades, under the guidance of Ray A. Kroc, has spread across the world.

The Ray A. Kroc Story

Ray A. Kroc was to become an American legend, yet he was a poor pupil in school. He dropped out of high school having opened his own music store, but when World War I broke out, he joined the Red Cross and became an ambulance driver. Unknown to him at the time, there was another underage driver, by the name of Walt Disney, who was also to become an American legend. How remarkable that these two were to go, in the years to come, into such successful businesses centering on themes for children.

After the War, Kroc became a professional piano player, he started to sell paper cups and in 1924 he went to Florida to deal in real estate. Stranded in 1926 when the land estate boom crashed, he returned to Chicago, and there too finally gave up the idea of becoming a musician and went back to selling paper cups. He formed Fold-a-Nook, his own company, only to have this go bust in 1954. Ray returned to selling while all the time noting the development of fast-food outlets and the approach of the McDonald brothers in particular. He wanted a big part of this action and saw a void in the fast-food market.

After meeting the brothers, Ray A. Kroc foresaw great potential in expanding the McDonald name nationwide. He was given a free hand by the McDonalds and formed a new McDonald's franchise company called McDonald's System Incorporated.

In 1960, Kroc changed this to McDonald's™ Corporation, by which it is now known. The McDonald brothers sold their entire rights to Ray A. Kroc in 1961 for 2.7 million dollars.

Media Magic

Kroc moved fast, entering the children's market, which he called "Media Magic." The McDonald brothers had had a franchiser named Goldstein who for years had proposed entering the children's market without much response from the McDonalds. Now he had someone who was interested in his ideas. Ray gave Goldstein full backing for his idea, which was to advertise on television using a circus vehicle he had

seen used in a show called "Bozo Circus." Goldstein enthusiastically sponsored the show himself.

Television was ideal for McDonald's™, especially as children were fast becoming McDonald's™ most important customers. Goldstein promoted "Bozo" the clown from the Circus to become the children's star; but in 1963, the television executives at the Washington station decided to axe the show. Goldstein was undeterred, and asked a promotion agency, Kal-Elrlich and Merrick, to come up with ideas that would preserve McDonald's™ image among children. Something had to be done very quickly. Bozo the clown had become McDonald's™ spokesman and Merrick decided the only solution was to engage another clown in a television commercial. The way forward was to establish McDonald's™ own clown and produce its own commercials.

The agency proposed naming the clown Archie McDonald, a reference to the famous golden arches seen outside McDonald's™ restaurants, but there was already an Arch McDonald in Washington. Willard Scott, who had played Bozo the clown, named the new clown Ronald McDonald, and went on to play the character.

Ronald McDonald made his debut in Washington, D.C., in October 1963. Janet Vaughn designed the costume. The hat consisted of a tray with a styrofoam burger and bag of fries, a milk shake, shoes shaped like buns, and a nose fashioned out of a McDonald's cup. The belt buckle was made of a styrofoam hamburger. The commercial featured Ronald McDonald magically pulling hamburgers out of his belt. Ronald McDonald's appearance marked the first occasion a "character" was used in commercials in the USA.

By 1965, Ronald McDonald became the national spokesman for the McDonald's™ restaurant chain. To this day the clown is of great appeal to children around the world.

McDonald's™ Characters

It was not until the late 1960s that McDonald's Corporation established their marketing department in response to the massive expansion project led by Ray A. Kroc.

Starting with the All-American Meal in 1961, McDonald's™ Corporation ran several meal combination promotions which were primarily aimed at the adult market. They had done little in the way of appealing to budget-minded families and kids. In 1969, McDonald's™ began the search for a new advertising agency.

Needham, Harper, and Steers were appointed. They put forward the idea of using television commercials. At this time fast-food commercials were practically nonexistent. McDonald's™ restaurants ran their first commercial on television in 1970 to the surprise of everyone because no food was promoted; instead seven "employees" danced around a McDonald's™ restaurant singing a song. Needham produced a theatrical theme for the commercial using up-and-coming actors who later went on to become movie or television stars.

Using the theatrical theme, Needham created McDonaldland, filling it with a host of storybook characters. These characters were: Hamburglar, Mayor McCheese, Grimace, and Officer Big Mac. All these characters are very famous with children worldwide today because of the Happy Meal™ promotions.

In 1975, a Mayor McCheese bag promotion was designed specifically for children. The bag featured special Mayor McCheese graphics, in brown and gold. Advertised as "The Honorary Meal of McDonaldland," it

included a regular cheeseburger, regular order of fries, a box of McDonaldland cookies, and a premium in the form of a McDonaldland Citizenship wall certificate. The promotion, although reasonably successful, was not repeated.

In the same year McDonald's™ ran the Captain Cook bag promotion. It was similar to Mayor McCheese, but included a Filet-o-Fish sandwich. Needham's characters, along with Ronald McDonald, became playground equipment for children obtained from McDonald's™ restaurants throughout America. Playgrounds became the centerpiece of McDonald's™ strategy for dominating the children's market.

Happy Meal™ Promotions

It was in 1977 that McDonald's™ Corporation made an important move on the promotion scene aimed at children worldwide: the introduction of the Happy Meal™ is seen today as one of the most remarkable promotions in marketing history.

Dick Brams, known as the father of the Happy Meal™, was Assistant Advertising Manager at St. Louis' McDonald's™ restaurant in 1974. He had been toying with the idea of kids' meals for some time, and when he was promoted to Advertising Manager for the district of San Francisco, he put forward his idea to McDonald's™. Ray A. Kroc instructed Dick Brams to try out his idea.

Brams asked two advertising agencies, Stolz Agency and Bernstein-Rein-Beasberg Agency to put forward their proposals for marketing kids' meals. Stolz proposed a promotion called FUN-TO-GO, while Bernstein-Rein-Beasberg's promotion was named Happy Meal™.

Happy Meal™ featured a regular Hamburger or Cheeseburger, fries, McDonaldland cookie sampler, and a premium, all of which came in a special box with McDonaldland graphics, puzzles, games, and other activities. Included with the meal was a drink.

Both promotions were tested over a limited period, and after evaluating Test Markets McDonald's™ Corporation decided on the Happy Meal™ concept.

The very first Happy Meal™ promotion started in 1978, in Kansas City and was called "CIRCUS WAGON." It featured a toy box with a round top like a lunch box, although it was soon replaced with a box better designed for stacking in McDonald's restaurants.

Happy Meals™ with their themes had a great impact on McDonald's™. It was to become their most important promotion, and still is to this day.

There were to be several Happy Meal™ themes each year in the USA. They became so popular that McDonald's™ decided to go international with them in 1980. Happy Meal™ promotions made their international debut in Australia, the Caribbean, Hong Kong, Latin America, and New Zealand, featuring a hamburger/cheeseburger, fries and a soft drink. There were seven cartons with generic premiums (toys).

The UK enjoyed its first Happy Meal™ promotion in 1985. The premium was "Fast Macs," using the McDonaldland characters created by Needham, along with Ronald McDonald, the clown from the 1960s' McDonald brothers' first restaurant.

Simon Marketing, a promotion firm from California, began their association with McDonald's™ Corporation in 1976. At that time they marketed games and were approached by McDonald's™ Los Angeles Cooperative agency to develop a game to be associated with McDonald's™. This was to be the very first scratch-card game and was also to be McDonald's™ restaurants' first-ever game. Winners were to learn on the spot if they had won. The test area for this game was Los Angeles. It brought so many new customers into McDonald's™ restaurants, that news of its success soon spread to other McDonald's™ cooperatives throughout the USA. They all wanted their own game.

As with Happy Meal™, McDonald's™ wanted a game with which they could go national. Simon Marketing were asked in 1981 to produce a national game. It had to be associated with McDonald's burger. The first national game was called "Big Mac." Total prizes were worth a staggering $8 million. The promotion was such a success, Simon Marketing went on to produce many more games for McDonald's Corporation worldwide.

One will find Simon Marketing's name on many toy promotion inserts (this being the paper illustrating the entire collection) within the clear packages.

Collecting McDonald's™ Collectibles

McDonald's™ characters, Happy Meal™ toys, and their prolific promotions are today the number one toy to collect for future investment.

There are many companies which develop promotional concepts, including Happy Meals™. Simon Marketing is the primary concept developer for Europe, Latin America, Africa, and sometimes for Asia. They are also very active in the USA.

Wedo is a primary supplier to Simon Marketing in Europe and parts of Africa and the Middle East. They also have subsidiary companies in other parts of the world. One such subsidiary, Creata Promotions, is a primary concept company, as well as supplier for Australia and New Zealand.

Other subsidiaries are: Creative Premiums Ltd. in Hong Kong, Creative Workshop in Canada, Banett Ltd. in the UK, and Toymarketing International Inc. USA. Others in the USA are Frankel and MB Sales.

The copyright date on the toy or insert card does not always relate to the year of release and can often refer to the date the Happy Meal™ toy theme went into planning and design.

At the bottom of the Happy Meal™ theme box or bag, one will find a small drawing of the week's premium or the week number of each promotion. There may be a colorful design or theme on the box that shows the weekly toy to collect. This is sometimes shown in 3-D. In the UK, only one theme bag has been issued in any one year, for example: 1994 World Cup, 1995 Water Fun, 1996 Batman Bike.

A Happy Meal™ promotion set is deemed to be in mint condition only if it has the correct boxes or bag. Europe has up to eight toys in a Happy Meal™ promotion, while an American set one may contain up to 21 toys.

In many American sets there are "under-three toys," this being a safety toy with no moving parts. The UK's first under-three toy was issued in 1994 with the

promotion Lego™. No other under-three toys have been issued in the UK since then.

Germany successfully tested the kids' meal concept in 1984 in Bremen with "Spaceships." They began by naming them Kindermenu in 1986 until the present term, "Junior Tüte," was first given to the German test promotion "Augsburg" in 1988. German restaurants do not use cartons. They began with a white bag, which was usually "themed." In 1990–91, they changed to numbered generic bags.

Latin Americans refer to Happy Meals™ as "La Cajita Feliz." Mexico's first national Happy Meal™ toy promotion was in 1989, and was named "Sailors."

Japan is involved in an extensive Test program. This is the only country with both national and Test Happy Meals™ on their International Happy Meal Calendar.

With respect to packaging, the UK and USA have four cartons, which are designed to serve as a theme backdrop with punch out pieces to enhance the 3-D effect. Graphics on boxes or cartons in each of these countries differ.

Mexico, Central, and South America usually have only one theme carton with Spanish graphics. Canadian cartons are the same as in the USA, only they will be engraved in English and French. Australia uses one box, not necessarily themed.

Many premiums may be the same, but are contained in different packages with multilingual graphics and color variations. International markets often develop creative themes that are not run in the USA.

In 1995, McDonald's™ collectibles were advocated by reputed auction houses to be the most collectible toys anywhere in the world.

Happy Hunting

Key to Price Guide

A price guide appears with most premiums and purchases throughout this book:

A Band: $2–6
B Band: $7–13
C Band: $14–20
D Band: $21–30
E Band: $31 + over

Acknowledgments

The authors would like to express their appreciation to: McDonald's™ Restaurants Ltd in the UK for their kind permission to publish this book; to McDonald's™ managers and their crews, especially at Reading and Slough Restaurants, for their super service; to McDonald's™ Australia, Hong Kong, Japan, Singapore, Russia; to Simon Marketing, London; to Helen Farrell, McDonald's Archives USA; our fellow collectors Bill and Pat Poe; Florida chapter Collectors Club; to Joyce Losonsky and Dianna Arazy.

A very special thanks must go to our good friend, Tony Thomas, who on his travels around the world has kept us abreast of intelligence and brought Happy Meal™ toys and memorabilia to the UK Collectors' Club.

To all our friends in this happy collecting world of McDonald's™ - have great fun.

Ray, Ruby, Lesley, David

FEELING GOOD

When you are hungry, where do you go?
To McDonald's of course, the one that you know.
Big Mac and Fries, washed down with Coke,
Or salad and tea, for the weight-watching folks.
Dads and Moms with their young girls and boys,
All waiting patiently for their "Happy Meal" toys.
Seeing their little faces light up.
What will it be? A Lion or Pup.
Music to cheer you on a gray day,
Flags and balloons free, nothing else to pay.
All this with fast service and a smile,
Not another quite like it, for at least a mile.
Thank you McDonald's, I've been your guest,
Carry on doing what you know best.

Advent Calendar

UK
December 1, 1989

This was the first Happy Meal promotion to be issued on a national basis in the UK. These premiums were issued over a period of four weeks before Christmas. Each premium came in a clear polybag with an insert card, showing the three toys to collect (the three Xmas Baubles were available for just one week, three to collect); on the reverse of the insert card were instructions on how to use each premium. Insert cards were marked with the following instructions: "These items are Christmas decorations and children handling them will need adult supervision."

Each premium was a hanging decoration, except the McDonaldland Sleigh, which could either hang, or could be folded in half to make a rocker. The Jumping Ronald and the sleigh were made of thin cardboard, with a tissue paper insert that opened out. The three baubles were made of a shiny shatterproof material.

Insert card marked: © 1989 McDonald's Corporation. Printed in West Germany.

AD02

Showing insert card

AD01

Premiums

AD01 "Jumping" Ronald McDonald **[D]**
AD02 McDonald Sleigh **[D]**
AD03 McDonald's Xmas Bauble, Red –
        Ronald (not shown) **[C]**
AD04 McDonald Xmas Bauble, Purple –
        Grimace (not shown) **[C]**
AD05 McDonald Xmas Bauble, Silver –
        Hamburglar (not shown) **[C]**

One box was issued

AD06 Advent Calendar **[D]**

AD06

Advent Calendar Box

UK
1993

AD07

This Advent box is designed like the UK Happy Meal box, a little bit smaller, but made up in the same way. The Advent box has 24 doors and windows with the number of each day for December. Behind each door or window there is a Christmas scene.

Box marked: © 1993 McDonald's Corp. Printed in Belgium. Simon Marketing Int. GmbH D-63268 Dreieich.

Free give away

AD07 Advent Box **[A]**

Airport

Holland
March, 1995
Japan
July, 1995
UK
April 26 – May 25, 1996

AP01

AP02

AP09

AP04

Japan has moved away from their plain *generic bags* (see Peanuts Japan April 95 pages 187–88) and have released some very colorful McDonaldland characters instead (see Disneyland Adventures Japan August 1995 page 75). As you can tell by the name of this promotion, the vehicles are used at an Airport, with McDonaldland characters. All premiums are made from a hard plastic and are all push toys on wheels. All the vehicles are a one-piece premium, except *Birdie in the Helicopter*, which is a two-piece toy. Premiums are all poly-bagged with insert cards, with the instructions on the back of the insert card. Premiums measure between 2¼ and 3½ inches long. *Ronald's Baggage Loader* ladder can be moved up and down. *Birdie in the Helicopter* moves; just place the red spinner on top, push the helicopter forward, and watch the spinner spin off. (This premium is the only one in the set to have a smaller insert card with a WARNING to keep away from eyes and faces.) *Hamburglar* is driving a red tow truck, for planes, and *Grimace* is the pilot to the jumbo plane. You can back-up Hamburglar's truck onto the front of the plane, which in turn will push and lock a spring-loaded device.

AP03

Pressing the red button on top of the jumbo will shoot *Hamburglar* forward.

Airport was also issued in Latin America, the Middle East and North Africa on June 7, 1995.

Japan premiums marked: © 1995 McDonald's Corp. China SN.

UK – Holland premiums marked: © 1995 McDonald's Corp. Macau.

Premiums

AP01 Baggage Loader [**A**]
AP02 Helicopter [**A**]
AP03 Jumbo Plane [**A**]
AP04 Plane Towing Truck [**A**]

Four Holland – UK boxes were issued

AP05 Departure Area [**A**]
AP06 Control Tower [**A**]
AP07 Observation Deck [**A**]
AP08 Loading Bay [**A**]
AP09 One bag (Japan) generic, McDonaldland characters

AP05   AP06   AP07   AP08

Aladdin

UK

November 19 – December 6, 1993

AL04

AL01

AL02

14

Another masterpiece by Walt Disney, a very colorful and fast-paced animated movie, and full of surprises, starting with the totally out of this world Genie, the voice of comedian Robin Williams. Aladdin, a street-smart peasant, found the lamp in the Cave of Wonders, and with the help of the Genie, Aladdin tries to win the heart of the Princess Jasmine. But the Genie cannot help him when it comes to making someone fall in love. So this is where the hilarious fun starts. Aladdin also has to keep the lamp from the evil sorcerer, Jafar, who also craves the magic lamp's power.

Each premium in this promotion had a special feature. *Aladdin and Jasmine on the Magic Carpet* was a pull-back action toy: *Jafar* had a button; when pressed his arms raised to reveal a black cloth cape. *The Sultan* was a hard plastic figure that wobbled from side to side, and finally the bottom of *The Magic Lamp* turned to make the *Genie*

AL03

appear from the top. Premiums were packed in polybags with insert cards.

Premiums marked: © Disney, China.

Each of the boxes could be made into a play scene for each toy.

This Happy Meal promotion tied in with the release of the Walt Disney video *Aladdin* in the UK.

Aladdin also ran in Holland on December 8–January 11, 1993; New Zealand in July–August 1993.

Premiums

AL01   Aladdin and Jasmine on Magic Carpet **[A]**

AL02   Jafar **[A]**

AL03   Sultan **[A]**

AL04   The Magic Lamp **[A]**

Four boxes were issued

AL05   Sultan's Palace **[A]**

AL06   Cave of Wonders **[A]**

AL07   Throne Room **[A]**

AL08   Prince Ali Parade **[A]**

AL06   AL05   AL07   AL08

Aladdin and The King of Thieves

USA • Canada

August – September, 1996

Aladdin and the King of Thieves is the third animated film in the series to be released on video by Walt Disney, *Aladdin* being the first, followed by *The Return of Jafar*.

Each premium is a two-piece toy. *Abu, Iago,* and *Maitre D'Genie* have wheels and are push-alongs, the rest have no moving parts. Backdrops measure 3¾ inches long and 4 inches tall and each has a plastic scene accessory attached to it. All premiums came in a printed sealed polybag numbered one to eight in English, French, and Spanish. Premiums marked: © Disney China/Chine. Backdrops marked: © Disney, Printed in China.

AL19

AL20

AL21

AL22

AL23

AL24

AL25

AL26

AL28

AL30

Under-3 Toy
Abu

AL27 under-three

AL31

Premiums

AL19 Cassim [**A**]

AL20 Abu and Carpet [**A**]

AL21 Jasmine [**A**]

AL22 Iago [**A**]

AL23 Genie [**A**]

AL24 Sa'Luk [**A**]

AL25 Aladdin [**A**]

AL26 Maitre D'Genie [**A**]

AL27 Abu (under-three) [**A**]

Two bags were issued

AL28 Palace (USA) [**A**]

AL29 Palace (Can) (not shown) [**A**]

AL30 Ala/Jasm (USA) [**A**]

AL31 Ala/Jasm (Can) [**A**]

Alvin and The Chipmunks

USA
March 8 – April 12, 1991

AC01

AC03

AC02

AC04

This was a regional promotion in Texas and Minnesota, USA, in 1991. Each character is made from soft hollow rubber and its accessories from a hard plastic. The costumes to each premium are designed to match different times in history. *Alvin* with his electric guitar is fashioned in the 1960s rock era, *Brittany* with her juke box has a dress from the 1950s, *Simon* with the video camera is fashioned for the 1990s with a space age image, and *Theodore* with his rap machine is themed on the 1980s. The under-three premium is *Alvin with a juke box*, a one-piece premium made from rubber. Each premium was in a polybag with insert card and discount vouchers for Alvin-themed purchases. Accessories marked: © 1990 M-B Sales Premiums marked: ® © 1990 Bagdasarian Prod except Brittany which was marked: ™ © 1990 K.R. Prod. Inc. China.

Alvin and the Chipmunks also ran in Mexico (with Spanish design box) and Puerto Rico, both in May 1991, and Singapore in March 1992.

Premiums
AC01   Alvin   [**B**]
AC02   Brittany   [**B**]
AC03   Simon   [**B**]
AC04   Theodore   [**B**]
AC05   Alvin and Juke Box (under-three)
          (not shown)   [**B**]

One bag was issued
AC06   Alvin (not shown)   [**B**]

Amazing Wildlife

USA • Canada
April 1 – 28, 1995

Each premium was a soft plush toy about 4 inches long and safety tested for children of all ages. "Recommended for children age one and over, not to be used in playpens or cribs," was printed on the polybags. This promotion was a tie-in with the National Wildlife Federation in Washington D.C., and on each Happy Meal box there was a choice of a FREE issue of Ranger Rick © Magazine or Your Big Backyard © Magazine. Each premium marked: National Wildlife Federation ®, M-B Sales, © 1994 McDonald's Corp. Made in China. *Siberian Tiger and Polar Bear* marked: Imported by Simon Marketing Inc.

AW01

AW02

AW03

AW04

Premiums
AW01   Asiatic Lion   [**A**]
AW02   Chimpanzee   [**A**]
AW03   Koala   [**A**]
AW04   African Elephant   [**A**]
AW05   Dromedary Camel   [**A**]
AW06   Galapagos Tortoise   [**A**]
AW07   Siberian Tiger   [**A**]
AW08   Polar Bear   [**A**]

Four bags were issued
AW09   Indian and African Forest   [**B**]
AW10   Africa and Australia   [**B**]
AW11   Galapagos Island and Saudi Arabia   [**B**]
AW12   Arctic and Siberia   [**B**]

AW05

AW06

AW07

AW08

AW09

AW10

AW11

AW12

An American Tail

USA

November 28 – December 24, 1986

AT01

This colorful animated film, presented by Steven Spielberg and directed by Don Bluth, is about a young Russian mouse and his family in the late nineteenth century, who decide to leave Russia for America, where, they were led to believe, there was plenty of food and especially no cats. On the sea voyage during a bad storm, Fievel falls overboard. Eventually he is washed ashore in New York harbor. He starts his long journey to find his family, meeting enemies and friends on the way.

Each premium was a 24-page paperback book, about 7 inches square in size. It told previously unreleased stories, exclusive to McDonald's, which were a follow-up to some of the scenes from the film. This promotion was a tie-in with the release of the film in the USA over Thanksgiving weekend.

All four books carry the McDonald's "M" logo on the front and back covers. They were also marked inside the cover: © 1986 Universal City Studios, Inc. and U-Drive Productions Inc. Printed in the USA.

AT03

AT02

Premiums

AT01   Fievel's Boat Trip   [**A**]
AT02   Fievel's Friends   [**A**]
AT03   Fievel and Tiger   [**A**]
AT04   Tony and Fievel   [**A**]

Two boxes were issued (not shown)

AT05   Mouse in the Moon   [**B**]
AT06   Slippery Solutions   [**B**]

AT04

An American Tail

Christmas Stockings • USA

December, 1986

These were released over the Christmas period in 1986 to coincide with the release of the film in theaters. McDonald's usually promote a plush toy at Christmas; in 1985 this was a Reindeer from the film *Santa Claus, The Movie*. In this case they were red plush Christmas stockings measuring 7 inches from tip to toe with a white fluffy band at the top, and an appliquéd motif on the front. They all had a white zipper.

Label marked: ™ © 1986 Universal City Studios, Inc. and U-Drive Productions Inc. All Rights Reserved. SEARS © 1986 McDonald's Corporation. Made in Korea.

Purchases

AT07   Fievel on Sled (not shown)   [**B**]
AT08   Fievel Seated on Ball (not shown)   [**B**]
AT09   Fievel Dancing   [**B**]
AT10   Fievel with Candy Cane (not shown)   [**B**]

AT09

Animaniacs

USA • Canada • Puerto Rico
May 6 – June 2, 1994

AN02

AN03

AN01

AN04

AN05

AN06

AN08

AN07

Each premium was a hard plastic action vehicle. When pushed along, they all moved in different ways. Each featured characters from the Steven Spielberg and Warner Bros television program, which was shown on the Fox Kid's Show. The under-three premium was the same as in the set, but it had the zebra stripe around the packet. Each premium came in a printed polybag. Premiums marked: ™ and © 1993 Warner Bros. China.

The boxes had puzzles on one side. The other side could be punched out to make a mask of one of the characters. This promotion took place over a period of four weeks. Two premiums were issued per week with one box.

Canada used exactly the same premiums, but the packaging was in French and English.

Premiums

AN01 Bicycle Built for Trio [**A**]
AN02 Dot's Ice Cream Wagon [**A**]
AN03 Goodskate Goodfeathers [**A**]
AN04 Mindy and Buttons Wild Ride [**A**]
AN05 Pinky and The Brain Mobile [**A**]
AN06 Slappy and Skippy's Chopper [**A**]
AN07 Upside-Down Wakko [**A**]
AN08 Yakko Ridin Ralph [**A**]
AN09 Bicycle Built for Trio (under-three)
(not shown) [**A**]

Four boxes were issued

AN10 Yakko Mask [**B**]
AN11 Dot's Mask [**B**]
AN12 Wakko Mask [**B**]
AN13 Squit Mask [**B**]

AN10

AN11

AN12

AN13

Animaniacs

UK

July 14 – August 8, 1995

AN14

AN15

AN16

AN17

This Happy Meal promotion in the UK contained four of the American premiums, but with slight variations. *Bicycle Built for Trio, Upside-Down Wakko,* and *Goodskate Goodfeathers* were all the same, but with slight color differences. *Dot's Ice Cream Wagon* has a picture of a popsicle on the side of the wagon, whereas the American premium has ice cream written on the side. All the premiums are made of a hard plastic and move in the same way as the American toys.

Three of the boxes have a mask to make on one side of one of the characters. The other three sides make a play scene. The other box make a complete play scene.

Each premium came in a polybag with a colored insert card.

These premiums marked: ™ and © 1993 Warner Bros MACAU, except *Dot's Ice Cream Wagon* which was marked: ™ and © 1995 Warner Bros MACAU. *Animaniacs* also ran in Germany and Israel in June 1995 and Latin America in 1995.

Four of the American premiums were issued in Australia February 24 – March 23, 1995, these premiums were: *Yakko Ridin' Ralph, Mindy and Button's Wild Ride, Dot's Ice Cream Wagon,* and *Pinky and the Brain Mobile.* These premiums were packed the same as the American ones. They even stated "Collect all eight," although only four were issued. One generic box was issued. This box was the same as issued in the *Darkwing Duck* promotion in Australia, in July 1994. (See page 67.)

Premiums

AN14 Bicycle Built for Trio [**A**]
AN15 Dot's Ice Cream Wagon [**A**]
AN16 Upside-Down Wakko [**A**]
AN17 Goodskate Goodfeathers [**A**]

Four boxes were issued

AN18 Film Studio Set/Dot's Mask [**A**]
AN19 Beach Scene [**A**]
AN20 Park Scene/Wakko's Mask [**A**]
AN21 City Scene/Yakko's Mask [**A**]

AN18

AN19

AN20

AN21

Animaniacs

USA • Canada
November 1 – 28, 1995

AN30

AN31

This promotion coincided with the release of the new Animaniacs animated series which was shown on the Fox Kid's Show on TV in the USA, and introduced new characters like the Hip Hippos. They were all new premiums, except that there were four issued as under-threes from the first Animaniacs promotion in USA May–June 1994. Each under-three was re-packaged into yellow and burgundy-colored, striped polybags. All premiums came in a printed polybag, numbered one to eight with multi languages: Spanish, French, and English. This promotion used some very large, colorful premiums. The premiums measure between 2¾ and 4¼ inches in height and between 2¼ and 4 inches in length (when closed), and are made from a hard plastic. All the premiums are push-along on wheels, except *Slappy and Skippy* and *Wakko, Yakko, and Dot*. They are just standing toys. Each premium is a one-piece toy with extendible plastic tubing within the premium, so that it can be pulled apart to create a bigger premium.

Premiums marked: ™ and © 1994 Warner Bros. China/Chine.

Packaging marked: © 1994 McDonald's Corp. etc.

AN32

Premiums

AN22 Pinky and The Brain [**A**]
AN23 Goodfeathers [**A**]
AN24 Dot and Ralph [**A**]
AN25 Wakko and Yakko [**A**]
AN26 Slappy and Skippy [**A**]
AN27 Mindy and Buttons [**A**]
AN28 Wakko, Yakko, and Dot [**A**]
AN29 Hip Hippos [**A**]

Four under-threes were issued

AN30 Mindy and Buttons Wild Ride
AN31 Goodskate Goodfeathers
AN32 Yakko Ridin Ralph
AN33 Bicycle Built for Trio

Four boxes were issued

AN34 Costumes [**B**]
AN35 Props [**B**]
AN36 Sound Dept. [**B**]
AN37 Make Up [**B**]

AN33

AN34

AN35

AN36

AN37

AN23

AN24

AN22

AN25

AN28

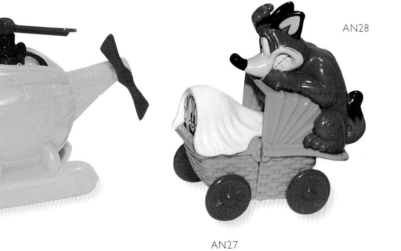

AN26

AN27

AN29

The Aristocats

UK

March 25 – April 21, 1994

This Happy Meal promotion was released to tie-in with the re-release of the Walt Disney film *The Aristocats*, at the theaters in the UK. The film was set in Paris, France in the nineteenth century. Duchess, a very prim and proper cat, lived in a well-to-do house with her three kittens. The butler of the house was not fond of cats and decided to get rid of them. He packed them in a sack and with the sack tied to the back of his motorcycle he rode out of Paris to dispose of them. He threw the cats into a stream, but they escaped, and were befriended by an ally cat, called Thomas O'Mally, and this is where the adventure really begins.

Each premium is made of hard plastic, *O'Mally* is a wind-up premium, that flips over, and *Duchess* is a push-along toy, with a moving head. The butler's motorcycle joins to the kitten's sidecar to make one toy, and as this is pushed along the kittens move up and down in the sidecar. Each toy came in a polybag with a colored insert card. All premiums marked: © Disney CHINA.

Aristocats also ran in Hungary, Holland, Scandinavia, Switzerland, Italy and Greece in April 1994; Belgium and France in July 1994.

AR01

AR02

AR03

AR04

Premiums

AR01   O'Mally   [**A**]

AR02   Edgar on Motorcycle   [**A**]

AR03   Kittens in Sidecar   [**A**]

AR04   Duchess   [**A**]

Four UK boxes were issued

AR05   Cats Club   [**A**]

AR06   Paris Street   [**A**]

AR07   Railway Track   [**A**]

AR08   Dressing Room   [**A**]

AR08   AR05

AR07   AR06

Asterix

Belgium • France • Germany • Holland
September – October, 1994

AS01

AS02

AS03

AS04

AS07

AS08

These characters are from a very popular European cartoon series on TV. This promotion was to coincide with the release of the new animated full length film, *Asterix in America*, at theaters. Asterix is so popular in Europe that they named a theme park after him. Asterix first appeared in 1959 in a comic strip book of the same name but only appeared as a cartoon in the late 1960s. Asterix and Obelix are Gauls from an ancient village in France, not yet conquered by the Romans, due to a magic potion that is mixed by their Druid. This gives them super-human strength. Obelix fell into the potion when he was a baby, and this gave him super-human strength.

Each character is made of a molded hard plastic. *Asterix* is in a boat on

wheels. When the boat is pushed along the sail pivots slightly around. *Obelix* is on wheels, when pulled back he shoots forward, and with the force his hat lifts back. *Idefix*, the dog, has a wind-up tail. Lie him down and watch him roll over and over. *Delphin* the Dolphin is a water squirter, when his top fin is pressed down it squirts water. It also has a wind-up tail which flaps up and down, which then enables it to swim in the water.

Premiums marked: Asterix ® © 1994 Goscinny–Uderzo China.

Germany's promotion was a "JT," (Junior-Tüte or a Happy Meal) no boxes were issued. This JT ran in October 1994.

Holland ran in October 12 – November 15 1994.

Premiums

AS01   Asterix [**A**]
AS02   Obelix [**A**]
AS03   Idefix [**A**]
AS04   Delphin [**A**]

Four boxes were issued

AS05   Indians in Forest (not shown) [**A**]
AS06   Sea Shore (not shown) [**A**]
AS07   Village (Dog) [**A**]
AS08   Obelix at Sea (Dolphin) [**A**]

Babe

USA • Canada

June 14 – July 7, 1996

Babe, a movie by Universal Pictures was based on a book published in 1983 by Dick King-Smith called *The Sheep-Pig*. Dick King-Smith is an author of many children's books based on farm life. *The Sheep-Pig* won the Guardian Children's Fiction Award in 1984. Now there is a computer-generated movie about a small pig won at a fair by Farmer Hogget. *Babe* was destined for the farmer's Christmas dinner, until *Babe* and a few of his friends helped chase away some sheep-rustlers and saved many sheep for the farmer, so the farmer kept him. *Babe's* dream was to become a sheep-pig, so he became very good friends with *Fly*, the farmer's sheepdog, who showed him all the tricks of the trade of sheep herding.

All seven premiums are a soft stuffed toys. Babe was issued twice and there were no under-threes issued. They measured between 3–4½ inches long and came in a printed polybag written in French, Spanish, and English.

Babe, Cow, and *Fly* premiums marked: Babe Imported by Simon Marketing Inc. Los Angeles CA. ™ and © 1995 U.C.S. © 1995 McDonald's Corp. Made in China.

Dutchess, MAA, Mouse, and *Ferdinand* premiums marked: Babe. M-B Sales, Westmount, IL. ™ and © 1995 U.C.S. © 1995 McDonald's Corp. Made in China.

PG01

PG02

PG03

PG04

PG05

PG06

PG07

PG09

PG10

Premiums

PG01 Babe [**A**]

PG02 Cow [**A**]

PG03 Maa (Sheep) [**A**]

PG04 Fly (Sheepdog) [**A**]

PG05 Ferdinand (Duck) [**A**]

PG06 Dutchess (Cat) [**A**]

PG07 Mouse [**A**]

PG08 Babe (re-issued) (not shown) [**A**]

Two bags were issued

PG09 Babe (sitting) [**A**]

PG10 Babe (standing) [**A**]

Back to the Future

USA

April 10 – May 7, 1992

BF01

BF03

BF02

BF04

Premiums

BF01   Doc's DeLorean   [**A**]

BF02   Marty's Hoverboard   [**A**]

BF03   Verne's Junkmobile   [**A**]

BF04   Einstein's Traveling Train   [**A**]

Four boxes were issued

BF05   Dinosaurs   [**B**]

BF06   Hill Valley Hotel   [**B**]

BF07   Medieval Times   [**B**]

BF08   Roman Times   [**B**]

Each premium was a molded hard plastic vehicle that had moving wheels, and an animated character. © 1991 McDonald's Corp. (c) 1991 UCS and Amblin.

All the characters and vehicles in this promotion were taken from the TV series *Back to the Future* shown on American television.

There was a problem with *Doc's DeLorean*, with some children pulling off wheels and swallowing them. While the toy was not recalled, parents were notified through in-store and drive-through signs that the toys were not to be put in the mouth. This toy could be replaced with one of the other toys or a generic toy if parents brought them in. Most customers, however, opted to keep the *DeLorean*.

Back to the Future ran in Panama in November 1992 and one generic bag was issued.

BF05   BF06

BF07   BF08

Back to School

Hong Kong
August 16, 1991

BS01

BS02

BS03

BS04

BS05

The five premiums can be clipped together

This test market promotion consisted of a set of five premiums. Each premium is made from a hard plastic and features McDonaldland characters on them. All five premiums can be clipped together onto the Ronald timetable. The premiums measure approximately 1¾–5½ inches long. The packaging is unknown. Each premium marked: "M®" logo, © 1991 McDonald's Corporation. It included a warning "Suitable for children age three and over." *Ronald* is a timetable, *Hamburglar* is a Set Square, *Grimace* is a 5-inch ruler, *Fry Guy* is a pencil clipper, which can be hung around your neck and *Birdie* is a stencil.

Hong Kong, Macau and China as a *self-liquidator* on August 16 1991 (no special packaging used). Japan ran as a test market in July 1991 and was re-run in August 1991 and August 1992.

Premiums

BS01   Time Table   [**A**]

BS02   Set Square   [**A**]

BS03   Ruler   [**A**]

BS04   Pencil Clipper   [**A**]

BS05   Stencil   [**A**]

One bag was issued

BS06   Generic Bag

Bambi

USA

July 8 – August 4, 1988

BB02

BB03

BB04

BB01

BB05

BB07

ach premium was a hard plastic posable figure, with limbs that move. Three under-three premiums were released with this promotion, and these were *Thumper* and two *Bambis*. *Bambi* came in two variations, one figure with the butterfly on the tail and the other one without. These premiums were one-piece figures that do not move.

Premiums marked: © Disney China. This promotion was tied-in with the re-release of the popular Walt Disney film Bambi.

Premiums

BB01	Bambi	[**B**]
BB02	Flower	[**B**]
BB03	Friend Owl	[**B**]
BB04	Thumper	[**B**]
BB05	Bambi with Butterfly (under-three)	[**C**]
BB06	Bambi without Butterfly (under-three) (not shown)	[**C**]
BB07	Thumper (under-three)	[**C**]

Four boxes were issued (not shown)

BB08	Fall	[**C**]
BB09	Spring	[**C**]
BB10	Summer	[**C**]
BB11	Winter	[**C**]

BB18
EUROPE

BB02
USA

Bambi

Europe
July, 1993

Australia
May, 1995

BB13

BB14

BB12

BB15

BB17

BB20

Once again, similar to the USA promotion, all four European premiums have movable limbs and are made from a hard plastic. The only difference is that *Bambi* and *Flower* have a color variation; Bambi is more of an orange color than the USA version and *Flower* has slightly different markings. The packaging would have been different. © Disney China.

Bambi ran in Belgium, Denmark, Finland, France, Greece, Italy, Holland, Norway, Portugal, Spain, Sweden, and Switzerland in July 1993.

Each premium in the Australian promotion was a one-piece solid hard plastic figure that did not move.

Each premium came in a clear polybag with: "M" logo. © 1994 McDonald's Australia Ltd. Contents made in China by Creata Promotion. Safety tested for children aged three and over, printed on them. One themed box was issued.

Premiums marked: McDonald's © Disney China.

Australian premiums

BB12 Bambi [**A**]
BB13 Flower [**A**]
BB14 Friend Owl [**A**]
BB15 Thumper [**A**]

Europe premiums

BB17 Bambi [**A**]
BB18 Flower (see p. 27) [**A**]
BB19 Friend Owl (not shown) [**A**]
BB20 Thumper [**A**]

One Australian box was issued

BB16 Winter/Spring [**A**]

BB16 Front

BB16 Back

Barbie Set 1

USA

August 2 – 29, 1991

BA01

BA02

BA03

BA04

BA05

BA06

This promotion was the first Happy Meal to have 16 different premiums, eight for boys and eight for girls. It also had toys for the under-threes. The boy's premiums were *Hot Wheels*. (See *Hot Wheels* USA August 1991 page 109).

Each premium is a miniature hard plastic Barbie, exclusive to McDonald's. Made for McDonald's. © 1991 Mattel, Inc. Made in China.

The under-three toys are *Costume Ball Barbie* and *Wedding Day Midge*. Although these premiums are the same as two of the others, they come with a zebra stripe around the packet.

Although a set of *Barbie* was tested back in 1990, this was the first national promotion set of *Barbie* to be released in the USA. All premiums were packed in clear polybags with insert cards enclosed and included one dollar off coupon when buying *Ice Capades Barbie* doll or *My First Barbie* doll from retailers.

BA11

BA12

BA07

BA08

Premiums

BA01 All-American Barbie [**A**]

BA02 Costume Ball Barbie [**A**]

BA03 Lights and Lace Barbie [**A**]

BA04 Happy Birthday Barbie (Black) [**A**]

BA05 Hawaiian Barbie [**A**]

BA06 Wedding Day Midge [**A**]

BA07 Ice Capades Barbie [**A**]

BA08 My First Barbie (Hispanic) [**A**]

BA09 Costume Ball Barbie
(under-three) (not shown) [**B**]

BA10 Wedding Day Midge
(under-three) (not shown) [**B**]

Two boxes were issued

BA11 At Home [**B**]

BA12 On Stage [**B**]

Barbie set 1

UK
January 31 – February 27, 1992

Each premium is a miniature hard plastic Barbie, which was exclusive to McDonald's. Made for McDonald's © Mattel, Inc. Made in China.

This was the first promotion in the UK to have eight premiums in one set: four for girls and four for boys. The boys' premiums were *Corgi Racers* (UK January 1992).

Fantasy Barbie, *Hawaii Barbie*, and *Weekend Barbie* were released in the first promotion of *Barbie* in America, with slightly different names. The *Wedding Day Barbie* in this British set is slightly different: it has blond hair. In America this *Barbie* had red hair and the name was also different; it was known as *Wedding Day Midge*. All premiums were packed in clear polybags with insert cards.

Barbie also ran in Mexico, Latin America, Belgium, Denmark, Finland, France, Greece, Italy, Norway, Portugal, Spain, Sweden, and Switzerland in February 1992. Holland ran it in January 9 – February 19 1992. Iceland in 1992. Panama and Puerto Rico in August 1991.

Holland and France issued four Hot Wheels that came from the USA in 1991 promotion: Camaro Z-18, 55 Chevy, 57 T-Bird and 63 Corvette.

BA50

BA51

BA52

Premiums
BA50   Weekend Barbie [**B**]
BA51   Fantasy Barbie [**B**]
BA52   Hawaii Barbie [**B**]
BA53   Wedding Fantasy Barbie [**B**]

Two boxes were issued
BA54   Wedding and Hawaii Catwalk [**B**]
BA55   Fantasy and Weekend Catwalk
        (not shown) [**B**]

BA54

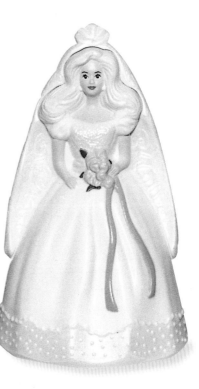

BA53

Barbie Set 2

USA

August 7 – September 3, 1992

BA13

BA14

BA15

BA16

BA17

BA18

This promotion was a set of 16 different premiums, eight for boys and eight for girls. The boys' premiums were *Hot Wheels Mini Streex*. USA August 1992.

Each premium is a miniature hard plastic Barbie as in set one, but all new designs. Three of the premiums have special features: *Rollerblade Barbie* has wheels, *My First Ballerina* pivots around and *Snap "n" Play Barbie* has a dress, but when removed, it reveals a different costume.

Made for McDonald's © 1992 Mattel, Inc. Made in China.

One under-three premium was issued with this promotion, *Sparkle Eyes Barbie*. This is the same as the other premium, but it was issued in packages with the zebra stripe around the package edge.

All premiums were packed in printed polybags, but only three Barbies came with a free Barbie Catalog for girls enclosed: *Ballerina*, *Sparkle Eyes* and *Rose Bride*.

Premiums

BA13	Birthday Surprise Barbie (Black)	[**A**]
BA14	My First Ballerina	[**A**]
BA15	Rappin "Rockin" Barbie	[**A**]
BA16	Rollerblade Barbie	[**A**]
BA17	Rose Bride Barbie	[**A**]
BA18	Snap "n" Play Barbie	[**A**]
BA19	Sparkle Eyes Barbie	[**A**]
BA20	Sun Sensation Barbie	[**A**]
BA21	Sparkle Eyes Barbie (under-three) (not shown)	[**B**]

Two boxes were issued

BA22	Beachfront Fun	[**B**]
BA23	Magic World	[**B**]

BA19

BA20

BA22

BA23

Barbie Set 2

UK
July 16 – August 12, 1993

Germany
October, 1993

BA55

BA57

BA58

BA56

BA56

Each premium is a miniature hard plastic *Barbie*, exclusive to McDonald's. Made for McDonald's © 1993, Mattel, Inc. Made in China.

In this set *Sea Holiday Barbie* has a blue material skirt, which could be taken off to reveal *Barbie* in a swim suit, and *My First Barbie* doll pivots around.

As with the first set of *Barbie* in the UK (1992), this promotion had eight premiums, four for girls and four for boys. The boys' premiums were *Hot Wheels-Attack Pack* (UK July 1993).

All premiums were packed in clear polybags with insert cards. Insert cards had a one pound off coupon offer if you purchased a *Barbie*, *Ken*, or *Barbie's Friend* doll costing £5 or more from a Woolworths store.

Germany issued the same premiums, Barbie and Attack-Pack, but in different packaging (German). A Happy Meal in Germany is called a JT (Junior-Tüte). No boxes were issued. Holland ran this promotion in September 9 – October 10, 1993 and had four boxes. France issued this promotion in 1993.

Sea Holiday Barbie
without dress

Premiums

BA55 My First Barbie [**B**]
BA56 Sea Holiday Barbie [**B**]
BA57 Crystal Heart Barbie [**B**]
BA58 Hollywood Hair Barbie [**B**]

Two boxes were issued

BA59 Limousine/Stage [**B**]
BA60 Sea Cruiser/Dressing Room [**B**]

Barbie Set 3

USA • Canada

August 6 – September 2, 1993

BA29

BA25

BA26

BA27

BA28

BA30

BA31

BA32

E ach premium is a miniature hard plastic Barbie with hair that can be styled. All premiums were issued in printed polybags, with insert cards with Barbie products shown and a dollar off any one *Paint-N-Dazzle Barbie* doll of fashion and a dollar off any one *Mermaid Barbie* or *Mermaid Skipper* doll and also if you spent over $10 on any Barbie products between August 6, 1993 and December 31, 1993 you could send off for a free videotape called *The Secret of How Barbie Dolls are Made*. The under-three premium released with this set was a re-release of the *Rose Bride Barbie* that first appeared in set two in 1992, with zebra stripes around the edge of the packing. In Canada only four Barbies were issued. *Western Stampin' Barbie* and *Romantic Barbie* were the same, but the third and fourth Barbies, *Birthday Party Barbie*, were white, not black, and *Paint-N-Dazzle Barbie* had brown hair instead of fair hair. These ran with Attack-Pack (see *Hot Wheels Attack-Pack UK July 1993* page 113) (Canadian packaging in English and French.) The USA promotion ran with *Hot Wheels-Die Cast Cars* (USA August 1993). Made for McDonald's © Mattel Inc. China.

Premiums

BA25 Birthday Party Barbie (Black) **[A]**
BA26 Hollywood Barbie **[A]**
BA27 My First Ballerina **[A]**
BA28 Paint-N-Dazzle Barbie **[A]**
BA29 Romantic Barbie **[A]**
BA30 Secret Hearts Barbie **[A]**
BA31 Twinkle Lights Barbie **[A]**
BA32 Western Stampin' Barbie **[A]**
BA33 Rose Bride Barbie
     (under-three) (not shown) **[B]**

Canadian Premiums

BA34 Birthday Party Barbie (White) **[A]**
BA35 Paint-N-Dazzle Barbie
     (Brown Hair) **[A]**

One bag was issued

BA36 Congratulations **[A]**

BA35

BA34

BA36

Barbie and Friends Set 4

USA • Canada
August 5 – September 2, 1994

BA41   BA40

This set contained eight premiums, for ethnic communities of the USA. Two black dolls were issued, ordered as optional by restaurant managers within their areas.

Each premium is a hard plastic figure, with hair that can be styled. (Except *Ken*).

The under-three toy issued with this set is a soft rubber *Purple Barbie Ball*.

There is a variation in *Camp Teresa* (BA41). *Camp Teresa* was issued in Columbus G.A., USA. She has blue sunglasses, a blue shirt under her jacket instead of pink, and a blue "fishing pole" patch on the left leg of her yellow trousers. This promotion was run with *World of Hot Wheels* (USA

August 1994), for boys. All premiums were issued in printed polybags. (Canadian packaging in English and French.) Premiums are identical to USA; this set contained *Camp Teresa* with patch. Made for McDonald's © Mattel, Inc. Made in China. Singapore March 1 – April 30 1995 and New Zealand October 1994, four premiums only, BA37, BA39, BA40, BA42.

New Zealand issued BA38, BA43, BA44, BA45 in 1995. Japan ran the promotion in January 1994 with all 16 premiums, this included the Hot Wheel cars, all issued in USA packaging.

Premiums

BA37 Bicycling Barbie [A]
BA38 Jewel and Glitter Shani (Black) (not shown) [A]
BA39 Camp Barbie [A]
BA40 Camp Teresa [A]
BA41 Camp Teresa (with patch) [C]
BA42 Locket Surprise Barbie (not shown) [A]
BA43 Locket Surprise Ken (not shown) [A]
BA44 Jewel and Glitter Bride Barbie [A]
BA45 Bridesmaid Skipper [A]
BA46 Purple Barbie Ball (under-three) [A]
BA47 Camp Site Bag was issued with this promotion [A]
BA48 Afro-American Locket Surprise Barbie [B]
BA49 Afro-American Locket Surprise Ken [B]

BA47

BA45   BA40

BA44

BA37   BA39

BA46

BA49   BA48

Barbie 95

USA

August 1 – 28, 1995

BA68   BA69   BA70   BA71

All premiums have real hair (except *Ken*) and all have accessories, except *Hot Skatin' Barbie*, *Cool Country Barbie*, and *Butterfly Princess Teresa*. *Ken* has a water jet ski. *Dance Moves Barbie*, *Lifeguard Barbie*, and *Ice Skatin' Barbie* have marked stands: Made for McDonald's ® © Mattel, Inc. China/Chine.

The *Bubble Angel Barbie* has wings that you can dip into soapy water to make bubbles. *Cool Country Barbie* is a one-piece toy; the horse has movable legs. Most (but not all) of the dolls have movable limbs and can turn at the waist. *Dance Moves Barbie's* stand will allow Barbie to be spun around. *Ice Skatin' Barbie* can be turned by a small wheel. Premiums marked:
© 1994 Mattel, Inc. China/Chine.

Packaging marked: © 1994 Mattel Inc. © 1994 McDonald's Corporation. In certain areas of the USA, restaurant managers could order optional black dolls, in this case *Lifeguard Barbie* and *Lifeguard Ken* (BA75 and BA73).

A variation has been found on the stands of *Ice Skatin' Barbie*. *Ice Skatin' Barbie* has a light blue-gray stand from the East Coast and Florida area, while the turquoise stand came from the West Coast. This promotion ran with Hot Wheels (see Hot Wheels USA 1995 page 109). There was one dual bag issued: Barbie on one side, Hot

BA72   BA74   BA76   BA78

Wheels on the other. On the side of the bag, you could make your own bracelet. For the first time McDonald's used a new packaging, still in printed polybags, (this set is numbered from one to eight, and Hot Wheels nine to 16), except on the front of the packet, and contains French, Spanish, and English.

BA78   BA77

Premiums

BA68	Hot Skatin' Barbie (Black)	[**A**]
BA69	Dance Moves Barbie	[**A**]
BA70	Butterfly Princess Teresa (Hispanic)	[**A**]
BA71	Cool Country Barbie	[**A**]
BA72	Lifeguard Ken (White)	[**A**]
BA73	Lifeguard Ken (Black)	[**B**]
BA74	Lifeguard Barbie (White)	[**A**]
BA75	Lifeguard Barbie (Black)	[**B**]
BA76	Bubble Angel Barbie	[**A**]
BA77	Ice Skatin' Barbie (Light blue-gray stand)	[**A**]
BA78	Ice Skatin' Barbie (Turquoise stand)	[**A**]
BA79	Li'Candystripes (under-three)	[**A**]

One dual bag was issued (Hot Wheels)

BA80	Ice Skatin'-Hot Skatin' Barbie	[**A**]

BA73   BA75

BA79

BA80

Barbie 95

UK

September 8 – October 6, 1995

BA81

BA82   BA83   BA84

Barbie 95 promotion ran with Hot Wheels 95 at the same time, making this two premiums per week, for four weeks, (see *Hot Wheels* UK 1995 page 112). There were four dual boxes used, Barbie one side, Hot Wheels the other. These Barbies have not been released in America, but their names and style are very similar to four of the premiums issued in America's Barbie 1995 promotion.

Once again each Barbie has real hair,

a first for a UK Barbie promotion, and all are one-piece premiums (except *Winter Action*, which is two-piece), unlike the American Barbies. All are made from a hard plastic and stand approximately 4½ inches high. There was also a competition in all participating McDonald's restaurants. All you had to do was join the dot to dot to complete the picture, color in the picture, and then answer a tie-breaker in no more than 15 words,

"My favorite Barbie/Hot Wheels Happy Meal toy is." Each entrant would receive a free regular soft drink for a properly completed form. Two prizes could be won, one "Zoom Tracer Desk" for the younger winner and a "Happy Meal Magic" for the older winner.

Premiums marked: Made for McDonald's © 1995 Mattel, Inc. Made in China. All premiums came in a printed polybag with insert cards.

BA85   BA86   BA87   BA88

Premiums

BA81 Butterfly Barbie [**A**]

BA82 Dance'N Moves [**A**]

BA83 Cut'N Style [**A**]

BA84 Winter Action [**A**]

Four dual boxes were issued

BA85 Ballroom (City) [**A**]

BA86 Stage (Race Track) [**A**]

BA87 Hair Salon (Car Show) [**A**]

BA88 Ski Slope (Desert Road) [**A**]

Barbie 95

Japan

January – February, 1995

Japan's Barbie promotion consisted of four Barbies that had already been released in America. These were from two different sets. *Camp Barbie* and *Jewel Glitter Bride Barbie* came from *Barbie and Friends* USA 1994. *Secret Hearts Barbie* and *Twinkle Lights Barbie* came from Barbie Set 3 USA 1993. The premiums came in clear polybags with a folded insert card of five sheets, showing clear instructions, as well as other products manufactured by Mattel, Barbie/Hot Wheels. As the insert card is in Japanese, the Barbie names may be different. We have used the American names here. This promotion also ran with Hot Wheels (see *Hot Wheels Japan 1995* page 111). Premiums marked: Made for McDonald's © Mattel Inc. China.

Premiums

BA89   Camp Barbie (not shown)   [**A**]

BA90   Secret Hearts Barbie (not shown)   [**A**]

BA91   Twinkle Lights Barbie (not shown)   [**A**]

BA92   Jewel and Glitter Bride Barbie
            (not shown)   [**A**]

BA93   Generic Bag   (not shown)

Japanese insert card showing the Hot Wheels that were issued along with the Barbie doll.

Japanese Insert Card

Barbie 96 Dolls of the World

USA • Canada
July, 1996

BA104   BA105

BA106   BA107

BA111   BA112

BA110 under-three

McDonald's, being one of the main sponsors for the Atlanta 1996 Olympic Games produced this promotion with Olympic-themed boxes and Barbies in national costumes from around the world. Five premiums only were issued in the USA and identical ones issued in Canada (except for a color variation on the last premium BA109, where she is wearing red bottoms and has a blue base compared to the USA which has blue bottoms and a red base). Canadian boxes were also issued. All Barbie dolls stand about

5 inches tall and are made from a hard plastic and all have real hair (except *Kenyan Barbie*). The *Mexican Barbie* did not move compared to the other Barbies that either moved their arms, hips or waists. All Barbies came with a base (except *Dutch* and *Mexican Barbie*). Each Barbie came in a printed polybag in multi languages: English, French, and Spanish. Each bag was numbered from one to five.

Premiums marked: © 1995 Mattel Inc. China/Chine. (*Kenyan Barbie* not marked except on her base: Made for McDonald's ® © 1995 Mattel Inc. China/Chine).

Five Hot Wheels were also issued with Barbie for boys, plus two Hot Wheels boxes. Hot Wheels cars were *Krackle Car*, *Hot Hubs*, *Roarin Rods*, *Flame*, and *Dark Rider*.

Premiums

BA104 Dutch Barbie [**A**]

BA105 Kenyan Barbie [**A**]

BA106 Japanese Barbie [**A**]

BA107 Mexican Barbie [**A**]

BA108 USA Barbie [**A**]

BA109 Canadian Barbie [**A**]

BA110 Under-three [**A**]

Two boxes were issued

(Create your own Barbie play world diorama.)

BA111 Medal Ceremony [**A**]

BA112 Medal Ceremony (Canadian) [**A**]

BA113 Olympic Track
          (Carrying USA Flag) (not shown) [**A**]

BA114 Olympic Track
          (Carrying Canadian Flag) (not shown)
          [**A**]

BA108   BA109

Barbie 96

UK

September 6 – October 3, 1996

BA95   BA96   BA97   BA98

This Barbie UK promotion also ran with four Hot Wheels (see *Hot Wheels 96 UK* page 112) for boys. All four Barbies had been re-issued from a previous USA promotion (see *Barbie 95 USA* page 35), except that two of these Barbies have variations. Re-packaged with insert cards, each had enclosed a leaflet showing Barbie's friends by Mattel. *Ocean Fun Barbie* (BA97) was called *"Lifeguard Barbie"* in the American set and she was wearing a different color costume, i.e. red jacket and bodysuit with blue shorts and white T-shirt. She is holding black binoculars and she had a gray dolphin fixed to the base of her stand. The other variation is *Hot Skatin' Barbie* (BA98). In the USA set she came without a stand. Each Barbie measures between 4 and 5 inches tall and they all have real hair and they each had either movable arms, waists, or legs. *Dance-N-Moves*, *Ocean Fun*, and *Hot Skatin'* are two-piece premiums. Pressing the yellow button on *Dance-N-Moves* (BA95) base will make her twist at the waist. Four dual Hot Wheels/Barbie boxes were issued. Premiums marked:
Made for McDonald's ® © Mattel Inc. China/Chine.

Premiums

BA95   Dance-N-Moves **[A]**

BA96   Cool Country **[A]**

BA97   Ocean Fun/Killer Whale **[A]**

BA98   Hot Skatin' **[A]**

Four dual boxes were issued (Hot Wheels/Barbie)

BA99   Dance Studio (City Street) **[A]**

BA100 Country Manor with Horses (Petrol Station) **[A]**

BA101 Beach Scene (Garage Repair) **[A]**

BA102 Park, Skate Boarding etc. (Building) **[A]**

BA99   BA100   BA101   BA102

Barnyard McDonald's Farm

USA
April – May, 1986

BY01

BX02

BX05

BY04   BY03

BY06   BY07

This regional promotion ran in Tennessee and Missouri and was also known as "McDonald's Farm." All premiums are made from a hard plastic, and have movable limbs. These were not exclusive to McDonald's restaurants, as most retail toy stores sold them as well. The premiums were made by Playmates Co. and came in a clear polybag. The premiums and the polybags came with no McDonald's markings on them at all. Three of the toys only had "Made in Hong Kong" imprinted on them, *Sheep*, *Pig*, and *Cow*. The rest had no markings. In some New England states, the translite showed only five premiums. The *Roosters* may have been sold instead of the *Hen* in some States. Two boxes were issued, *Barn* and *House*. Both of these boxes had an extra flap attached to them that laid flat on the table. This flap created a playmat barnyard or a front garden that had a path leading up to the front door.

Premiums

BY01	Cow	[**C**]
BY02	Farmer	[**C**]
BY03	Hen	[**C**]
BY04	Pig	[**C**]
BY05	Rooster	[**C**]
BY06	Sheep	[**C**]
BY07	Wife	[**C**]

Two boxes were issued

BY08	Barn (not shown)	[**B**]
BY09	House (not shown)	[**B**]

Batman Returns

USA

June 12 – July 9, 1992

BM01

BM04

BM03

BM02

BM05

Each premium is a hard plastic molded action vehicle. The premiums each have a special feature. The front of the *Batmobile* flies off when a button is pressed. The tail on the *Catwoman Cat Coupé* moves from side to side when pushed along. The *Batman Push and Go Car* is activated by pushing down the *Batman*, then it whizzes along. And finally, when the *Penguin Roto Roadster* is pushed along, the umbrella at the front rotates. Premiums marked: © 1991 DC Comics, Inc. © McDonald's Corp. China.

This promotion was released to tie-in with the release of the new movie *Batman Returns*, starring Michael Keaton, Danny DeVito and Michelle Pfeiffer.

Canadian Happy Meals are called "Treat of the Week" and are a Point of Purchase (P.O.P.) for 69 cents each.

Premiums

BM01 Batman Push and Go Car [**A**]

BM02 The Batmobile [**A**]

BM03 Catwoman Cat Coupé [**A**]

BM04 Penguin Roto Roadster [**A**]

One bag was issued

BM05 Batman is Hero [**A**]

Batman Returns Plastic Cups

Prior to the *Batman Returns* premiums being issued, a set of six plastic, 7-inch drinking cups with lids was issued, plus two extra cups on a special order. A *Batman Returns* brown bag was issued. (Two extra cups and brown bag not shown).

Each cup was issued with a soft plastic lid. With each cup, a combination of three different colored lids was issued: silver, black, and light green. The lids could be used as a Frisbee, 4¼ inches in diameter, and are made from a soft plastic. On the front of each Frisbee ® Batdisc™ is the Bat logo with Batman Returns ® written underneath and with McDonald's ® stamped above the Bat logo.

Inside the Batdisc is written: "Frisbee is a Reg ™ of Kransco." © 1991 McDonald's Corp. T.M. and © 1991 DC Comics Inc. "Caution May contain small parts, not for children under three. Recommended for children 8 and over."

Cups marked: The Collectibles ® Made in Canada. Batman and all related elements are trademarks of DC Comics Inc. © 1991.

BM51   Batman   [**A**]

BM52   Catwoman   [**A**]

BM53   Penguin   [**A**]

BM54   Batmobile   [**A**]

BM55   Penguin in Duck Boat   [**A**]

BM56   Selina Kyle and Bruce Wayne   [**A**]

Silver, black and light green Frisbee Batdiscs

Batman Returns Neck Pens

Australia
1993

Each premium is a pen which fits into a pen holder. Three are characters, and the fourth is the *Batmobile*. Each pen top is made of a semi-hard rubber. *Batman* and *Catwoman* have a black pen and cord, *Penguin* has a gray pen and cord, and finally the *Batmobile* has an orange pen and cord.

© McDonald's Aust. Ltd ™ and DC 1992 China.

Each premium came in a clear polybag, with a color card insert.

BM27   BM28   BM29   BM30

Premiums

BM27   Batman   [**A**]

BM28   Penguin   [**A**]

BM29   Catwoman   [**A**]

BM30   Batmobile   [**A**]

Batman The Animated Series

USA • Canada
October 29 – November 25, 1993

BM06

BM08

BM07

BM09

BM10

This promotion contained eight premiums, four figures with movable limbs and four action vehicles. © 1993 DC. China.

Batman, *Robin*, *Joker*, and *Catwoman* were later used in a Happy Meal promotion in the UK in January 1994.

The Batman figure was also used as the under-three premium. It came with a zebra stripe around the packet and is a solid figure with no moving parts. The cape is fixed to the body.

This promotion was released to tie in with the new animated TV program.

When all four boxes were joined together, they created a Gotham City play scene. Canadian premiums were the same, except that the packaging carried a maple leaf under the "M" and had dual language, French and English.

BM11

BM12

BM13

Premiums
BM06 Joker [**A**]
BM07 Poison Ivy [**A**]
BM08 Robin [**A**]
BM09 Two-Face [**A**]
BM10 Bat Girl [**A**]
BM11 Batman [**A**]
BM12 Catwoman with Panther [**A**]
BM13 Riddler [**A**]
BM14 Batman (under-three) (not shown) [**B**]

Four boxes were issued
BM15 Crazy Carnival [**B**]
BM16 How Does Your Gotham
        City Grow? [**B**]
BM17 The Great Catnapping Caper [**B**]
BM18 Two-Face and His Two-Way Ray [**B**]

BM17

BM15

BM18

BM16

Batman

UK
January 28 – February 24, 1994

BM20

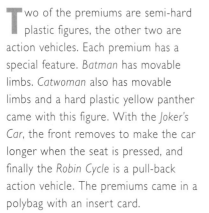

BM19

BM21

BM22

Two of the premiums are semi-hard plastic figures, the other two are action vehicles. Each premium has a special feature. *Batman* has movable limbs. *Catwoman* also has movable limbs and a hard plastic yellow panther came with this figure. With the *Joker's Car*, the front removes to make the car longer when the seat is pressed, and finally the *Robin Cycle* is a pull-back action vehicle. The premiums came in a polybag with an insert card.

This promotion was released to tie-in with the new Saturday morning TV program in the United Kingdom, which was called *Batman The Animated Series.* © 1993 DC. China.

Germany issued the same premiums in September 1994, but in different packaging and for the very first time Germany issued Happy Meal boxes, which were labeled "Junior Box." A free give-away was also handed out. This was a 10-page comic booklet, approximately 6 x 8 inches in size, promoting Batman figures and videos.

Batman also ran in Holland, Belgium, Switzerland in March 30 – May 3 1994. Greece, France, Italy, Scandinavia, Denmark ran it in January – February 1994. Singapore ran this promotion in February 1995.

Premiums
BM19 Batman [B]
BM20 Robin [A]
BM21 Joker [A]
BM22 Catwoman with Panther [A]

Four UK boxes were issued
BM23 Gotham City [A]
BM24 Bat Cave [A]
BM25 City Museum [A]
BM26 Penthouse Suite [A]

UK Translite

BM26

BM24

BM23

BM25

Batman Forever

USA • Canada

June 1 – 30, 1995

Batman Forever by Warner Bros is the third Batman movie made since the start of the 1990s. The movie features new stars and new high-tech gadgets as well as a new film director, Joel Schumacher, compared to the first two films, *Batman* and *Batman Returns*. Val Kilmer starred as Batman, Chris O'Donnell as Robin, Tommy Lee Jones as Two-Face, and Jim Carrey as the Riddler.

This promotion from McDonald's was aimed at the adult collector, due to the rating of the movie, PG. *Batman Forever* was released in theaters on June 29. With this promotion, all items on offer were special packaging for the McDonald's special *Great Gotham Meal*, and featured a fantastic set of four, high-quality chiseled glasses. Each had a picture of the character on the front and a scene from Gotham City on the back. For $1.75 each, they came with any burger or muffin purchased. Four paper cups, two large, and two medium, were offered with Coca-Cola ™ and ®. Two paper cups were offered, one with *Batman* and *Robin* on it, and on the other, the *Riddler* and

BM37

BM38

BM39

BM40

Two-Face. Both cups came in two sizes, medium, and large (USA measure). One bag was issued as a part of the special packaging, and burger wrappers and fries cartons were also issued with *Batman Forever* markings on them. All Canadian packaging is marked with a maple leaf and made in Canada. All American packaging is made in America. The Gotham Glasses marked

with: (character's name) McDonald's "M" logo, manufactured for McDonald's, Batman Forever. Made in France, ™ and © 1995 DC Comics All Rights Reserved. Paper cups marked: Coca-Cola Ltd © 1995 McDonald's Corp. DC, Comics ™ and © 1995.

There was a Batman Forever Gotham Glass Collection promotion in Australia and Hong Kong in July 1995.

Purchases

BM33   Batman Glass   [**C**]
BM34   Riddler Glass   [**C**]
BM35   Robin Glass   [**A**]
BM36   Two-Face Glass   [**C**]

Four paper Coca-Cola cups were issued

BM37   Cup Medium (Batman – Robin)   [**A**]
BM38   Cup Large (Batman – Robin)   [**A**]
BM39   Cup Medium
            (Riddler – Two-Face)   [**A**]
BM40   Cup Large (Riddler – Two-Face)   [**A**]

One bag was issued

BM41   Batman Forever

Four fries cartons were issued

BM42   Fries Cartons   [**A**]

BM42 Fries Cartons

BM41

BM33

BM34

BM35

BM36

Batman Forever

UK

June 30, 1995

BATMAN

BM44　　BM43　　BM43　　BM44

46

UK Translite

BM45 **Give-away Batman Mask**

UK Trayliner

UK Ceiling Dangler

This promotion coincided with the release of the *Batman Forever* film in the UK, at theaters from July 14. Because *Batman Forever* was certified as PG in the UK, there were no Happy Meal toys produced, due to the fact that McDonald's restaurants cater for three to seven year olds. Original author Bob Kane first thought of the caped crusader at the age of 13 and Batman was seen 55 years ago, in 1939 in the DC comic book. Robin appeared in 1940 for a trial period, and the comic book sales doubled. The re-designed Batmobile for *Batman Forever* with a tail spoiler was taken from the Batmobile that appeared in the comic book in 1941. Two-Face appeared in 1942 and has never been played by a real life actor, until this film. The Riddler appeared in 1948 then disappeared for 20 years.

McDonald's "Batman Forever Challenge" had three million prizes to give away. The main prize was a MGF Sports Car or a visit to Warner Bros Studios in California, plus TVs and many food offers with over two million medium Coca-Cola's ™ © to be won. There was a breakfast offer with free regular coffee or regular orange juice and a supersize offer on an Extra Value or Super Hero Meal with large fries and drinks at no extra cost. No purchase was necessary to enter the challenge.

Each cup came in two sizes. It showed *Batman* and *Two-Face* on the outside and on the lip of each was a yellow tag to push and turn to find out if you have won.

DC Comics ™ © 1995 All Rights Reserved.

Purchases

BM43　Medium Cup　[**A**]

BM44　Large Cup　[**A**]

One generic bag was issued

One free give-away

BM45　Batman Mask　[**A**]

Batman Forever Action Cards

New Zealand
July, 1995

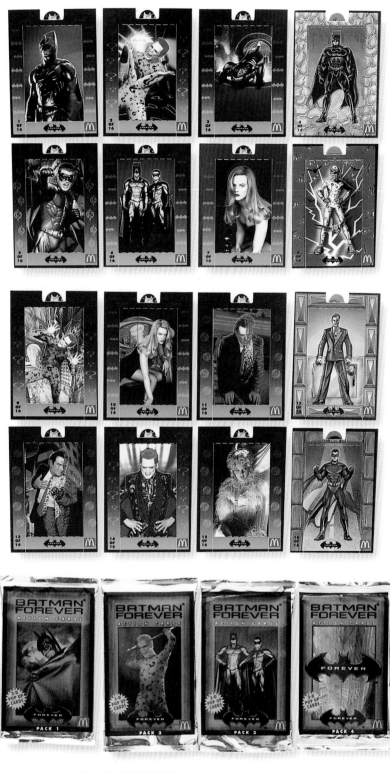

A good promotion from New Zealand, released over a four week period, one pack per week. Each pack contains four 3-D pop-up cardboard cards, each measuring 3½ x 2½ inches, making a grand total of 16 cards to collect. On the back of each card are some interesting facts about each character. *Card 1.* An eligible bachelor from Gotham City, Bruce Wayne is the wealthy owner of Wayne Enterprises. *Card 2.* The Riddler, original name Edward Nygma, once worked for Wayne Enterprises as an inventor. *Card 3.* The state-of-the-art Batmobile, with more ingenious devices than a jet fighter and which can travel almost as fast! *Card 4.* A portrait picture of Batman. *Card 5.* Robin, who was once an acrobat, lost his family recently in a circus accident. *Card 6.* Bruce Wayne comes up against the Riddler, Batman, and Two-Face with the help of Robin, and some high-tech weapons. *Card 7.* Dr. Chase Meridian, a criminal psychologist. *Card 8.* A portrait picture of the Riddler. *Card 9.* The Riddler has countless more riddles to baffle Batman and Robin. *Card 10.* Dr. Chase Meridian is captivated by the mysterious dark stranger, Batman, *Card 11.* Harvey Dent, once a district attorney until an ugly courtroom accident scarred half his face, is now known as Two-Face. *Card 12.* A portrait of Two-Face. *Card 13.* Two-Face with deep evil eyes and an outrageous dress sense. *Card 14.* The Riddler has a great ambition to find out who is behind the Bat mask. *Card 15.* Sugar, one of Two-Face's sidekicks. *Card 16.* A portrait picture of Robin.

Each pack of cards came in a silver foil packet and each card is numbered one to 16. Each card marked: Warner Bros. A Time Warner Entertainment Company © 1995 Warner Bros. All rights reserved. DC Comics ™ © 1995.

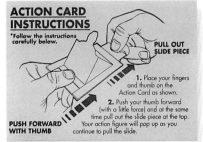

ACTION CARD INSTRUCTIONS
Follow the instructions carefully below.

PULL OUT SLIDE PIECE

1. Place your fingers and thumb on the Action Card as shown.
2. Push your thumb forward (with a little force) and at the same time pull out the slide piece at the top. Your action figure will pop up as you continue to pull the slide.

PUSH FORWARD WITH THUMB

Premiums

BM46   Action Cards Pack One, 1 to 4 **[A]**
BM47   Action Cards Pack Two, 5 to 8 **[A]**
BM48   Action Cards Pack Three, 9 to 12 **[A]**
BM49   Action Cards Pack Four, 13 to 16 **[A]**

One box was issued

BM50   Generic Box

Batman Forever (Badges)

Australia

July 7 – August 3, 1995

This promotion was released in Australia to coincide with the showing of the film at local theaters. Each badge is a two-picture 3-D hologram and each has the portrait of a main character with their names displayed underneath. If you tilt the badge in the light, another picture will appear with the character in an action pose. Each badge is made from plastic, and there is a hole in the top of each for a chain or there is a plastic clip on the reverse side.

Premiums marked: Batman™ Forever™ © 1995 DC Comics All Rights Reserved China.

All premiums came in a clear sealed polybag with black print.

BM52   BM53   BM54   BM55

Premiums

BM52 Batman [**A**]

BM53 Robin [**A**]

BM54 Two-Face [**A**]

BM55 Riddler [**A**]

One box was issued

BM56 Generic box (not shown) [**A**]

48

Batman Bike Accessories

UK

May 24 – June 20, 1996

This is a worthwhile set for Batman collectors to obtain. All four premiums are quite large, the *Mirror* being the longest at about 8½ inches. The *Water Bottle* is 7 inches long, *Accessories Case* 6 inches long, and the *Hooter* 5 inches tall. All are one-piece toys, (except the *Water Bottle*) and are made from a hard plastic (except *Hooter* which is soft rubber). The last time any bike accessories were issued in the UK was *I Like Bikes* in June 1991. There was a Batman coloring competition in some participating restaurants. Premiums came in a polybag with an insert card showing fixing instructions on the reverse.

Premiums marked: © 1995 DC Comics. All Rights Reserved China. Simon Marketing Inc. Gmbh, D-63268 Dreieich.

BM58

BM59

BM60

BM61

Premiums

BM58 Batman Rearview Mirror [**A**]

BM59 Riddler Hooter [**A**]

BM60 Batcar Water Bottle [**A**]

BM61 Bike Accessories Case [**A**]

One bag was issued (not shown)

BM62 Batman – Robin [**A**]

Beach Series

Australia

January 6 – February 2, 1995

BT16

BT17

BT18

BT19

This Beach Series started the New Year off in January of 1995 in Australia. Each premium is made from a hard plastic. The pink *Starfish Sand Mold* had embossed "M"s on each of its five tentacles, and an embossed smiling face in the center. The starfish measures 4½ inches across. The *Yellow Spade* is embossed with starfish and the McDonald's name along the handle, and on the front of the spade is an embossed picture of Ronald McDonald placing an "M" logo flag onto his ready-made sand castle. The spade measures 6¾ inches long. The *Sand Bucket* is a plain red, 3½-inch high plastic bucket

with a yellow handle, which was embossed with "M"s placed on top of each other along the complete length of the handle. The *Purple Rake* has starfish embossed along the handle with the McDonald's name, and at the rake end is an embossed picture of *Grimace* holding a spade. The *Purple Rake* measures 6¾ inches in length.

Premiums marked: © 1995 McDonald's. Made in China.

Each premium came in a clear sealed polybag with black print: "M ™" logo, © 1995 McDonald's Australia Ltd. Contents made in China by Creata Promotion.

Premiums

BT16   Starfish Sand Mold [**A**]
BT17   Spade Yellow [**A**]
BT18   Sand Bucket [**A**]
BT19   Rake Purple [**A**]

One box was issued

BT20   Generic box (not shown)

Beach Time
Beach Toy

UK • Europe
August 2, 1991

USA
June 1 – 28, 1990

BT06

BT01

BT03

BT02

BT04

BT05

BT08

BT09

BT10

E ach premium is an inflatable beach toy. In Europe (not in England) there was a fifth premium issued. This was a watertight neck purse made from a hard plastic with a string cord. © 1991 McDonald's Corporation. Simon Marketing Int'i GmbH-D-6072 Dreieich CE.

A warning is printed on each of the inflatable premiums. It reads: "Warning! Only to be used in water in which the child is within its depth and under supervision."

The four USA premiums were part of a Happy Meal promotion, Beach Toy 1990. This American set had four additional toys. These premiums were marked in the same way except that they did not have the CE mark.

Premiums

BT01   Birdie Seaside Submarine [**B**]

BT02   Fry Kid Super Sailor [**B**]

BT03   Grimace Bouncin' Beach Ball [**B**]

BT04   Ronald Fun Flyer [**B**]

BT05   Neck Purse (Europe only) [**B**]

One colored plastic bag was issued with this UK promotion

BT06   Ronald Swimming

USA Premiums

BT07   Ronald and Grimace Beach Pail
         (not shown) [**A**]

BT08   Birdie Shovel and Sand Spinner [**A**]

BT09   Fry Kids Sand Castle Pail [**A**]

BT10   Ronald Squirt Rake [**A**]

Four USA bags were issued (not shown)

BT11   Grimace [**C**]

BT12   Hamburglar [**C**]

BT13   Ronald/Stars [**C**]

BT14   Ronald/Treasure Chest [**C**]

Beauty and the Beast

UK
October 11, 1992

BE01

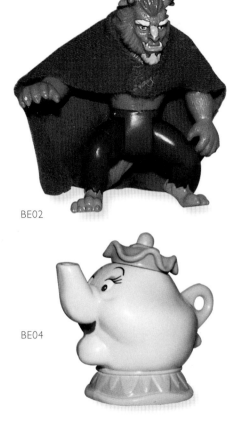

BE02

BE03

BE04

Each premium has its own special feature. *Belle* is a three-piece premium. She has a changeable head and two dresses. *Mrs Potts* the teapot is a pull-back action toy that spins around and the lid pops up and down. *Cogsworth* the clock is a wind-up toy that moves along on wheels and rocks from side to side at the same time, and finally *The Beast* is a hard plastic figure with movable limbs and a material purple cape.

Premiums marked: © 1992 McDonald's Corp. © Disney.

This promotion tied-in the theatrical release of the Walt Disney film *Beauty and the Beast*, based on the Grimms' fairy tale of the same name. This promotion ran for eight weeks.

Beauty and the Beast also ran in Spain, Norway, Holland, Greece, Finland, Denmark, and Belgium in December 1992. France ran it November – December 1992.

Premiums

BE01 Belle [**C**]
BE02 The Beast [**C**]
BE03 Cogsworth [**B**]
BE04 Mrs Potts [**B**]

Four boxes were issued

BE05 Village Street [**C**]
BE06 Ballroom Entrance [**C**]
BE07 Kitchen [**C**]
BE08 Castle and Surrounding Woods [**C**]

BE08   BE06   BE07   BE05

Beauty and the Beast

Germany
November – December 1992

BE09

BE10

This set contains two premiums. *The Beast* is a plush soft figure approximately 5½ inches tall, with a rubber PVC head, and *Belle* is a hard plastic figure with a large yellow satin dress. Her dress can be removed.

There are no markings on the premiums, but the bags have Simon Marketing printed on them. These premiums were sold as a set only, and was a self-liquidator.

Purchases
BE09   The Beast [**C**]
BE10   Belle [**C**]

Belle without Dress

Berenstain Bears

USA

October 31 – November 29, 1987

BR03

BR01

BR02

BR04

The Berenstain Bears were first issued as a test promotion in Evansville in 1986 (November 28 – December 24). They differed from the photographs shown. The test premiums had four to the set, but the hands and feet were painted, had flocked heads, and were made of a soft rubber. No under-three premium was issued with this set. The *Sister* premium came with a sled instead of a truck and her arms were straight by her sides. *Mama Bear* wore a one-piece jump suit (not a skirt as in the second set). *Brother Bear's* yellow scooter had green handles, and finally *Papa Bear* had a dark orange wheelbarrow. Four boxes were issued with this test set, which had a Christmas theme to them. The accessories to this test set carried no McDonald's identification.

The Berenstain Bears ran nationally on October 31 – November 29 1987; they are made of a hard rubber and their hands and feet are unpainted.

Two under-three premiums were issued. Both were one-piece premiums with no flocking on their heads. Each came with a punch-out card with accessories printed on them. *Mama Bear* wears a skirt. All accessories are marked with McDonald's. Four boxes were issued, with a fall theme.

The Berenstain Bears have been around for 25 years, but appeared on a CBS TV show for the first time in 1985. Stan and Jan Berenstain (husband and wife) have written and published nearly 50 books, and appeared in five TV specials leading up to 1985. © 1986 S & J Berenstain. China. Berenstain Bears also ran in Japan in February, 1988.

Premiums

BR01   Sister with Red Wagon   [**A**]
BR02   Papa with Wheelbarrow   [**A**]
BR03   Brother on Scooter   [**A**]
BR04   Mama with Yellow Shopping Cart   [**A**]
BR09   Mama Bear under-three
       (not shown)
BR10   Papa Bear under-three
       (not shown)

Four boxes were issued (not shown)

BR05   Barn Dance   [**C**]
BR06   General Store   [**C**]
BR07   School   [**C**]
BR08   Tree House   [**C**]

Berenstain Bears Books

USA
January 26 – February 22, 1990

In this national promotion eight books were released, two books a week, one a storybook and the other an activity book. As with the "An American Tail" promotion issued in the USA in November 1986, the storybooks had 24 color pages and measured approximately 7 inches square. The story and activity books were exclusive to McDonald's. The activity books measured 8 x 10 inches and all eight books carried the "M" logo on the front cover. Printed inside of cover: © 1990 Stanley and Janice Berenstain. Printed in the USA. Brought to you by McDonald's ® in Cooperation with the American Library Association. The two badges were issued as a test in South Bend, Indiana.

BR13

BR17

Premiums (Storybooks)
BR11   Life with Papa (not shown)   [**A**]
BR13   Attic Treasure   [**A**]
BR15   Substitute Teacher (not shown)   [**A**]
BR17   The Eager Beavers   [**A**]

Four boxes were issued (not shown)
BR19   Sharing Brings Good Things   [**C**]
BR20   Teamwork Saves the Day   [**C**]
BR21   Thank Goodness . . . Bears   [**C**]
BR22   What To Do Depends on You   [**C**]

Activity Books
BR12   Life with Papa (not shown)   [**A**]
BR14   Attic Treasure (not shown)   [**A**]
BR16   Substitute Teacher (not shown)   [**A**]
BR18   The Eager Beavers (not shown)   [**A**]

Two bags were issued (not shown)
BR23   Teamwork Saves the Day   [**C**]
BR24   What To Do Depends on You   [**C**]

Big Buddies

New Zealand
November 6 – 30, 1993

BG03

BG02

BG04

BG01

Each premium is a hard plastic figure, all with moveable head, feet, and arms. The figures range between approximately 3½ and 5 inches tall. They were issued as clean-ups.
  Premiums marked: © 1993 McDonald's Corp. China.

Premiums
BG01   Ronald McDonald   [**A**]
BG02   Grimace   [**A**]
BG03   Birdie   [**A**]
BG04   Hamburglar   [**A**]

One box was issued
BG05   (not shown)

Bobby's World

USA • Canada • Puerto Rico
March 4 – 31, 1994

BW01

BW01

BW04

BW03

BW05

BW02

BW03

Premiums

BW01 Wheeler/Spaceship [**A**]

BW02 Inner Tube/Submarine [**A**]

BW03 Skates/Roller Coaster [**A**]

BW04 Wagon/Race Car [**A**]

BW05 Inner Tube (under-three) [**A**]

Four boxes were issued

BW06 Cheap Skates/Bobby Skating [**B**]

BW07 Drag/Bobby in Wagon [**B**]

BW08 Planet/Bobby on Big Wheels [**B**]

BW09 Wave/Bobby in Pool [**B**]

This national promotion is based on the Fox TV Saturday morning kids' show. Each premium is made from hard plastic and is a two-piece toy. All the characters are push-along and run on wheels. Their heads can be turned around. Each character fits into a shell in the shape of a *Spaceship*, *Roller Coaster Submarine*, or *Race Car*. The under-three is a one-piece premium, no wheels, with *Bobby on an inner tube*. It is made from soft rubber and has a small hole in the snorkel. The toy can be used as a water squirter. Premiums marked: © /TM FCN'94 China.

Packed in printed polybags. Bags are marked: ™ and © 1994 Fox Children's Network Inc. Bobby is a trademark of Alevy Productions. © 1993 McDonald's Corporation, China.

BW07   BW08

BW06   BW09

Buckets of Fun

UK
1987

BK03

BK01

BK02

BK04

All four buckets featured McDonaldland characters. Each bucket is made from a hard plastic with a colored lid and spade. *Fun Fair* has a red lid, handle, and spade. *Garden* has a green lid, handle, and spade. *Picnic* was issued with a yellow lid, handle, and spade. *Beach* has a blue lid, handle, and spade. Each bucket could be bought with any food purchase. One bucket was issued per week. Buckets were safety tested for children age three and older. Premiums were made in Germany by *Wedo Promotion*. © 1987 McDonald's Corporation and McDonald's Hamburglar Limited. All Rights Reserved.

Happy Pail 1 (USA, 1983) promotion appeared before the UK premiums, but is very similar. It was regional in upper New York State. Each premium came with: a pail, lid, handle, and shovel. The lid and handle color matches the pail. The lid has four holes in it. Premiums marked: © 1983 McDonald's Corporation. Genpak Corporation, Glens Falls, NY, Mammoth Containers.
1) *Ronald and Mayor under Beach Umbrella* (pink pail, shovel, and lid)
2) *Ronald in Inner Tube* (white pail, shovel, and lid)

3) *Airplane Pulling Banner* (yellow pail, shovel, and lid).

Happy Pail 2 (Olympic, May 18 – June 17, 1984) added an Olympic theme to this American national promotion. The lids have four open vent holes in them. Each pail came with lids and handles the same color. All pails came with a yellow shovel.

1) *Athletics* (beige lid and pail)
2) *Cycling* (yellow lid and pail)
3) *Olympic Games* (white lid and pail)
4) *Swimming* (blue lid and pail)
A contribution for each Happy Pail 3 (May 30 – July 6, 1986) Meal sold was donated to the Ronald McDonald Children's Charities and Ronald McDonald House.
1) *Beach* (blue handle and lid, yellow shovel)
2) *Parade* (orange handle and lid, red rake)
3) *Picnic* (yellow handle and lid, yellow shovel)
4) *Treasure Hunt* (red handle and lid, yellow shovel)
5) *Vacation* (green handle and lid, red rake)

Purchase

BK01	Fun Fair	[**A**]
BK02	Garden	[**A**]
BK03	Picnic	[**A**]
BK04	Beach	[**A**]

No special packaging
(Green plus Blue Spade plus Blue Lid not shown)

Cabbage Patch Kids

USA • Canada
November 27 – December 31, 1992

CA01

CA02

CA03

CA04

CA05

CA06

CA11
(without sock)

CA12

Each premium is a molded hard plastic figure with wool hair. The under-three premium is a hollow rubber figure that does not move. This promotion was run over the Christmas period. It ran with Tonka for boys (USA 1992). This promotion also ran in Canada over the same period. This was Canada's first Happy Meal and was a set that contained four premiums, but some of the figures and the names varied. Premiums were packed in printed polybags. The Canadian set had English and French packaging details.

Singapore issued the same five premiums as the USA, CA01, CA02, CA03, CA04, CA05 in October 1994, but they issued a box.

New Zealand's premiums were issued in 1994. They are identical to the Canadian set, CA09, CA10, CA11, CA12 plus under-three, except for the packaging. New Zealand's are packed in clear polybags with inserts and a coupon for any *Cabbage Patch Kid* doll. © 1992 OAA. INC.

Canada issued premiums, in November – December 1992 and New Zealand, Central America, Mexico, and Puerto Rico issued only four premiums in June 1994.

Premiums USA

CA01　Mimi Kristina "All Dressed Up"　[**A**]

CA02　Ali Marie "Tiny Dancer"　[**A**]

CA03　Jennifer Lauren "Fun On Ice"
　　　　(black)　[**A**]

CA04　Lindsey Elizabeth
　　　　"Holiday Dreamer" (with sock)　[**A**]

CA05　Jessica Wallace "Holiday Pageant"　[**A**]

CA06　Anne Louise (under-three) USA　[**A**]

One bag was issued with this promotion, a dual bag for both Cabbage Patch Kids and Tonka

CA07　Christmas Decor (USA)　[**A**]

CA19 and CA20 Boxes (Canadian, dual
　　　　language)

CA09　Jennifer Rita "Tiny Dancer"
　　　　(The same as CA02 USA)　[**A**]

CA10　Christina Maria "Happy Birthday"
　　　　(The same as CA01 USA)　[**A**]

CA11　Emily Elizabeth "Sweet Dreamer"
　　　　(Like CA04, but without sock)　[**A**]

CA12　Jamie Christina "Fun On Ice"　[**A**]

CA21　Melanie Merrill under-three
　　　　(Canada) (The same as USA
　　　　under-three)　[**A**]

CA07

Note: There are two versions of Holiday Dreamer (CA04), one with sock (USA), and one without sock (Canada) CA11.

Cabbage Patch Kids

USA

December 2 – 29, 1994

CA14

CA16

CA13

CA15

CA17

E ach premium is a hard plastic figure with movable arms and legs and hair made from wool. All the dolls are dressed in Christmas fancy dress costumes. © 1994 OAA. Inc.

The under-three premium to this set is a hollow rubber figure that does not move. This was the same under-three premium used in the first set of *Cabbage Patch Kids* in 1992, but in different colors. © 1992 OAA Inc. This promotion was issued over the Christmas period: it ran with Tonka for boys – USA December 1992.

Premiums

CA13   Mimi Kristina "Angel" [**A**]

CA14   Kimberley Katherine
            "Santa's Helper" [**A**]

CA15   Abigail Lynn "Toy Soldier" (Black) [**A**]

CA16   Michelle Elyse "Snow Fairy" [**A**]

CA17   Sarajane under-three [**A**]

One dual bag was issued, for both Cabbage Patch Kids and Tonka

CA18   Cabbage Patch Kids/Tonka

Camp McDonaldland

USA

June 30 – July 5, 1990

CM01

CM02

CM03

CM04

Each premium is made from a hard plastic and comes with a Camp McDonaldland logo stamped on it. The under-three is the same as *Ronald's Collapsible Cup* except the packaging has the black and white zebra strip around the edge of the package. All premiums came in a printed polybag. Some of the *Fry Kid Utensils* (CM03 knife-purple, fork-turquoise, spoon-yellow) came with five bandages plus a 25 cent coupon enclosed. The 25 cent coupon was for plastic bandages called Happy Strips ™ by Curad ® Kid Size ™. Each bandage is decorated with McDonaldland characters with activities on the box and all-assortment size bandages. The *Fry Kid Utensils* (CM05 knife-green, fork-yellow, spoon-blue) came without bandages and was issued in clean-up weeks in 1990 and 1991.

Premiums marked: © 1989 McDonald's Corporation, China.

Camp McDonaldland also ran in Hong Kong and Taiwan in September 1990, Singapore in October 1990. Japan ran it as a Test Market in May 1990 and ran it in May 1991. Australia's promotion was called "Bush Camp Kit" and this promotion ran in September – October 1991 with a special bag.

Premiums

CM01 Grimace Canteen [**A**]

CM02 Birdie Canteen Mess Kit [**A**]

CM03 Fry Kid Utensils [**A**]
         (with or without bandages and
         coupon)

CM04 Ronald Collapsible Cup [**A**]

CM05 Fry Kid Utensils (not shown) [**B**]
         (without bandages and coupon)

One under-three cup was issued

CM06 Ronald Collapsible Cup
         (not shown) [**B**]

Four boxes were issued

CM07 At The Lake [**C**]

CM08 Camping Out [**C**]

CM09 Nature Walk [**C**]

CM10 Playtime At Camp [**C**]

Two bags were issued (not shown)

CM11 Playtime [**C**]

CM12 Nature Walk [**C**]

CM07

CM08

CM09

CM10

Carnival

USA

September 7 – October 4, 1990
Re-issued March – April 1991

CN02

CN01

CN04

This was a regional promotion in Florida, Illinois, Ohio, Joplin, and Charlestown. Each premium is made from a hard plastic and each part is interchangeable. *Birdie*, *Grimace*, and *Hamburglar* all have five pieces to each premium. *Ronald* has only four pieces in the packet. All premiums are packed in clear polybags with insert cards. Premiums marked: © 1990 McDonald's Corp. China.

Carnival also ran in Guatemala in July 1991, Japan ran a test market in March 1991 and in January 1992, Mexico in February 1991, Costa Rica in April 1991, and Panama in March 1991.

CN05

Premiums

CN01 Birdie on Swing [**B**]

CN02 Grimace on Merry-Go-Round [**B**]

CN03 Hamburglar on Ferris Wheel [**B**]

CN04 Ronald on Carousel [**B**]

One under-three was issued

CN05 Grimace on Rocker (under-three) [**C**]

One USA box was issued

CN07 Ronald – Train [**A**]

CN03

CN07

Changeables

USA

December 26, 1987 – January 29, 1988

CH01

CH05

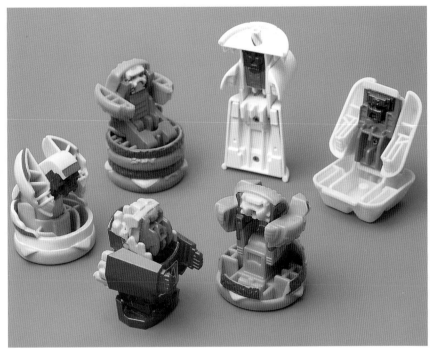

CH06

CH02

CH03

CH04

Each premium is either a food item or package that transforms into a robot. The faces are painted, but the hands are not.

This promotion came in two variations, the first set to be issued contained five premiums. The *Shake* was issued in the second set making the promotion a set of six. This was a regional promotion, and it ran in different parts of the USA during the year of 1987.

Premiums marked: © 1987 McDonald's Corporation.

Two boxes were issued, one with each Happy Meal variation, and one showing the Milk Shake CH07.

Premiums

CH01   Big Mac Sandwich [**A**]
CH02   Chicken McNuggets [**A**]
CH03   Egg McMuffin Sandwich [**A**]
CH04   Large French Fries [**A**]
CH05   Quarter Pounder with Cheese [**A**]
CH06   Milk Shake [**B**]

Two boxes were issued

CH08   Box (not shown)
The boxes were identical apart from the added *Milk Shake*.
See *New Food Changeables* page 174.

CH07 Front

CH07 Back

Changeables

Australia
1991

CH10

CH11

CH12

CH13

Each premium has been issued in other promotions from the USA and UK, but with slight color changes and different names. *Mega Mac*, *Robofries*, and *Burgertron* were first seen in *New Food Changeables* USA May 1989 and *Mega Mac* and also *Robofries* in *McRobots* UK April 1990. *Shakernetic* first appeared in the USA. *Changeables* appeared in December 1987 but without the legs and hands painted in. It also had a different two-tone color head.

Premiums came in a clear polybag with an insert card, with instructions on the reverse.

Premiums marked: © 1990 McDonald's Australia China.

Inserts Cards marked: © 1991 McDonald's Australia Ltd.

Premiums

CH10   Mega Mac   [**A**]
CH11   Shakernetic   [**A**]
CH12   Robofries   [**A**]
CH13   Burgertron   [**A**]

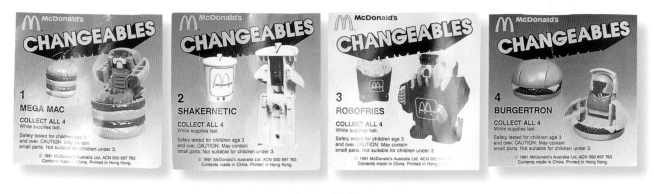

Insert Cards

Chip 'N' Dale Rescue Rangers

USA

October 27 – November 23, 1989

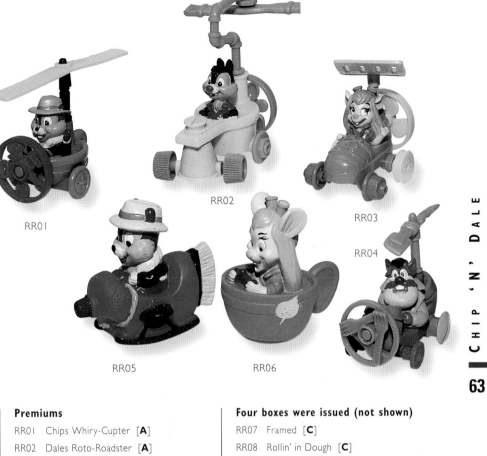

RR01

RR02

RR03

RR04

RR05

RR06

Each premium is a push-along action vehicle in three parts. The parts can be interchanged to create different vehicles. Two under-premiums were issued with this promotion. These were hollow plastic premiums which did not move.

Premiums marked: © Disney China.

This Happy Meal promotion was issued to tie in with the new Disney TV show, *The Rescue Rangers*. The program featured the characters *Chip 'N' Dale*, plus two mouse companions, *Gadget* and *Monterey Jack*. The Gadget mobiles, as they were called, were made by Gadget, and were made out of common household items.

Premiums

RR01   Chips Whiry-Cupter   **[A]**
RR02   Dales Roto-Roadster   **[A]**
RR03   Gadget's Rescue Racer   **[A]**
RR04   Monterey Jack's Propel-a-Phone   **[A]**
RR05   Chips' Rockin' Racer (under-three)   **[B]**
RR06   Gadget's Rockin' Rider
       (under-three)   **[B]**

Four boxes were issued (not shown)

RR07   Framed   **[C]**
RR08   Rollin' in Dough   **[C]**
RR09   Yolk's on Him   **[C]**
RR10   Whale of a Time (not shown)   **[C]**

Cinderella (Christmas Plush Toy)

USA

December, 1987

CI02

CI01

Cinderella plush toys were available over the Christmas period in the USA as purchases. This classic Walt Disney movie was first released in 1950, and was the first full-length animated feature film since *Bambi* in 1942. From a French fairytale, Cinderella is put upon by her greedy stepmother and her two spoiled stepsisters. One day they receive an invitation to the palace ball, and jealously they prevent Cinderella from attending. The fairy godmother and two mice *Jacque* and *Gus*, help Cinderella's dream come true. Each mouse is a soft, stuffed plush toy, measuring 3½ inches high, and comes sealed in a clear polybag, within a 4-inch-high, octagonal box. Each box and mouse has a gold cord, so they can be hung up. Purchases marked: © The Walt Disney Company. Made in China. Simon Marketing Inc., Los Angeles, CA. Within each box is a special offer leaflet: subscribe to the Disney channel and receive a free 14-inch Mickey Mouse. Mickey Mouse T-Shirt offer and $3 off, when you purchase the Walt Disney's *Lady and the Tramp* video.

Purchases

CI01   Jacque   **[B]**
CI02   Gus   **[B]**

Circus

USA
March 8 – April 12, 1991

UK
December 12, 1991

CP03

CP02

CP04

CP01

CP05

CP06

CP07

CP08

There were two promotions, one in the UK called "Circus" and the other promotion occurred in the USA. This was known as "Circus Parade." Each premium is a geared action toy. Moving parts enable them to be pushed along. Premiums marked: © 1989 McDonald's Corp.

Circus Parade was a regional promotion in St. Louis. It was issued March 8 – April 12 1991. All the premiums were the same; they came in clear polybags with card inserts which read *Circus Parade*, and not just *Circus* as the translite read. One bag was issued; when cut it created a circus ring.

Circus also ran in Switzerland, Sweden, Spain, Norway, Holland, Italy, Finland, Denmark, Belgium in March 1991. France ran this promotion in April 1991, Puerto Rico ran it in August 1991 and Singapore in November 1993.

Premiums

CP01   Ring Master – Ronald [**B**]

CP02   Bare Back Rider – Birdie [**B**]

CP03   Elephant Trainer – Fry Guy [**B**]

CP04   Playing Calliope – Grimace [**B**]

Four UK boxes were issued

CP05   Circus Caravan [**C**]

CP06   Circus Ring [**C**]

CP07   Circus Entrance [**C**]

CP08   Circus Train [**C**]

One USA bag was issued (not shown)

CP09   Circus [**A**]

64

Connectibles

USA

August 29 – September 5, 1991

CB01

CB02   CB03   CB04

These premiums are quite difficult to obtain because they were used as a clean-up after the Barbie and Hot Wheels promotion and most stores received only one or two premiums. Each toy is made from a hard plastic and the vehicles are identical to the ones used on the Muppet Babies promotion in 1991. Each vehicle joins together to form a train. All premiums are packed in clear polybags with card inserts. There was no special Happy Meal box or bag issued.

© 1990 McDonald's Corp. China. (accessories only)

© 1991 McDonald's Corp. China. (characters only)

Premiums

CB01   Birdie on a Tricycle [C]

CB02   Grimace on a Wagon [C]

CB03   Hamburglar in an Airplane [C]

CB04   Ronald McDonald in a
          Soap-Box Racer [C]

Connect-a-Car

UK

October – November, 1991

CN01

CN02   CN03   CN04

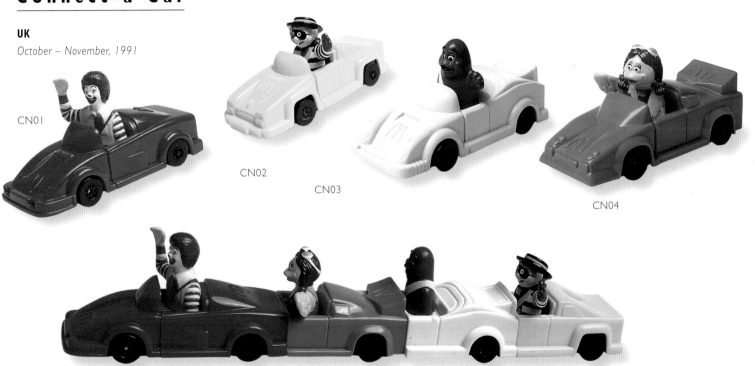

Each premium is a large molded car, which separates into two parts, so the front end of the car can be attached to the back end of another. Premiums marked: © 1991 McDonald's.

This was not a Happy Meal promotion. These cars could be purchased with any food or drink purchase. The promotion was issued over a period of four weeks, with a different car each week. Each premium was polybagged with an insert card.

The promotion did not have any special packaging.

Purchases

CN01   Ronald in Red Roadster [C]

CN02   Hamburglar in Yellow Cabriolet [C]

CN03   Grimace in White Speedster [C]

CN04   Birdie Pink in Sports Coupé [C]

Corgi Racers

UK
January 31 – February 27, 1992

Translite shown

This promotion was run with Barbie for girls. This was the first promotion to have eight premiums, in England. (See Barbie set 1 UK January 1992 page 30.)

This set of cars has recently been found in two stores in 1995, in a boxed set called "Corgi Auto-City … Transporter Set," complete with a red and white transport truck and with two traffic lights, one M6 motorway sign, and a miniature man and four road cones. Woolworths had a slightly different version of the Transporter set, with the cars, lorry, and road cones. Box set marked: © 1993 Mattel Inc. Mattel UK Limited.

Premiums

CO01 Ferrari [**D**]
CO02 Mercedes [**D**]
CO03 BMW [**D**]
CO04 Porsche [**D**]

Two boxes were issued (not shown)

CO05 Race Track 1 Start [**B**]
CO06 Race Track 2 Finish [**B**]

Each of the boxes made part of a race track. Each premium was a die-cast car. Corgi. Made in China.

CO01   CO02   CO03   CO04

Crazy Vehicles

USA
August 29 – September 5, 1991

CV01   CV02   CV03   CV04

Each premium is a large hard molded plastic vehicle which can split into three pieces and connect in different ways. Premiums marked: © 1990 McDonald's Corp. China.

This was a regional promotion that was released as a clean-up after the Barbie and Hot Wheels promotion in 1991. Stores received only one or two of the premiums.

There was no special packaging to the promotion. *Crazy Vehicles* ran in Venezuela in August 1991, Panama in November 1991, New Zealand in February 1992, Japan in March 1993, and Puerto Rico in May 1993.

Premiums

CV01 Birdie in Pink Airplane [**C**]
CV02 Grimace in Green Car [**C**]
CV03 Hamburglar in Yellow Train [**C**]
CV04 Ronald in Red Buggy [**C**]

Darkwing Duck
(Adventures of)

Australia
June – July, 1994

Darkwing Duck, by Walt Disney, is an animated cartoon series made for TV. The main character is a crime-busting duck out to rid the world of villains with his sidekick *Launchpad* and his daughter *Gosling*. Darkwing Duck has a saying, "Let's get dangerous!" or "a major villain," in this case *Megavolt*.

These premiums are made from a hard plastic with no moving parts. The packets are clear plastic polybags marked with: "M" logo. © 1994. McDonald's Australia Ltd. Contents made in China by Creata Promotion. Safety tested age three and over, not for children under three etc. One box issued, not themed but just a generic box. The premiums marked: 94 McDonald's, © Disney China.

DW07

DW06

DW08

DW09

Premiums
DW06 Darkwing [**A**]
DW07 Gosling [**A**]
DW08 Launchpad [**A**]
DW09 Megavolt [**A**]

Name the Musical Instruments
One box was issued
DW10 Front (Generic)
DW10 Back

Darkwing Duck

New Zealand
June – July 24, 1994

These premiums are made from a hard plastic. All the premiums have a *Darkwing Duck* character concealed inside. The character appears when the premium is opened. Launchpad and Gosling's vehicles' seats flip over to show the characters, and the satchel, with books sticking out from the top, has Honker inside.

Premiums marked: © Disney China.

Premiums
DW01 Darkwing in Thunderquack [**A**]
DW02 Launchpad in Motorcycle [**A**]
DW03 Gosling in Sidecar [**A**]
DW04 Honker in Satchel [**A**]

One box was issued
DW05 (not shown)

DW01

DW02

DW03

DW04

Dink The Little Dinosaur

USA

September 14 – October 11, 1990

DD01

DD02

DD03

DD04

DD05

DD06

This was a regional promotion in the United States, and was Test Marketed in Oklahoma and Texas in September – October 1990. These characters originated from a cartoon serial shown on Saturday morning, on American TV. Each character is made from a soft hollow rubber, and measures between 1½ to 4 inches in height. Each premium came in polybags, with a cardboard backdrop (Diorama) which had useful information about the dinosaur on the back. One box was issued for all six dinosaurs. Premiums marked: © 1989 Ruby – Spears, Inc. China.

Premiums

DD01   Crusty the Giant Sea Turtle   [**B**]

DD02   Amber the Corythosaurus   [**B**]

DD03   Scat the Compsognalthus   [**B**]

DD04   Shyler the Edaphosaurus   [**B**]

DD05   Flapper the Pterodon   [**B**]

DD06   Dink the Apatasaurus   [**B**]

One box was issued

DD07   Dink   [**B**]

DD07 Front

DD07 Back

Dino-motion
Dinosaurs

USA • Canada
February 5 – March 4, 1993

DM03

DM04

DM05

DM06

DM01

DM02

DM07

E ach premium is a press-and-play action figure, which is cable-controlled. Each figure has different moving parts. Premiums marked: © Disney China.

The under-three premium released with this promotion is a hollow rubber figure that does not move. You can fill it with water and squirt! Premiums marked: © Disney China.

This promotion was issued to tie in with the Walt Disney TV program *Dinosaurs* on ABC television. Some markets ran Disney Dinosaur Video sweepstakes at the same time.

Canadian Happy Meal is called "Treat of the Week" and is a Point of Purchase (P.O.P.) sold at 69 cents each.

Premiums
DM01 Baby Sinclair [**A**]
DM02 Charlene Sinclair [**A**]
DM03 Earl Sinclair [**A**]
DM04 Fran Sinclair [**A**]
DM05 Grandma Ethyl [**A**]
DM06 Robbie Sinclair [**A**]
DM07 Baby Sinclair (under-three) [**A**]

Four boxes were issued
DM08 A Tree-Mendous Lunch [**B**]
DM09 Baby Food [**B**]
DM10 Bob Labrea High School [**B**]
DM11 Cave Sweet Cave [**B**]

DM09

DM08

DM11   DM10

Dinosaurier Memory

Germany
April, 1994

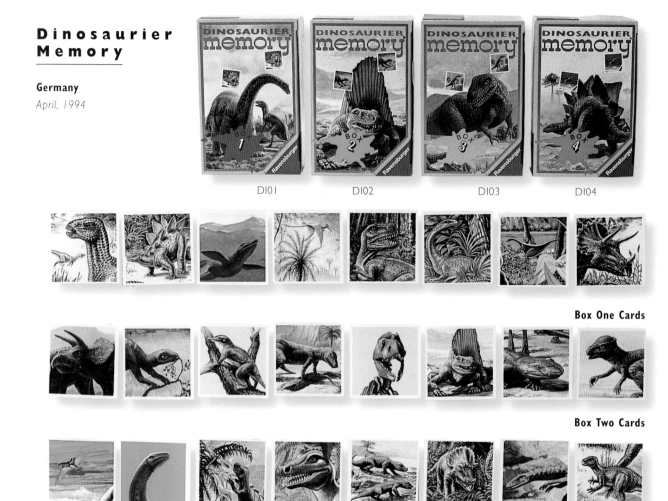

DI01   DI02   DI03   DI04

Box One Cards

Box Two Cards

Box Four Cards
Leaflet Showing
Cards to Box 3

This promotion from Germany consisted of four boxes of cards, one available each week, and in each box were 16 cards (eight cards, two of each), each with a different picture of a dinosaur. Each card measures just over 1½ inches square, with a picture on one side and Ravensburger printed on the other. Each box contains a leaflet, showing useful information on each dinosaur, and information on other dinosaur products available, plus instructions on how to play the game. Each pack is shuffled and placed face down. Each player in turn will turn over two cards. If they match, the player removes the cards. With no match, the cards go back face down onto the table, ready for the next player.

Cards marked: Ravensburger.

Boxes marked: Exclusive for McDonald's Corp. Deutschland. Made by Kids-Promotion, 85567 Grafing.

© 1994 by Ravensburger Spieleverlag.

Instructions

Premiums

DI01	Apatosdaurus	[A]
DI02	Dimetrodon	[A]
DI03	Tyrannosaurus Rex	[A]
DI04	Stegosaurus	[A]
DI05	Junior Tüte Bag (not shown)	

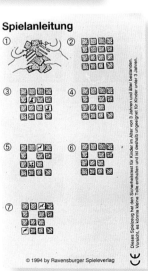

Spielanleitung

© 1994 by Ravensburger Spieleverlag

Disney Fun Rides

New Zealand

December 1993 – January 1994

FR01   FR02   FR03

The New Zealand premiums were used in the British set of Euro Disney August 1992, except with different characters, and in different colors. They all move in the same way. All the premiums came in clear polybags with card inserts. © Disney China. Disney Fun Rides also ran in Japan in August 1993, and in Singapore in October – November 1994. Singapore called their promotion "Mickey's Toon Town."

Premiums

FR01   Mickey Mouse in Red Fire Truck   [**A**]

FR02   Donald Duck in Boat   [**A**]

FR03   Minnie Mouse in Teacup   [**A**]

FR04   Goofy in Train   [**A**]

One box was issued

FR05   (not shown)

FR04

Disney's Goof Troop (Squirters)

Australia

February 3 – March 23, 1995

GT01

GT04

GT03

GT02

Four Walt Disney Goof Troop squirters, each made from soft hollow PVC and standing between 2½ and 3 inches high. Premiums are not dated, but marked: © Disney China (Drain after each use). Squirters came in a clear, sealed polybag with instructions to "squeeze and then release toy slowly when underwater so it fills up with water, remove toy from water and start squirting!" Polybags marked: "M™" logo © 1995 McDonald's Australia Ltd. Contents made in China by Creata Promotion.

Premiums

GT01   Goofy   [**A**]

GT02   Pete   [**A**]

GT03   PJ   [**A**]

GT04   Max   [**A**]

One bag was issued

GT05   Generic

Disney's Goof Troop

Australia

January 9 – February 7, 1994

Walt Disney's cartoon characters from children's TV, the Goof Troops, are one-piece solid plastic figures that stand about 2–2¼ inches tall. Premiums marked: © 1994 Disney Made in China.

Packaging was a clear polybag with black writing: "M™" logo, © 1994 McDonald's Australia Ltd. Contents made in China by Creata Promotion.

Note: These premiums are very similar to the ones issued in cereal packets in the USA, except that the cereal toys are smaller in size (except Pete who is the same size and Goofy who has no skateboard) and they are not dated, unlike the McDonald's ones.

GT06   GT07   GT08   GT09

Premiums

GT06 Goofy **[A]**

GT07 Pete **[A]**

GT08 PJ **[A]**

GT09 Max **[A]**

Disney's Gummi Bears

Australia

May, 1994

GU01   GU02   GU03   GU04

The Gummi Bears from children's TV is an animated cartoon by Walt Disney featuring these lovable little bears who live in the forest and who are surrounded by mystery and magic. With the help of a magic potion called "Gummiberry Juice" that lets them bounce here, there and everywhere, they fight for what's right in everything they do.

Each premium is a one-piece solid plastic figure standing approximately 2 inches tall. Premiums marked: 1994 McDonald's © Disney China.

Packaging is a clear printed polybag with black writing (like Goof Troop Aust 1995): "M™" logo © 1994 McDonald's Australia Ltd. Contents made in China by Creata Promotion.

Note: These premiums are the same as those issued in cereal packets in the USA, except that the cereal toys are marked with: "Kellogg Co. 1991."

Premiums

GU01 Cubbi **[A]**

GU02 Tummi **[A]**

GU03 Gruffi **[A]**

GU04 Sunni **[A]**

Disney Insiders
Disneyland Paris

UK

January 19 – February 15, 1996

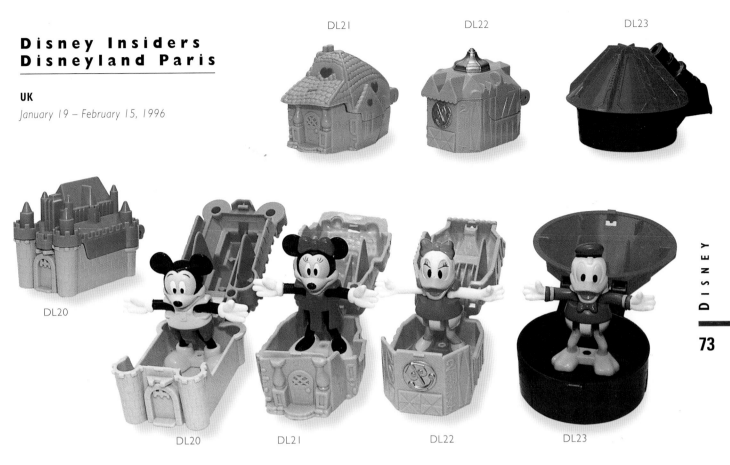

DL21   DL22   DL23

DL20

DL20   DL21   DL22   DL23

This UK promotion is very similar to the Japanese set, "Disneyland Adventures," that ran in August 1995 to celebrate 40 years of Disneyland, except that the UK promotion was based on Disneyland in Paris and featured slight color changes. The first week's premium was *Mickey Mouse in a Castle*. The castle's base is pink; in Japan this was gray. Mickey Mouse in Japan had blue shorts and red shoes, but due to a costume change at Disneyland Paris in 1996, the UK Mickey Mouse does not. Week two was *Minnie Mouse in House* which is identical to the Japanese one, except her house. In Japan, the pillars holding up the porch roof are painted in cerise pink, and the two hearts on the side of the house are not painted pink, unlike the UK version. Week three was *Daisy Duck in Small World* and the only difference to this premium is that in the Japanese version of the house, the symbol on the front was not painted gold. Week four was *Donald Duck in Space Mountain*. Donald Duck's figure is identical to the Japanese one, except that in Japan, Donald was in the Cave of Wonders. All premiums are sealed in a polybag with an insert card, showing all four characters.

Figures marked: © Disney China.

Houses marked: © Disney Disneyland Paris ® China.

DL24   DL25   DL26   DL27

Premiums

DL20   Mickey Mouse in Castle [**A**]

DL21   Minnie Mouse in House [**A**]

DL22   Daisy Duck in Small World [**A**]

DL23   Donald Duck in Space Mountain [**A**]

Four UK boxes were issued

DL24   Main Street [**A**]

DL25   Dumbo Ride [**A**]

DL26   Cup and Saucer Ride [**A**]

DL27   Space Mountain [**A**]

Disneyland Adventures
Disneyland 40th

USA

June 1 – June 28, 1995

DL03

DL04

DL01

DL02

DL05

DL06

DL07

DL08

DL09

DL10

This promotion was released to celebrate 40 years of Disneyland in California and each premium is a viewer with pictures of each of the main events in Disneyland. Premiums are made from a hard plastic and all run on wheels. They came in numbered, printed polybags. The under-three is Winnie the Pooh with green and yellow stripes around the edge of the packet. It is the same as the main premium, except that the under-three is not a viewer, it is a plastic train with moving wheels.

Premium one: Brer Bear/Splash Mountain, Aladdin and Jasmine at Aladdin's Oasis, Simba in the Lion King Celebration, Mickey Mouse/Space Mountain, Roger Rabbit in Mickey's Toontown, Winnie the Pooh on Big Thunder Mountain Railroad, Peter Pan in Fantasmic! and finally King Louie on the Jungle Cruise. Each premium is marked with Disneyland 40th, plus the name of the ride. © Disney China/Chine. Roger Rabbit marked: © Disney – Amblin China/Chine.

A variation has been found on Winnie the Pooh, in the New York area. The premium has a black cabin to the train. The green cabin for Winnie the Pooh was found in most other States.

Premiums

DL01 Brer Bear [**A**]
DL02 Aladdin [**A**]
DL03 Lion King [**A**]
DL04 Mickey Mouse [**A**]
DL05 Roger Rabbit [**A**]
DL06 Winnie the Pooh (green) [**A**]
DL07 Peter Pan [**A**]
DL08 King Louie [**A**]
DL09 Winnie the Pooh (black) [**B**]
DL10 Winnie the Pooh (under-three) [**B**]

Four boxes were issued

DL11 Splash Mountain – Fantasmic [**B**]
DL12 Aladdin Oasis – Jungle Cruise [**B**]
DL13 Lion King – Mickey's ToonTown [**B**]
DL14 Space Mountain – Big Thunder [**B**]

DL11

DL12

DL13

DL14

Disneyland Adventures 40 Years of Disneyland

Japan
August, 1995

This is one of our favorite sets from Japan, celebrating 40 years of Disneyland. Four very sturdily made buildings from Disneyland and four main Disney characters. Each of the four figures may contain small parts, because each premium has spring-loaded arms and legs so they are not suitable for under-threes. The packaging is clear polybags with an insert card with the main character/building on the front, written in Japanese. Each figure comes in its own sealed clear polybag within the main packaging, and all the premiums have another smaller insert card inside (written in Japanese). This is a warning about the small parts and their unsuitability for very young children. The figures stand approximately 3 inches high and the buildings are approximately 3½ inches long and 2¾ inches high.

All the buildings are hinged at one end, and open up into equal halves. The figures are then placed into allocated slots inside the building. Fold in the arms and bend the character's body forward and then close the lid. There is a catch on the lid; when you press the building just under the catch, the figure will spring out like a jack-in-the-box. On each base of each building is marked: 40 years Adventures Disneyland.

All premiums plus Buildings marked: © Disney China.

Generic bags have been issued from Japan featuring McDonaldland characters. These have taken the place of the white generic bag (see Peanuts Japan 1995 page 188). Because they are generic, you could also obtain any combination of bags from different participating McDonald's restaurants. (also see Trayliner).

DL15

DL16

DL17

DL18

Premiums

DL15 Daisy Duck – The Sultan's Palace [**A**]
DL16 Mickey Mouse – The Magic Kingdom
         Castle [**A**]
DL17 Donald Duck – The Cave of
         Wonders [**A**]
DL18 Minnie Mouse – Mickey's House [**A**]
DL19 Generic bag

New Generic Japanese Bags

Dragonettes

UK

January 29, 1993

DR04

DR01

DR02

DR03

E ach premium is a semi-hard plastic model dragon, holding a different object.

Premiums marked: 1988 © McDonald's. China.

This promotion was tied in with the celebration of the Chinese New Year, when a Chinese-style dish was on promotion each of the four weeks. The promotion was aptly called "Tastes of the Orient."

In some entrances to McDonald's restaurants (UK) you may have seen two full-size cardboard cut-outs of

Chinese characters for a limited number of weeks.

Dragonettes also ran in Germany August 27 – September 20 1992, as a JT (Junior Tüte), no boxes were issued. Europe ran this promotion in 1993. Holland in March 18 – April 28 1993. Israel May 1994. Hong Kong as a self-liquidator in 1988. Japan also issued these premiums with minor variations, i.e. Gigi (DR04) had a yellow wand with a red tip and Richie (DR01) had no double foot peg.

Foyer cardboard cut-out

Dragonettes counter display

DR07

DR06

DR08

DR05

Premiums

DR01 Richie with Ball [**A**]

DR02 Puff with Fire Cracker [**A**]

DR03 Lucky with Fortune Cards [**A**]

DR04 Gigi with Magic Wand [**A**]

Four UK boxes were issued

DR05 Chinese Lantern [**B**]

DR06 Chinese Junk Boat [**B**]

DR07 Street Scene [**B**]

DR08 Pagoda [**B**]

Drive and Fly Classics Speedies

UK
December 15, 1994 – January 15, 1995

Europe
March, 1995

Holland
January 4 – February 7, 1995

E ach premium is a wind-up vehicle. Ronald's Car moves around in circles, and the wheels clasp at periodic intervals. Grimace's plane moves along then flips over. The Green Tram moves around in circles; at the same time, the top moves up and down. Birdie's Three Wheeler moves in the same way as the airplane.

Premiums marked: © 1994 McDonald's Corporation. China.

The Europe promotion was called Classics. Holland's promotion was called Speedies, and they ran it January 4 – February 7 1995. Middle East and North Africa ran it in January 1995.

Premiums

FD01   Ronald in Red Car [**A**]

FD02   Grimace in Purple Plane [**A**]

FD03   Hamburglar in Green Tram [**A**]

FD04   Birdie in Silver Three-Wheeler [**A**]

Four UK boxes were issued

FD05   Park and Road [**A**]

FD06   Hanger and Runway [**A**]

FD07   Tramway [**A**]

FD08   Old Fashion Street [**A**]

FD01

FD02

FD03

FD05   FD07

FD04

FD06   FD08

Duck Tales I

USA
February 5 – March 10, 1988

This promotion featured gadgets or adventure toys from the Walt Disney animated Duck Tales starring Scrooge McDuck. The under-three was the only premium to come polybagged.

Premiums
(premiums and boxes not shown)
DT01 Duck Code Quacker/Whistle
       (orange) [**B**]
DT02 Magnifying Glass
       (green with decal) [**B**]
DT03 Telescope (yellow with either a
       horizontal or vertical decal) [**B**]
DT04 Wrist Watch Decoder
       (blue with decal) [**B**]
DT05 Magic Motion Map (under-three)
       (paper) [**B**]

Four boxes were issued
DT06 City of Gold [**C**]
DT07 Cookie of Fortune [**C**]
DT08 Hula Hoopla! [**C**]
DT09 Westward Dough [**C**]

Duck Tales II

USA
1988

Australia
1988

DT10
DT11
DT12
DT13
DT28
DT29

Each premium is a hard plastic molded vehicle with a *Duck Tale* character. Each premium has moving wheels. *Scrooge McDuck* and *Webbigail* are *two* piece toys, the other two are just a *one* piece toy. The under-three premium is also a one piece toy, made of hard plastic. Premiums marked: © Disney. China.

This regional Happy Meal promotion featured characters from the weekday afternoon TV series called "Duck Tales" produced by Walt Disney.

Distribution: Texas, Michigan, Maryland, and New Jersey.

Note: With the Australia's premium all four characters could be detached from their vehicles, unlike the USA

promotion. Also the under-three *Huey* has silver paint on underside of skates, the American set did not. Box unknown. Packaging much like Duck Tales Australia 1996.

Duck Tails II ran in Germany on March 16 – April 16 1990 as a self-liquidator, and Belgium, Denmark, Finland, France, Italy, Holland, Norway, Sweden, and Switzerland on August 10, 1990. Packaging unknown.

Premiums (USA)
DT10 Scrooge McDuck in Red Car [**B**]
DT11 Webbigail on Blue Tricycle [**B**]
DT12 Launchpad in Orange Airplane [**B**]
DT13 Huey, Dewey, and Louie
       on Surf Ski [**B**]
DT14 Huey Skating (under-three) (not shown)

One USA box was issued (not shown)
DT15 Duck Tales press-outs [**A**]

Australian Premiums
DT26 Scrooge [**C**]
DT27 Webbigail [**C**]
DT28 Launchpad [**C**]
DT29 Huey, Dewey, and Louie on
       Surf Ski [**C**]
DT30 Huey (under-three) [**B**]

Duck Tales II

Australia

March – April, 1993

DT22

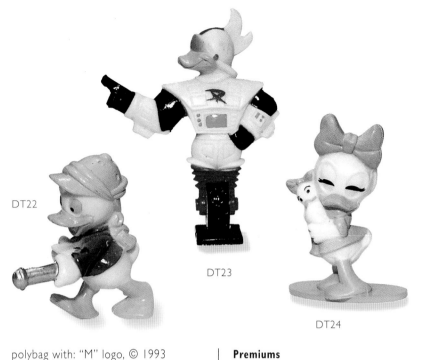

DT23

DT21

DT24

D isney's Duck Tales II has four more solid plastic figures, with *Gizmo Duck* standing the tallest at 2¾ inches high and *Nephew Louie* being the shortest at approximately 2 inches tall. *Scrooge McDuck* is carrying a bag of money. Louie has a backpack and torch. *Gizmo Duck* is on a unicycle and *Webbigail* is carrying a doll.

All premiums came in a printed polybag with: "M" logo, © 1993 McDonald's Australia Ltd. Contents made in China for Creata Promotion. The premiums have no McDonald's markings on them, only © Disney (not dated) markings.

Note: These same figures have been released before, in American cereal packets with the identification "© Disney Kellogg Co. 1991 China."

Premiums

DT21   Scrooge McDuck   [**A**]
DT22   Louie   [**A**]
DT23   Gizmo Duck   [**A**]
DT24   Webbigail   [**A**]

One box was issued

DT25   (not shown)

Duck Tales

Australia

December 15, 1995 – January 11, 1996

T his is the promotion that ran over the Christmas period in Australia in 1996 and featured some of the Duck Tales characters, with a bad guy, and one of the Beagle brothers. Each premium is made from solid plastic and stands approximately 2½ inches high. Each premium has a plastic ring attached that was used as a key ring. All premiums marked with: © Disney. All the toys came in a clear sealed polybag with black print and marked with: "M™" logo, © 1995 McDonald's Australia Ltd. Made in China by Creata Promotion.

DT16   DT17   DT18   DT19

Premiums

DT16   Scrooge McDuck   [**A**]
DT17   Webbigail   [**A**]
DT18   Louie   [**A**]
DT19   Beagle Boy   [**A**]

One box was issued

DT20   (not shown)

Packaging

Earth Days

USA • Canada
April 8 – May 5, 1994

ED02

ED03

ED06

ED04

ED01

This national promotion was released in association with the National Audubon Society, with an address to write to for more information on how to enjoy nature. The *Binoculars* and the *Tool Carrier with Shovel* came in printed polybags and the *Bird Feeder* and *Globe Terrarium* came in a clear polybag with insert cards. The *Binoculars* can be closed to form Earth and have a warning: "Do Not Look Into The Sun." It is made from a hard plastic. The *Bird Feeder* comes in three pieces and is made from a semi-hard plastic. The *Globe Terrarium* is a two-piece premium; when put together, it forms Earth with the different countries. It is made from a semi-hard plastic and included with the *Terrarium* is a small polybag of *Grow Your Own Meadow Mix* (USA origin

seeds and dirt) with a warning: "contains small parts, not for children under three," plus instructions on how to plant your Meadow Mix Terrarium. The *Tool Carrier* is a three-piece premium made from a semi-soft plastic. The *Shovel* and yellow handle are in a printed polybag of their own. On each premium packing is some information from the National Audubon Society on how to make the best use of your nature set. *Binoculars* and *Shovel* premiums marked: © 1993 McDonald's Corp. China. The *Tool Carrier*, *Bird Feeder*, and *Terrarium* marked: © 1993 McDonald's Corp. Made in USA.

Premiums

ED01   Binoculars   [**A**]

ED02   Bird Feeder   [**A**]

ED03   Terrarium   [**A**]

ED04   Tool Carrier   [**A**]

ED05   Tool Carrier (under-three)
       (not shown)   [**A**]

One bag was issued

ED06   Earth Days   [**A**]

Euro Disney

UK

August 21, 1992

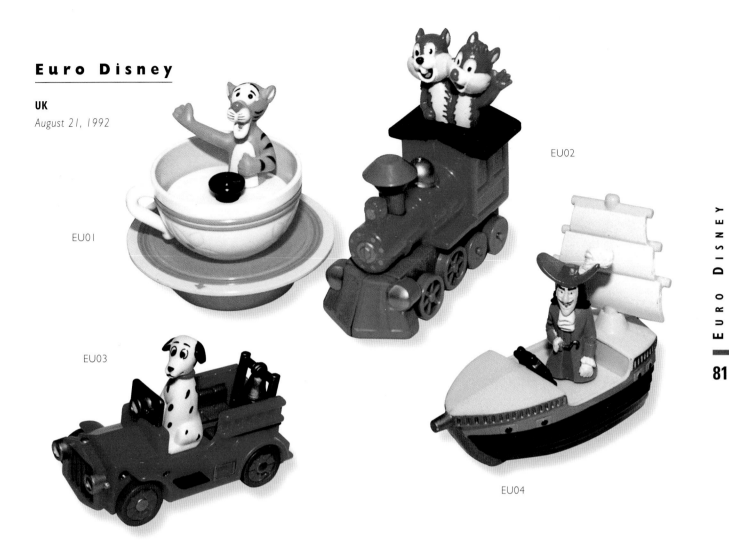

EU01

EU02

EU03

EU04

Each premium is a hard plastic molded action toy, containing a Disney character. Each toy has its own moving parts. The *Dalmatians* heads move, *Captain Hook* wobbles in the boat, *Tigger* turns around in the teacup, and finally *Chip 'N' Dale* bobs up and down in the train. © Disney Made in China.

This promotion ran for six weeks and was issued in conjunction with the opening of the Euro Disney Theme

Park near Paris on April 12, 1992.

These premiums were also used in New Zealand, but were called "*Disney Fun Rides*," December – January 1994, but they had different characters, and the colors varied.

Euro Disney also ran in Switzerland, Portugal, Sweden, Spain, Holland, Norway, Italy, Belgium, Denmark, Finland, France, Scotland, and Wales August 13 – September 23.

Premiums

EU01 Tigger in Teacup [**B**]
EU02 Chip 'N' Dale in Train [**B**]
EU03 Dalmatian in Fire Truck [**B**]
EU04 Captain Hook in Boat [**B**]

Four boxes were issued

EU05 Tigger (box not shown) [**C**]
EU06 Chip 'N' Dale [**C**]
EU07 Dalmatian (Pongo) [**C**]
EU08 Captain Hook [**C**]

EU06

EU07

EU08

Search and Win
(Euro Disney)

Early in 1992 a search-and-win competition was run at each of the participating McDonald's restaurants, with a family vacation to Euro Disney to be won. This competition was run through the aid of four scratch cards. A card was given each time you visited a McDonald's restaurant during this promotion. No purchase was necessary. France also issued these cards together with a china mug.

Translite shown

EU09

EU12

EU11

Premiums

EU09   Adventure Land – red card [**B**]

EU10   Fantasy Land – blue card
        (not shown) [**B**]

EU11   Frontier Land – green card [**B**]

EU12   Discovery Land – mauve card [**B**]

Space Mountain Prize Draw

This competition from McDonald's was to celebrate the opening of Space Mountain in Disneyland Paris, and allowed 100 families to enjoy a ride inspired by Jules Verne's novel *From the Earth to the Moon*, written over a hundred years before. This high-tech flight literally fires you from a 36-meter-long cannon, on the side of Space Mountain, through meteor showers. You lose the feeling of gravity while spinning.

Complete a prize draw entry form by June 15, 1995. You must be over the age of 16. No food purchase was necessary. An Extra Value Méal, (EVM) was on offer at the same time. Hand in the coupon found on the trayliners and receive large fries and large soft drink for the price of medium fries and soft drink.

Translite

Trayliner

Fast Macs
(McDonaldland Cars)

USA
Test 1994

UK
1994

USA • Canada
Re-Released 1985

FA01

FA02

FA03

FA04

FA06

FA07

This promotion was first released in the UK in 1984, but it was limited to certain areas. It was released again in 1985 throughout the UK. This was a self-liquidator. Each car has a pull-back action for propulsion. They are made of a hard plastic and measure about 2 inches in length. Each premium is marked with the character's name, and McDonald's Corp. © 1984 Made in Hong Kong. The cars came packaged in clear plastic bags. Printed on the bags: "safety tested for children three years and older, made in Hong Kong."

In 1984 in the USA, the above UK set was issued as a test in certain states. The cars came in blister packs and could be purchased for 59 cents each. They were redesigned for national distribution in 1985.

The USA and Canadian sets were released in 1985. They were variations on the British set. Two variations are shown below. *Ronald's Yellow Runabout* had no windshield, but the *Roadster* was the same as the UK version. The cars came packaged on blister cards. In Canada, these premiums could be purchased for 69 cents each with any purchase of food. The toys were made in Hong Kong or Thailand.

FA06

FA02

Purchases UK 1984

FA01   Ronald in Yellow Jeep [**E**]
FA02   Officer Big Mac in Police Car [**C**]
FA03   Mayor McCheese in Pink
　　　 Sun Cruiser [**E**]
FA04   Hamburglar in Red Sports Car [**C**]

Purchases USA and Canada 1985

FA05   Ronald in Yellow Runabout
　　　 (not shown) [**C**]
FA06   Officer Big Mac in Squad Car [**C**]
FA07   Birdie in Pink Sun Cruiser [**C**]
FA08   Hamburglar in Red Roadster [**C**]

Field Trip

USA

September 10 – October 7, 1993

FT01

FT02

FT03

FT04

FT06

A national promotion aimed at the young naturalist. Each premium is a two-piece item, and is made from hard plastic, except the *Explorer Bag*, which is a one-piece item that is made of vinyl. All premiums came in a printed polybag. The *Nature Viewer* stands 2½ inches high and has a red magnifier for a lid. The red lid carries a warning: "Do not look into the sun." Remove the red magnifier lid, and then place a specimen into the clear beaker, replace the red lid, and you are ready for viewing. There is an insert card with instructions, inside the packaging. Also carries a warning: "Do not keep little critters in the Nature Viewer for too long." The red magnifier lid is in its own, sealed polybag, within packaging. The *Leaf Printer* is a 4½ inch square, hard plastic frame with a hinged, orange lid, and one red crayon. Lift the orange lid, place a flat object, i.e. a leaf, on the green base and cover with a piece of paper. Close the lid, then rub over the top of the paper with the red crayon, and watch the outline of the object appear. The instructions are molded into the plastic on the reverse side of the *Leaf Printer*. The *Kaleidoscope* stands about 4½ inches high, and comes with a white removable cap. The instructions are on an insert card within the packaging. Remove the white cap, place a specimen, i.e. flower, or autumn leaf, into the clear container, replace the white lid, and view your specimen through the yellow eye piece. Turn the *Kaleidoscope* around to see the colors mix and change. The final premium is a 9½-inch-tall vinyl *Explorer Bag*, so you can carry all the goodies you have found. All premiums marked: © 1992 McDonald's Corporation. China. Printed polybags marked: © 1993 etc.

The *Nature Viewer* was also used as the under-three, but in a zebra striped packaging.

Premiums

FT01 Nature Viewer [**A**]
FT02 Leaf Printer [**A**]
FT03 Kaleidoscope [**A**]
FT04 Explorer Bag [**A**]
FT05 Nature Viewer (under-three)
      (not shown) [**A**]

One bag was issued

FT06 Field Trip [**A**]

The Flintstones

USA • Canada

June 3 – July 7, 1994

FL09

FL11

FL10

FL12

FL13

FL14

Each premium came in two parts. One is a hard, hollow plastic building, which has a back opening to the house, the second part is a vehicle. Each premium took the form of a building and vehicle from the movie. All the vehicles are push-along figures, with the characters seated in them.

The under-three premium is a hollow rubber figure that rocks.

All these premiums coincided with the release of the Steven Spielberg movie The Flintstones, taken from the early cartoon TV series, but featuring actors instead.

© UCS and Amblin. China.

Canadian premiums were the same, but with dual language on the packaging and on the stickers (French and English).

Premiums

FL09 Barney and Fossil Fill-up [A]

FL10 Betty, Bamm-Bamm, and
      RocDonald's [A]

FL11 Fred and Bedrock Bowl-o-rama [A]

FL12 Pebbles, Dino, and Toy-saurus [A]

FL13 Wilma and Flintstone's House [A]

FL14 Rocking Dino (under-three) [A]

One bag was issued

FL15 RocDonald's Drive-Thru [A]

FL15

The Flintstones

UK
July 15, 1994

Belgium • France • Germany
August, 1994

FL01

FL02

FL03

FL04

FL05   FL06

FL07   FL08

Each premium is a hard plastic model from the Steven Spielberg film *The Flintstones*.

RocDonald's has doors on each side. *Fred in Bronto-crane*: when Fred's head is pushed down the Bronto's head and tail move up and down. The other two are push-along action vehicles which have moving parts. *RocDonald's* and the *Bedrock Bus* each has a sheet of stickers for sticking to the models.

© U.C.S. and Amblin. TM H-B, Inc. China. The boxes all contained scenes from the film.

This promotion tied in with the release of the film at theaters. German premiums were issued with different insert cards.

Premiums		Four boxes were issued	
FL01	RocDonald's [A]	FL05	Town Bedrock [A]
FL02	Fred In Bronto-crane [A]	FL06	Quarry and Bowl-o-rama [A]
FL03	Wilma and Dino in Car [A]	FL07	Fred's House [A]
FL04	Bedrock Bus [A]	FL08	Barney's House [A]

Flintstones Gadgets

Australia
December 9, 1994

FL36

FL38

FL37

FL39

E ach premium is made from a hard plastic, except the *Mastodon* which is made from a hollow soft rubber. These premiums are from the Steven Spielberg film *The Flintstones* and feature gadgets used around the house. All are one-piece toys. *Mastodon* is a water squirter: place in a bowl of water, squeeze toy, then slowly release to draw water in through his trunk. Then remove the toy from the bowl and squeeze. *Dictabird* has a small button on its back. When pushed, his beak moves up and down. *Pigasaurus* is the waste-disposal unit under the sink. His head goes back to revel an empty stomach, and finally the *Lobster* lawn mower. When pushed along, his claws move in and out. One box was issued, an *Activity Box*. The premiums came in a printed polybag marked: © 1994 McDonald's Australia Ltd. Made in China by Creata Promotion.

Premiums marked: © U.C.S. and Amblin. TM H-B, Inc McDonald's made in China.

Four glass mugs were available, designed in the traditional Flintstone fashion. A glass cost 99 cents with any food purchase.

© 1993 McDonald's Corp. © U.C.S. and Amblin ™ H-B Inc.

All McDonald's outlets in North America were re-named RocDonald's for the duration of the Flintstones promotion. Special clothing was issued to staff: RocDonald's T-shirts, hats, and managers' sweat shirts.

Premiums

FL36   Mastodon [**A**]
FL37   Dictabird [**A**]
FL38   Pigasaurus [**A**]
FL39   Lobster [**A**]

One box was issued (not shown)

FL40   Activity Box [**A**]

Purchases

FL16   Four different fries cartons were issued, with a 7-inch paper cup for soft drinks.
FL17   Tree Mendous Mug Made in France [**C**]
FL18   Pre-Dawn Mug Made in USA [**C**]
FL19   Rocky Road Mug Made in USA [**C**]
FL20   Mammoth Mug Made in France [**C**]
FL21   Flintstone Summer 1994 AD T-Shirt [**C**]
FL22   Flintstone Pens (not shown) [**A**]

FL21

FL17   FL18   FL19   FL20

Flintstones Kids

USA
1988

FL23

FL24

FL25

FL26

FL27

With this promotion the Flintstones go back in time, to when they were kids. Once again this is an animated cartoon series for TV made by Hanna-Barbera Productions Inc. The regional promotion sold mainly in parts of Florida and in New England during 1988. Each premium is in two parts, the character and the vehicle. The characters are made from a semi-hard rubber and have no moving parts. The vehicles can be pushed along on wheels. They are approximately 3½ to 4 inches long and are made from a hard plastic. *Barney* sits in a Mastodon mobile, *Betty* has a Pterydactil mobile, *Fred* comes with a Green Gator mobile and finally *Wilma* has her Dragon mobile. One under-three was issued, *Dino*, made from solid rubber and

standing about 3 inches high. All premiums came in clear polybags with insert cards except the under-three premium, *Dino*, which came in a clear polybag with no insert card but was safety tested for children of all ages. "Recommended for children age one and over" was printed on the pack. The under-three has no markings on the packaging or the premium to say it is from McDonald's. All characters, vehicles and under-threes marked with: © 1988 H-B Prod. Inc China. Insert cards marked: © 1988 Hanna-Barbera Productions, Inc. and © 1988 McDonald's Corporation.

Flintstones Kids also ran in Guatemala (with bag), Venezuela, and Costa Rica in March 1991.

Premiums

FL23 Barney [**B**]
FL24 Betty [**B**]
FL25 Fred [**B**]
FL26 Wilma [**B**]

One under-three was issued

FL27 Dino [**C**]

One box was issued (not shown)

FL28 Drive in Country [**B**]

The Flintstones Stationery Series

Australia

September, 1994

FL29

FL30

FL32

FL31

T his promotion was a purchase for 99 cents each, and was *not* a Happy Meal.

Once again this promotion was released to coincide with the new Steven Spielberg film *The Flintstones*. All premiums are made from a hard plastic and are about 3 to 3½ inches long and between 1½ to 3½ inches high. The characters are fixed to the vehicles. The vehicles all have wheels and can be pushed along. As the title name suggests, these premiums are items that can be used in the office. *Fred's Flintmobile Eraser Holder* comes in three pieces: car, roof canopy, and eraser in the shape of a giant T-bone steak that sits on the top of the roof.

Bamm-Bamm's Bedrock Memo Holder is a two-piece premium. *Bamm-Bamm* is on a scooter, with Bedrock News printed on the side. He also comes with a yellow Memo pad (Printed Post-It ® Notes, produced by 3M Australia Ply Ltd.) with a large pink McDonald's "M" on it. *Pebbles Trike Embosser* is a one-piece premium. The bike saddle is hinged; pushing Pebbles forward will reveal a McDonald's "M". If you place a sheet of paper under the saddle and press down it will mark the paper with an "M." *Barney's Rubblemobile* is a one-piece premium and is used as a pencil sharpener. All premiums came in clear polybags with insert cards. No special Happy Meal box was issued except

four fries cartons, which are different from the ones used in America in June 1994. They are made a lot smaller in size than the American issue and the top edges of the cartons are cut differently. Australian cartons are printed Australia © 1993. The approximate size is 5½ inches wide and 6¾ inches high when flat.

American cartons printed in United States of America © 1993. Approximate size 5¾ inches wide and 7¾ inches high when flat.

Premiums marked: © U.C.S. and Amblin. TM H-B, Inc McDonald's made in China.

Purchases

FL29   Fred's Flintmobile [**A**]

FL30   Bamm-Bamm [**A**]

FL31   Pebbles Trike [**A**]

FL32   Barney's Rubblemobile [**A**]

FL33   Four fries cartons were issued. [**A**]

FL33

Floppy Puppets
(Gliedertiere)

Germany

December, 1993

From Germany, sold as a Junior Tüte (Happy Meal). No boxes were issued, just one Junior Tüte bag. Each animal is made from a hard plastic, with jointed limbs, which are held together by an elastic cord going through the center of each limb. The animals are standing on spring-loaded platforms. When the platform is pressed, this will make the head and limbs bend and dance. Each premium measures between 4 and 4½ inches tall. The premiums marked: © McDonald's Corp. Made by Kids Promotion 8018 Grafing.

FP02

FP03

FP01

FP04

Premiums

FP01   Elephant [**A**]
FP02   Dog [**A**]
FP03   Donkey [**A**]
FP04   Lion [**A**]

Food
Fun-damentals

USA

March 5 – April 1, 1993

Each premium is a hard plastic food or drink that converts into a character. All premiums came with a mini note pad and information on nutrition for parents and children. The under-three premium was a hollow rubber one-piece figure: © McDonald's Corp. China. This promotion was issued in cooperation with The American Dietetic Association. Ran in Singapore April 26 – May 26 1993, Mexico April 1994, Puerto Rico August 1994, Venezuela October 1994, Argentina November 1994.

FF01

FF02

FF03

FF04

FF05

FF06

Premiums

FF01   Milly Milk [**A**]
FF02   Otis Sandwich [**A**]
FF03   Ruby Apple [**A**]
FF04   Slugger Steak [**A**]
FF05   Dunkin Ear of Corn (under-three) [**A**]

One bag was issued

FF06   Rhyme Hungry [**A**]

Fraggle Rock 2

USA • Canada

March 11 – April 7, 1988

FG01

FG02

FG03

FG04

FG05

FG06

Each premium is a hard plastic vehicle, with characters seated inside. Each vehicle is shaped and colored as a vegetable. The under-three premiums is made of a semi-hard plastic. © Henson Associates Inc. 1988 China.

This promotion was taken from the Jim Henson's Saturday morning cartoon series *Fraggle Rock* shown on NBC television. Back in 1987, a test promotion was issued in the West Virginia areas. The premiums in this promotion were different. Two of the premiums did look the same, but the wheels were smaller. The other two premiums are a Bulldozer and a Forklift Truck. With this set, only one box was issued. Canadian premiums are the same, but in different packaging which carried the maple leaf under the "M."

Premiums

FG01 Gobo in his Carrot **[A]**

FG02 Red in her Radish **[A]**

FG03 Mokey in her Eggplant **[A]**

FG04 Wembly and Boober in a Pickle **[A]**

FG05 Gogo holding Carrot
(under-three) **[B]**

FG06 Red holding Radish (under-three) **[B]**

Four boxes were issued (not shown)

FG07 Radish Tops **[B]**

FG08 Party Picks **[B]**

FG09 Radishes in Cave **[B]**

FG10 Swimming Hole Blues **[B]**

From The Heart

USA

February 1 – 14, 1988

This Valentine promotion was regional in the southern states. Each premium consists of six scratch-and-sniff cards. *Ronald Frosting Cake* has the scent of chocolate and *Ronald* with the *Hot Chocolate* has the smell of cinnamon. Both Valentine premiums feature McDonaldland characters and each card measures about 3 x 4 inches in size (six cards laid flat, measure 18 inches long). Perforations allow the cards to be detached from each other. Cards came in polybags. The box is in the shape of a letter box. All six cards marked: © 1989 McDonald's Corporation Printed in the United States of America.

Premiums

FH01 Ronald Frosting Cake (not shown) **[B]**

FH02 Ronald Hot Chocolate (not shown)
[B]

One box was issued

FH03 Play Matchmaker **[B]**

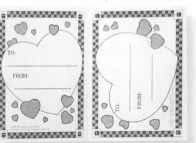

Back of each card

Fry Benders

USA

September 7 – October 4, 1990

FB02

FB01

FB04

FB03

This set first appeared as a regional promotion in Michigan then in 1991 it was re-issued as a clean-up in many areas. The premiums came in three parts and were made to look like genuine French fries.

All parts are interchangeable with each other. The main body is about 4 inches long when laid straight and is made from a soft yellow rubber, which you can bend into many positions. The other two accessories (hands and feet) are made from a hard plastic. *Freestyle* has the dark blue, yellow, and silver roller skates and a green "M" on back of her T-shirt. *Froggy* is the scuba diver with a yellow "M" on his tanks. *Grand Slam* plays baseball and has a yellow "M" on his cap. *Roadie* is the cyclist with a red "M" on his helmet and wheels that turn. One under-three premium, *Tunes*, on a red skateboard with yellow wheels, green helmet, and gloves, has a red boom box under his arm. He is a one-piece figure. The premiums are polybagged with insert cards. Main Fry Benders body-marked with: © 1989 McDonald's China.

Fry Benders also ran in Panama in January 1991, Japan in October 1991, Malaysia in October – November 1991, Singapore in May 1992, and Costa Rica in January 1993.

Premiums

FB01	Freestyle	[**B**]
FB02	Froggy	[**B**]
FB03	Grand Slam	[**B**]
FB04	Roadie	[**B**]
FB05	Tunes (under-three)	[**C**]

One box was issued (not shown)

FB06	Fry Bender-Cut-Outs	[**B**]

FB05

Funky Neon Cup

UK
1992

FN01

FN02

FN03

FN04

FN05

FN06

FN07

FN08

As the translite states, "Free Funky Neon Cup, when you buy any seriously large soft drink. 24oz size served with free neon cup at same price as 22oz."

The translite shows only four Funky Neon Cups, but there were eight different logos, one for each cup, and each of the eight cups came in four colors: yellow, orange, green, and pink. Now this made a grand total of 32 cups to collect. Each cup started with the words "I Like It" then the logo. All the cups are made from a PVC plastic and stand approximately 6½ inches tall with the McDonald's "M™" logo on the back of each cup. Cups marked on base: The Collectibles ® Made in Canada.

Translite shown

Purchases

FN01   It's Bad   [**A**]
FN02   It's Wet   [**A**]
FN03   Go Go Go   [**A**]
FN04   It's Choice   [**A**]
FN05   It's Boss   [**A**]
FN06   Chill Out   [**A**]
FN07   It's Cool   [**A**]
FN08   It's Xcellent   [**A**]

Funny Fry Friends

USA

December 22 – January 18, 1990

Holland

July 15 – August 25, 1991

FU01

FU02

FU03

FU04

FU05

FU06

FU07

FU08

Each premium is a three-piece semi-hard rubber figure with interchangeable feet and headgear that could be put together to make different characters, or friends.

Premiums marked: © 1992 McDonald's Corp. China.

Four of these premiums were released back in 1989 as a test run. These premiums were: *Gadzooks, Matey, Tracker* and *Zzz's.*

Funny Fry Friends also ran in German in January 1993 as a JT (Junior Tüte) and was called "Pommesfritzchen". It had four premiums only: *Gadzooks, Too Tall, Zzz's Fry Guy,* and *Rollin' Rocker* (same as USA), no boxes were issued.

The Guatemala premiums were: *Explorer (Tracker), Pirate (Matey), Vagabundo (Rollin' Rocker),* and *Dormilon (Zzz's)* and this promotion ran in 1990.

Hong Kong ran this promotion as a self-liquidator in January 1990. New Zealand, Malaysia, and Mexico ran it on January 2, 1990.

Premiums

FU01 Hoops, Basketball [**B**]

FU02 Rollin' Rocker [**B**]

FU03 Gadzooks, Groucho Character [**B**]

FU04 Matey, Pirate [**B**]

FU05 Tracker, Explorer [**B**]

FU06 Zzz's, Sleepy Fry Guy [**B**]

FU07 Too Tall, Clown on Stilts [**B**]

FU08 Sweet Cuddles, Baby Fry Girl [**B**]

FU09 Little Darling, Cowgirl (under-three) [**B**]

FU10 Lil' Chief, Indian (under-three) [**B**]

Four boxes were issued (not shown)

FU11 Cool Days at School [**C**]

FU12 City Sights [**C**]

FU13 Ski Holiday [**C**]

FU14 Snowy Day Play [**C**]

Funny Fry Friends

UK

February 15 – March 14, 1991

(UK Translite)

FU15

A ll four of these premiums were the same as the American toys.

This promotion ran in Belgium, Denmark, Finland, France, Italy, Norway, Spain, Sweden, and Switzerland in June 1991 (they were the same as the American toys).

FU16

FU17

Premiums

FU15   Too Tall Clown on Stilts [**B**]

FU16   Rollin' Rocker [**B**]

FU17   Hoops Basketball Player [**C**]

FU18   Sweet Cuddles Baby Fry Girl [**B**]

Four boxes were issued

FU19   Ski Holiday [**C**]

FU20   City Sights [**C**]

FU21   Cool Day at School [**C**]

FU22   Snowy Day at Play [**C**]

   (boxes not shown)

FU18

Funny Fry Friends

Australia
1992

FU23

FU24

FU26

FU25

FU27 under-three

Once again these *Funny Fry Friends* from Australia are a three-piece premium, (except the under-three, which is a two-piece premium). Each has interchangeable hats, feet and bodies and all are made from a semi-soft rubber. There is a variation in all the Australian premiums unlike the American and UK promotions. The main variation is that the Australian premiums are a lot smaller in size and measure between 3¾ and 2¾ inches high. Each premium has an "M" printed on the hats, except *Roll 'N' Rocker*. She has an "M" on her headphones. The American and UK premiums stand between 2¼ and 4 inches high.

This photograph gives an indication of the size differences between the Australian and American premiums.

Other variations: Australian *Tracker*: the snake's tail is different compared to the USA *Tracker* and the Australian *Tracker's* body is of a darker blue, like the one used for the *Gadzooks* (FU03), USA premium.

Australian *Snoozy*: the teddy bear on the hat and the rabbit on the slippers are also different from the USA premium (compare pictures).

Each premium was in a clear polybag with an insert card. Each insert card was numbered from one to four with instructions on the reverse. "Under Age 3 Toy" was printed on the under-three insert card and was therefore recommended for children age one and over. Premiums marked: © 1992 McDonald's Australia Ltd. China.

Premiums

FU23	Tracker	[**A**]
FU24	Roll 'N' Rocker	[**A**]
FU25	Too Tall	[**A**]
FU26	Snoozy	[**A**]
FU27	Hop-a-Long (under-three)	[**A**]
FU28	Generic box (not shown)	

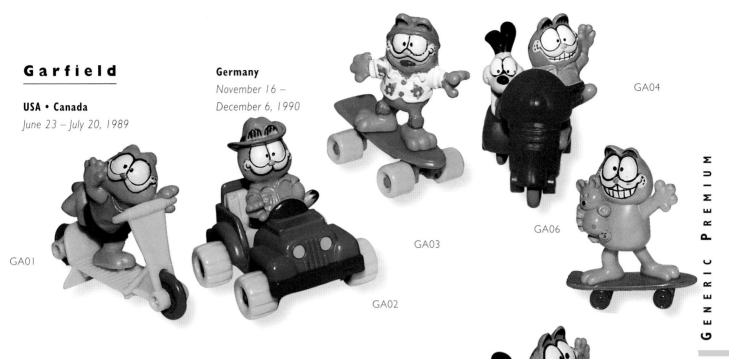

Garfield

USA • Canada

June 23 – July 20, 1989

Germany

*November 16 –
December 6, 1990*

GA04

GA03

GA06

GA02

GA01

Each premium is a hard plastic push-along vehicle, with a removable *Garfield* figure. The under-three premiums are one-piece figures that do not move. The *Garfield Safari* sack in this promotion was only a test.

© 1978 – 1981 United Feat. Synd. © McDonald's China. This promotion was taken from the Saturday morning TV series *Garfield* shown on CBS television. Garfield was created by Jim Davis.

The German premiums are identical to the USA premiums, except that *Garfield on Motorcycle with Odie* came with a blue motorcycle and yellow wheels instead, and was a self-liquidator. No boxes were issued.

Garfield was first released in July 1988 as a market test in Charlestown, South Carolina, and Erie, Pennsylvania. Premiums and vehicles were slightly different from this promotion.

Garfield also ran in the Philippines in 1989 and in New Zealand in April 1990 with a Ronald McDonald comic. Canada was sold as a Point of Purchase (P.O.P.) for 59 cents.

Garfield Market Test July 1988 USA (not shown)

This test promotion is very much like the later premiums of 1989 Garfield in that the figures are detachable from their vehicles. All premiums came in a polybag with an insert card and there was no under-three issued.

Premium 1 *Garfield* stands on a bright pink skateboard, with green wheels, with six spokes. He is also wearing a pink helmet without straps and a white flowered shirt.

Premium 2 *Garfield* is sitting on a green tricycle with a large front wheel and two small back ones, wheels colored purple. He is wearing a yellow cap, placed backward on his head, and blue overalls.

Premium 3 *Garfield* is sitting on a red scooter with green wheels and yellow handlebars. He is wearing a gray vest.

Premium 4 *Garfield* is sitting in a dark blue car with yellow trim and tires. He is wearing a purple hat and purple neck scarf.

GA12

Premiums

GA01 Garfield on Scooter **[A]**

GA02 Garfield in Four-Wheeler **[A]**

GA03 Garfield on Skateboard **[A]**

GA04 Garfield on Motorcycle with Odie **[A]**

GA12 Garfield on Blue Motorcycle
     with Odie (Germany) **[A]**

GA05 Garfield on Roller Skates
     under-three (not shown) **[B]**

GA06 Garfield with Pooky on
     Skateboard (under-three) **[B]**

Four boxes and one sack were issued

GA07 AHH, Vacation!!! **[C]**

GA08 Cat with a Mission **[C]**

GA09 Garfield Catches Lunch **[C]**

GA10 Mischief This Morning **[C]**

GA11 Safari Garfield (sack) (not shown) **[B]**

GA07

GA08

GA09

GA10

Generic Premium

UK
December, 1992

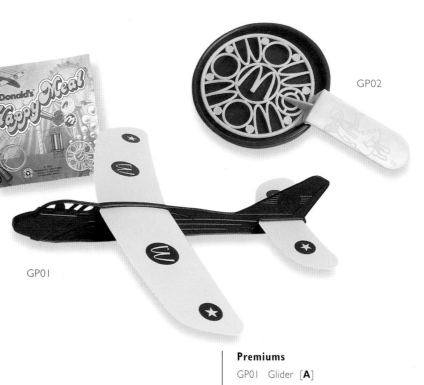

GP01

These premiums were issued in clean-up weeks around the UK, but only two of the premiums have been issued so far. The *Glider* is a three-piece toy with stickers. The wings are pushed through slots on the main body of the *Glider* and the body is made from a semi-hard plastic. The wings are made from a thin flexible plastic. Glider marked: © 1992 McDonald's Corporation made in Germany. The *Bubble Maker* is a two-part premium made from plastic. Mix a soapy solution in the red dish and use the yellow bubble ring to create bubbles. *Bubble Maker* marked: © 1992 McDonald's Corp. Simon Marketing Int. GMBH D6072 DREIECH made in Italy.

GP02

Both premiums came in a clear polybag with insert cards (the *Bubble Maker* came in a cellophane polybag). All four premiums were issued in Germany, 1992 as a Junior Tüte.

Premiums

GP01 Glider [**A**]
GP02 Bubble Ring Holder [**A**]
GP03 Skipping Rope (not issued) [**A**]
GP04 Crayons (not issued)

Two boxes were issued (not shown)

GP05 Ronald and Friends on Tricycle [**A**]
GP06 Ronald and Friends at the Beach [**A**]

Good Morning

USA
January 4 – 31, 1991

GM01

GM02

GM04

GM03

This national promotion ran in January 1991 and was based on items kids would use in the mornings. Week 1 premium is a Ronald McDonald yellow *Toothbrush*. Week 2 premium is the Ronald McDonald yellow play *clock* with a picture of Ronald in a plane on the clock face, and hands that glowed in the dark. The clock stands about 3 inches high. Week 3 premium is a 12oz white *Drinking Cup* with Ronald and a rabbit on it and the sun rising over the hill. Also given with the drinking cup was a 4oz box of

"Nestle's Juicy-Juice" with a 25 cents coupon. A 6oz can of Juice was used instead of the 4oz box in some parts of New England, because of state law. The Drinking Cup was used as the under-three, but out of its packaging. Week 4 is the McDonaldland character *Comb*, in five different color sections that join together and measure 4½ inches long when joined. The *Comb*, *Toothbrush*, and *Clock* came in printed polybags. Premiums marked: © McDonald's Corp. China.

Premiums

GM01 Ronald Toothbrush © 1989 [**A**]
GM02 Ronald Clock © 1989 [**A**]
GM03 Ronald Drink Cup and Fruit Juice (not shown) © 1990 [**A**]
GM04 McDonaldland Character Comb © 1990 [**A**]

One bag was issued

GM05 Good Morning (not shown) [**A**]

A Goofy Movie

UK

October 4 – 31, 1996

GO01

GO02

GO03

GO04

Walt Disney Pictures presents *A Goofy Movie*, shown at local theaters in the UK from October 18. It all began on the last day of school. For Max, this was the very last chance he had to impress Roxanne, the most beautiful girl in the school, so with help from his best friend PJ and the class clown Bobby, he devised a plan. The gymnasium came alive with music and flashing lights, Max jumped into action dressed as "Powerline," a rock idol with a difference. The whole school was captivated by the dancing and singing of Powerline, especially Roxanne. They soon got together and made a date to go and see Powerline in concert on TV. The head teacher was furious at Max's actions on stage and phoned Max's father, Goofy. Goofy arranged a fishing vacation for them both, to protect Max from any more trouble. Max was not at all happy with this idea of fishing, listening to Goofy's choice of music, or what Goofy had planned. As time passed by, Max thought it could not get any worse, until one day they met Big Foot in the forest. Goofy and Max had to hide in the car. Over the next few days, Max started to realise that his father was fun to be with and was quite a cool guy after all. After Max explained about the date with Roxanne and the concert with Powerline Goofy decided to let Max go to the concert.

All the premiums are one-piece toys made from a hard plastic. *Roxanne* is the only one with real hair. They all twist at the hips except *Roxanne* and *Max*. *Big Foot's* arms can be moved and *Max's* head can be turned. *Big Foot* leaves giant footprints when pressed in sand. All premiums measure between 4¼ and 5 inches tall and came in a sealed polybag with an insert card. Premiums marked: © Disney China.

Packaging marked: © Disney. © 1996 McDonald's Corporation.

Premiums

GO01 Goofy [**A**]
GO02 Roxanne [**A**]
GO03 Max [**A**]
GO04 Big Foot [**A**]

Four boxes were issued

GO05 Goofy Fishing [**A**]
GO06 School Entrance [**A**]
GO07 Night Show Stage [**A**]
GO08 Tent in Forest Clearing [**A**]

GO05

GO06

GO07

GO08

Gravedale High

USA

March 8 – April 12, 1991

GD02

GD01

GD03

GD04

GD06

GD05

This promotion was a regional in the Kansas City area. This animated TV series was created by NBC TV and was shown on NBC TV on Saturday mornings in America, and was also shown on children's afternoon TV in England. *Gravedale High* had the voice of a well-known American star, Rick Moranis, who played the normal, down-to-earth teacher, Max Schneider, who in the series had to teach a class of teenage monster misfits. Each premium is made from a hard plastic. *Frankentyke* is a miniature Frankenstein. Pull his arms down and his tongue sticks out. *Sid*, the invisible boy who seems to surf on water into the classroom, has a handle on the back of

his school locker, which is in the shape of a coffin. Press down and his gloves and shoes move. *Vinnie Stoker*, the smoothie in the classroom, sleeps in his school locker. Turn the orange knob at the end of his coffin to make him disappear back into the coffin. *Cleofatra* is a one-piece premium with a weighty base so she can rock to and fro. She was also used as the under-three premium but in different packaging. In certain states there was a translite showing only three premiums, saying "Collect all Three." *Frankentyke* was not included.

All premiums marked: © 1991 NBC made in China.

Premiums

GD01 Frankentyke [**B**]

GD02 Sid [**B**]

GD03 Vinnie Stoker [**B**]

GD04 Cleofatra [**B**]

One under-three was issued

GD05 Cleofatra [**B**]

One bag was issued

GD06 Crossword Puzzle [**A**]

Halloween McNugget Buddies

USA
October 8 – 28, 1993
Germany
February, 1995

HA03   HA04

HA01

HA02   HA05   HA06

This was a three-week promotion to tie in with Halloween. Each premium is a soft plastic McNugget dressed in Halloween costume. All the costumes can be interchanged to create different characters. Each premium is a three-piece toy, except *McBoo*. The under-three premium is *McBoo McNugget*. This is a two-piece premium and is the same as in the set, but came with the black and white zebra stripe around the package.

Panama also ran the *Halloween McNuggets* promotion but with one box, of a Spanish design. © 1992 McDonald's Corp. China.

Germany: Identical to the USA, but only five premiums were issued: *McBoo, Monster, Mummie, McNuggula,* and *Witchie,* as a Junior Tüte. No boxes were issued. Packaging was in German. This also ran in Mexico and Guatemala in 1993, as *Monster McNuggets*.

Premiums USA

HA01 McBoo McNugget [**A**]
HA02 Monster McNugget [**A**]
HA03 Mummie McNugget [**A**]
HA04 McNuggula McNugget [**A**]
HA05 Pumpkin McNugget [**A**]
HA06 Witchie McNugget [**A**]
HA07 McBoo McNugget
      (under-three USA) [**A**]

Three USA boxes were issued

HA08 Bobbing For What? [**A**]
HA09 Vampire Hotel [**A**]
HA10 Gory Laboratory [**A**]

HA10   HA08   HA09

Halloween Monster McNuggets

UK

November 10 – December 7, 1995

HA16

HA17

HA18

Identical to the USA McNugget Buddies (see page 101) issued in October 1993. These premiums stand approximately 2½ and 3½ inches high, and each head came in its own clear sealed polybag, within the main packaging. The premiums came in a clear polybag with an insert card. Toys marked: © 1992 McDonald's Corp. China. Insert card marked: © 1994 McDonald's etc.

HA19

Premiums

HA16 Monster [**A**]

HA17 Witchie [**A**]

HA18 McBoo [**A**]

HA19 McNuggula [**A**]

Four UK boxes were issued

HA20 House Garden [**A**]

HA21 Forest [**A**]

HA22 Ghost Train [**A**]

HA23 Haunted House [**A**]

HA20   HA21   HA22   HA23

Halloween 95
(What Am I Going To Be For Halloween?)

USA

October 1 – 28, 1995

HA26

HA27   HA28   HA29

HA30   HA31   HA32   HA33

What am I going to be for Halloween?) *Ronald* was issued in Week 3, and you had to guess his costume. Each came with two accessories that clip together to form a Halloween costume around the character. Accessories and figurines are made from a hard plastic. All the figurines are in their own, clear sealed polybag within the main packaging. Packaging is a printed polybag, with three languages: English, French, and Spanish. Each character stands between 2¾ and 3¼ inches high. *Hamburglar* is dressed as a Bat, *Grimace* is dressed as a Ghost, *Ronald* is dressed as a Monster, and *Birdie* is dressed in a Pumpkin outfit. The four audio tapes

that accompanied the figurines can be found on a special full-length album, "Ronald Makes it Magic," available on cassette or compact disc from "Kid Rhino, Part of Rhino Records Inc, USA." Each premium's packaging was numbered from one to eight. The under-three is *Grimace* inside a pumpkin. Push the pumpkin from the bottom, and *Grimace* will appear out of the top. The under-three was packed in a green and white zebra striped printed polybag.

All accessories and figurines marked: © 1995 McDonald's Corp. China/ Chine. Tapes marked: P and © 1995 McDonald's Corp, Kid Rhino, Part of Rhino Records Inc.

Premiums

HA26   Tape 1–Ronald Makes it Magic [A]
HA27   Tape 2–Travel Tunes [A]
HA28   Tape 3–Silly Sing-along! [A]
HA29   Tape 4–Scary Sound Effects [A]

HA30   Hamburglar [A]
HA31   Grimace [A]
HA32   Ronald [A]
HA33   Birdie [A]
HA34   Grimace (under-three) [A]

Four boxes were issued

HA35   Bat [A]
HA36   Ghost [A]
HA37   Monster [A]
HA38   Pumpkin [A]

HA34

HA35   HA36   HA37   HA38

Halloween Pails

USA

Regional promotion in October 11–31, 1985, Test Marketed in the New England area, central New York, and Boston. All pails were orange, and dated: © 1985. Each pail has a black handle and lids. Two of the pails had the same face, but different names: *McPunky* and *McPunk'n* (had same face), *McGoblin* and *McJack* (had same face). You only saw one pail with the same face in any one area. All earlier pails had their names printed on the side with the McDonald's "M" logo underneath. Your Happy Meal was normally issued in these pails.

In October 13–30, 1986, the Halloween Pails went national over the USA. They re-issued three of the pails from 1985, but the faces were printed slightly smaller. Once again, pail and lids were orange. The same pails from 1986 were re-issued in October 16–31, 1987, but with modified lids. Once again the pails were orange colored and had handles.

For the October 6–31, 1989 Halloween, two new pails were introduced: *McGhost* was a white pail and lid, *McWitch* had a green body and lid. The lid had a pointed hat design, unlike all the earlier pails, which had a pumpkin-shaped lid (like *McGhost*). Both these pails did not carry their names on the back. Each pail had a black handle. Pails marked on base: © 1986 McDonald's Corporation, and on back of pails: "Safety-tested for children of all ages. Recommended for children age one and over."

With the October 5–25, 1990 promotion, three new pails and colors were designed. And once again no names appeared on them. Pails marked on base: © 1986 McDonald's Corporation, and on back of pails: "Safety-tested for children of all ages. Recommended for children age one and over." Only the *Ghost* Pail glowed in the dark, and the translite to this promotion read: "Boooost Your Spirits! McDonald's Halloween Happy Meal, while supplies last."

HP12   HP13

HP21   aHP20   HP22

Three new designs appeared in the October 2–29, 1992 promotion, each with four parts: lid, cookie cutter, handle, and pail. All three pails had black handles and they all had lids that you turned and locked onto the pail. Each had a cookie cutter as a part of the lid, i.e.: *Pumpkin* had a green cookie cutter, and had an orange pail and lid. *Ghost's* pail and lid were white and the *Witch's* pail and lid were green. The handles attached to the lids, unlike the early pails which attached to the pail itself. Base of the pails marked: © 1986 McDonald's Corporation made in USA © 1991 McDonald's Corporation. The usual safety warning was printed on the back of the pails.

Yet again another three new designs for the Halloween Pails promotion in October 7–27, 1994. As the 1992 promotion, all premiums came in four parts: handle, cookie cutter, lid, and pail. All cookie cutters could be turned and locked to the lid, and all the lids are push-on. Pails marked on base: © 1986 McDonald's Corporation PAIL made in USA © 1993 McDonald's Corporation. Plus the safety warning on the back of each pail.

A colorful 5¼-inches-high *Halloween Cup* (HA25) was issued when you purchased a soft drink. Marked on base of cup is "Sweet Heart," and down the side of the cup marked: © 1983 McDonald's Corp. Printed in USA.

Premiums

HP01	McPunky	[**C**]
HP02	McPunk'n	[**C**]
HP03	McGoblin	[**C**]
HP04	McJack	[**C**]
HP05	McBoo	[**C**]
HP06	McBoo	[**B**]
HP07	McGoblin	[**B**]
HP08	McPunk'n	[**B**]
HP09	McBoo	[**A**]
HP10	McGoblin	[**A**]
HP11	McPunk'n	[**A**]
HP12	McGhost	[**A**]
HP13	McWitch	[**A**]
HP14	Neon Pumpkin	[**A**]
HP15	Glow-in-the-dark Ghost	[**A**]
HP16	Neon Witch	[**A**]
HP17	Ghost (not shown)	[**A**]
HP18	Pumpkin	[**A**]
HP19	Witch (not shown)	[**A**]
HP20	Ghost	[**A**]
HP21	Pumpkin	[**A**]
HP22	Witch	[**A**]

Happy Meal Band

UK
June 4, 1993

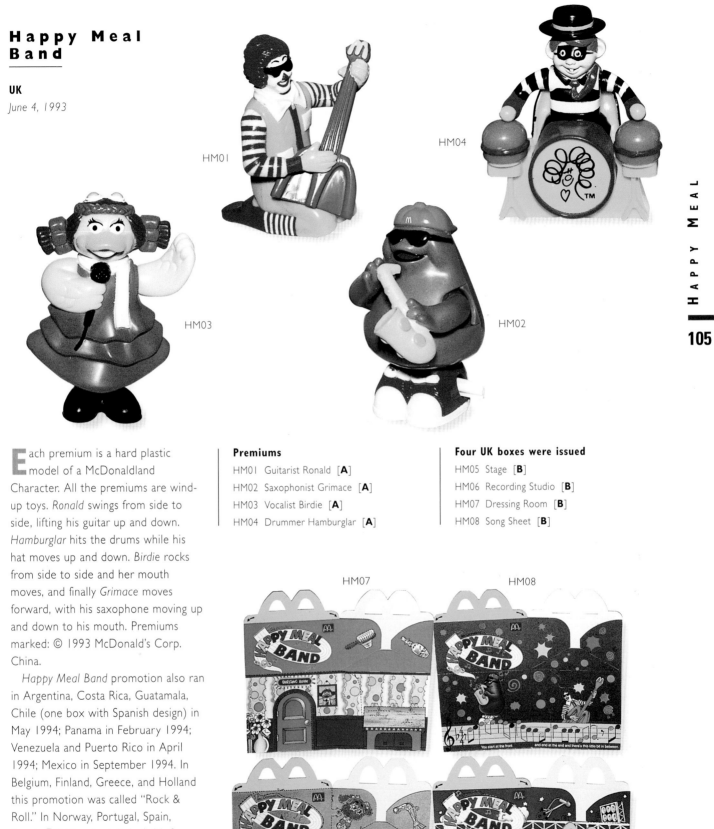

HM01

HM04

HM03

HM02

Each premium is a hard plastic model of a McDonaldland Character. All the premiums are wind-up toys. *Ronald* swings from side to side, lifting his guitar up and down. *Hamburglar* hits the drums while his hat moves up and down. *Birdie* rocks from side to side and her mouth moves, and finally *Grimace* moves forward, with his saxophone moving up and down to his mouth. Premiums marked: © 1993 McDonald's Corp. China.

Happy Meal Band promotion also ran in Argentina, Costa Rica, Guatamala, Chile (one box with Spanish design) in May 1994; Panama in February 1994; Venezuela and Puerto Rico in April 1994; Mexico in September 1994. In Belgium, Finland, Greece, and Holland this promotion was called "Rock & Roll." In Norway, Portugal, Spain, Sweden, Switzerland, Italy (with four boxes), and Denmark this promotion was called "McTwist," June 1993. Japan ran a Test Market in August 1993.

Premiums

HM01 Guitarist Ronald [**A**]
HM02 Saxophonist Grimace [**A**]
HM03 Vocalist Birdie [**A**]
HM04 Drummer Hamburglar [**A**]

Four UK boxes were issued

HM05 Stage [**B**]
HM06 Recording Studio [**B**]
HM07 Dressing Room [**B**]
HM08 Song Sheet [**B**]

HM07

HM08

HM06

HM05

Happy Birthday Happy Meal

USA
October 28 – December 1, 1994
New Zealand
1995

Each premium is a hard plastic molded action figure, which can be connected together to form a train. When all the premiums are put together it measures 42 inches in length. When pulled along, each premium has its own moving parts.

All the characters in this promotion had previously been used in Happy Meals over the past 15 years.

This set was issued to celebrate the 15th anniversary of the Happy Meal in the USA. It was the first time that different characters had been used in one Happy Meal promotion.

The under-three toy used in this promotion was *Ronald McDonald*. He was the same as above, but with a zebra stripe around the packet.

The *Barbie* premium was withdrawn after a few days. It came apart to reveal a sharp metal rod in the center.

Variations on the *Muppet Babies* have been found; *Kermit* with a white tie and *Kermit* with a blue tie.

New Zealand celebrates 10 years of the Happy Meal. These premiums are identical to the USA in 1994, including the packaging. Only 13 premiums were issued, no *Muppet Babies*. Two were available each week, for 1 dollar each, with any purchase. 10 cents was donated to children's charities from each Happy Meal, to support the *Ronald McDonald House*.

HB02

HB03

HB01

HB05

HB04

HB07

HB06

HB19

HB21

HB20

HB18

HB09

HB08

HB10

HB11

HB12

HB13

HB14

HB17

Premiums

HB01 Ronald McDonald © 1994
 McDonald's Corp. [**A**]

HB02 Barbie © 1993 Mattel, Inc. [**A**]

HB03 Hot Wheels © 1993 Mattel, Inc. [**A**]

HB04 E.T. E.T. ® ® and © 1994 U.C.S. [**A**]

HB05 Sonic The Hedgehog ™ and
 © 1994 Sega [**A**]

HB06 The Berenstain Bears © 1994
 S and J Berenstain [**A**]

HB07 Tonka © 1994 Tonka Corp. [**A**]

HB08 Cabbage Patch Kids © 1994
 O.A.A. [**A**]

HB09 101 Dalmatians © Disney [**A**]

HB10 The Little Mermaid © Disney [**A**]

HB11 Muppet Babies (Kermit, white tie)
 © 1994 Henson [**A**]

HB12 Peanuts © 1958, '65, '66, '72 UFS [**A**]

HB13 Tiny Toons © 1994 Warner Bros. [**A**]

HB14 Looney Tunes © 1994
 Warner Bros. [**A**]

HB15 The Happy Meal Guys
 © 1994 McDonald's Corp. [**A**]

HB16 Ronald McDonald (under-three) [**B**]

HB17 Muppet Babies (Kermit, blue tie)
 © 1994 Henson (not shown) [**C**]

HB15

**Four boxes were issued with this
promotion**

HB18 Ronald McDonald ®, Barbie ®,
 Hot Wheels ®, and Sonic the
 Hedgehog ™ [**B**]

HB19 Berenstain Bears ™, Cabbage Patch
 Kids ®, Peanuts ® and Tonka ® [**B**]

HB20 Tiny Toons ®, Looney Tunes ®,
 E.T. ® and The Happy Meal
 Guys ® [**B**]

HB21 Muppet Babies ™, 101 Dalmatians ®,
 The Little Mermaid ® and
 The Happy Meal Guys ® [**B**]

The Canadian set was called Favourites
Happy Meal (English and French).

Hook

USA

December 6 – January 2, 1991-2

HK02

HK04

HK03

HK01

Each premium was a bath toy. *Peter Pan* has a hollow rubber base, with a hard plastic figure and sail that floats. The *Mermaid* is a hard plastic wind-up figure that swims. *Captain Hook* is a hard plastic boat, figure, and sail that floats. Finally, *Rufio* is a hollow rubber squirt toy.

This promotion was released to tie in with the release of the film *Hook* by Steven Spielberg, starring Dustin Hoffman as Captain Hook, Robin Williams as Peter Pan, and Bob Hoskins as Smee, Captain Hook's mate.

This is a tale of Peter Pan, who finds himself returning to Never Never Land to rescue his children from the evil Captain Hook after they have been kidnapped and to rediscover his childhood. All premiums came in a printed polybag.

Premiums marked: © 1991 Tri-Star Inc Pictures Inc. © 1991 McDonald's Corp. China.

Hook also ran in Mexico in December 1991.

Premiums	
HK01	Peter Pan [**A**]
HK02	Mermaid [**A**]
HK03	Captain Hook [**A**]
HK04	Rufio [**A**]

Four boxes were issued	
HK05	Jolly Roger [**C**]
HK06	Never Tree [**C**]
HK07	Pirate Town [**C**]
HK08	Wendy's House

HK05

HK06

HK07

HK08

Hot Wheels

USA

August 2 – 29, 1991

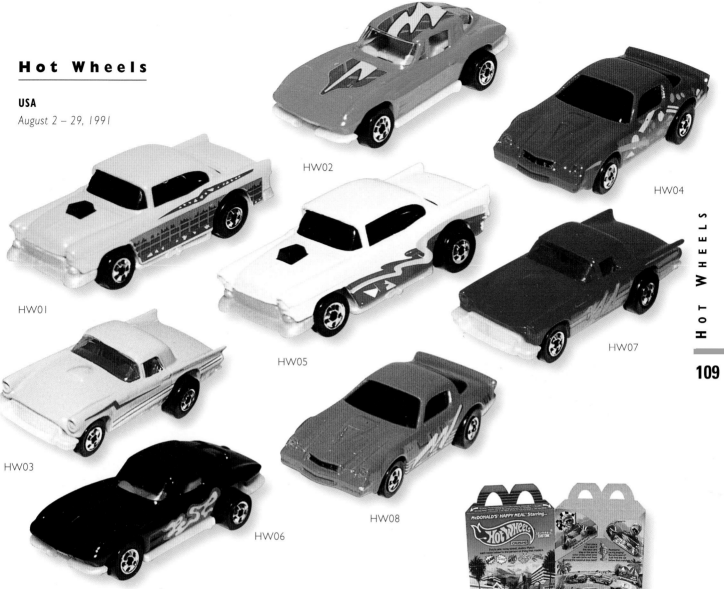

HW02

HW04

HW01

HW05

HW07

HW03

HW08

HW06

HW10

HW11

Each premium was a die-cast Californian Custom car; they were not exclusive to McDonald's, as they were available in retail stores. Each car came with a 2 dollars-off voucher, for a Hot Wheels purchase. Each car was polybagged with an insert card.

Premiums marked: Hot Wheels ® © Mattel Inc. Malaysia.

The under-three premium was a hollow plastic *Wrench* (yellow) and *Hammer* (red). This came packaged with a zebra stripe around the bag.

This promotion ran with Barbie for girls (see *Barbie Set 1 USA August 1991 page 29*).

Holland and France issued the *'55 Chevy*, *'63 Corvette*, *'57 T-Bird*, and the *Camaro Z-28* on January 9 – February 19, 1992 with Barbie Set 1 (see *Barbie Set 1 UK, January 1992 page 30*).

Premiums

HW01	'55 Chevy, Yellow © 1978	**[A]**
HW02	'63 Corvette, Green © 1979	**[A]**
HW03	'57 T-Bird, Turquoise © 1977	**[A]**
HW04	Camaro Z-28, Purple © 1982	**[A]**
HW05	'55 Chevy, White © 1978	**[A]**
HW06	'63 Corvette, Black © 1979	**[A]**
HW07	'57 T-Bird, Red © 1977	**[A]**
HW08	Camaro Z-28, Orange © 1982	**[A]**
HW09	Wrench and Hammer (under-three)	**[B]**

Two boxes were issued

HW10	Cruising	**[B]**
HW11	Racers	**[B]**

HW09

Hot Wheels 95

USA

August 1–28, 1995

HW54   HW55   HW56   HW57

HW58   HW59   HW60   HW61

HW62   HW63

This national promotion ran with Barbie 95 (see page 36) and had a dual bag, Barbie on one side and Hot Wheels on the other. There were eight premiums, plus the under-threes to each Hot Wheels and Barbie promotion. Each premium came in a numbered, printed polybag (Hot Wheels numbered nine to 16). This promotion is the first time that McDonalds have used three different languages on the front of the packaging, French, English, and Spanish, and each vehicle has a different name in each country.

Each premium is a push-along vehicle, with a die-cast base and a plastic top (see *World of Hot Wheels 94* page 116). Four of the vehicles from this set have a push button on the side of the car, which releases a spoiler on top of the car for more stability at high speeds. Vehicles are: Shock Force, Twin Engine, Blue Bandit and Back

Burner. The under-three is the Key Force Truck, in a green and yellow zebra stripe packet. This was first released in the promotion "Totally Toy Holiday": December– January 1994. One dual bag was issued with a "Save $2.00 instantly on any Hot Wheels ® Power Charger set or track System Starter set" coupon.

Premiums marked: Hot Wheels ® © 1994 Mattel Inc. China/Chine. Under-three marked: Hot Wheels ® © 1993 Mattel Inc. China. Packaging marked: © 1994 McDonald's Corporation (except under-three packaging, © 1995).

Premiums

HW54	Lightning Speed
HW55	Shock Force
HW56	Twin Engine
HW57	Radar Racer
HW58	Blue Bandit
HW59	Power Circuit
HW60	Back Burner
HW61	After Blast

One dual bag was issued

HW63	Finish Line

One under-three was issued

HW62	Key Force Truck

Hot Wheels 95

Japan
July, 1995

Premiums (not shown)

HW74   McDonald Thunderbird [**A**]

HW75   Hot Wheels Funny Car [**A**]

HW76   McDonald Funny Car [**A**]

HW77   Turbine 4-2 [**A**]

HW78   One generic bag

(see *Peanuts* Japan April 1995
page 188) [**A**]

In this Japanese Hot Wheel promotion, all these cars have been re-issued from two earlier American sets, except that the *McDonald Thunderbird* car (HW74) is blue in the Japanese set, and red in the American set (HW31). *Hot Wheels Funny Car* and *McDonald's Funny Car* came from Hot Wheels Diecast USA 1993, and the *Turbine 4-2* came from the World of Hot Wheels USA 1994. Premiums were polybagged with an insert card. Barbie also ran with this promotion. (See *Barbie 95 Japan* page 37.)

Japanese insert card

Hot Wheels 95

UK
September 8 – October 6, 1995

HW66

HW65

HW67

HW64

These vehicles have been re-issued from two previous Hot Wheels promotions from America. The packaging has been changed to polybags with insert cards. Insert cards marked: © 1995 McDonald's Corporation. © 1995 Mattel, Inc. All Rights Reserved. Premiums marked: Hot Wheels ® © 1993 Mattel, Inc.

China. *Hot Wheels Camaro*, *McDonald Dragster*, and *Hot Wheels Funny Car* came from the Hot Wheels Diecast USA 1993. *Flame Rider* came from World of Hot Wheels USA 1994.

This promotion also ran with Barbie, over the same four weeks. A coloring competition also ran. (See *Barbie UK 1995* for more details page 36.)

Premiums

HW64   Hot Wheels Camaro [**A**]

HW65   McDonald Dragster [**A**]

HW66   Flame Rider [**A**]

HW67   Funny Car [**A**]

Four dual boxes were issued

HW68   City (Ballroom) [**A**]

HW69   Race Track (Stage) [**A**]

HW70   Car Show (Hair Salon) [**A**]

HW71   Desert Road (Ski Slope) [**A**]

HW68   HW69   HW70   HW71

(Back of boxes will show Barbie)

Hot Wheels 96

UK

September 6 – October 3, 1996

This Hot Wheels UK promotion also ran with four Barbie dolls (see *Barbie UK 1996* page 39) for girls. All four cars have been re-issued from previous USA promotions and re-packaged with insert cards. All cars are identical in color to the USA ones except *Street Shocker* (HW79), which had a yellow body with black windows for the UK set and a green body with gray windows for the USA set. *Street Shocker*, *2-Cool*, and *Turbine 4-2* were first issued in World of Hot Wheels in 1994 and *Lightning Speed* first appeared in Hot Wheels 95. Each vehicle measures approximately 3 inches long. Four dual Barbie/Hot Wheels boxes were issued: and each box could be made into a diorama.

Premiums marked: Hot Wheels ® © Mattel Inc. China (*2-Cool, Turbine 4-2*).

Premiums marked: Hot Wheels ® © Mattel Inc. China. Chine. (*Street Shocker, Lightning Speed*).

Premiums

HW79   Street Shocker © 1993   [**A**]

HW80   2-Cool © 1994   [**A**]

HW81   Lightning Speed © 1994   [**A**]

HW82   Turbine 4-2 © 1994   [**A**]

Four dual boxes were issued Barbie/ Hot Wheels

HW83   City Street (Dance Studio)   [**A**]

HW84   Petrol Station (Country Manor with Horses)   [**A**]

HW85   Garage Repair (Beach Scene)   [**A**]

HW86   Building (Park, Skateboarding, etc.)   [**A**]

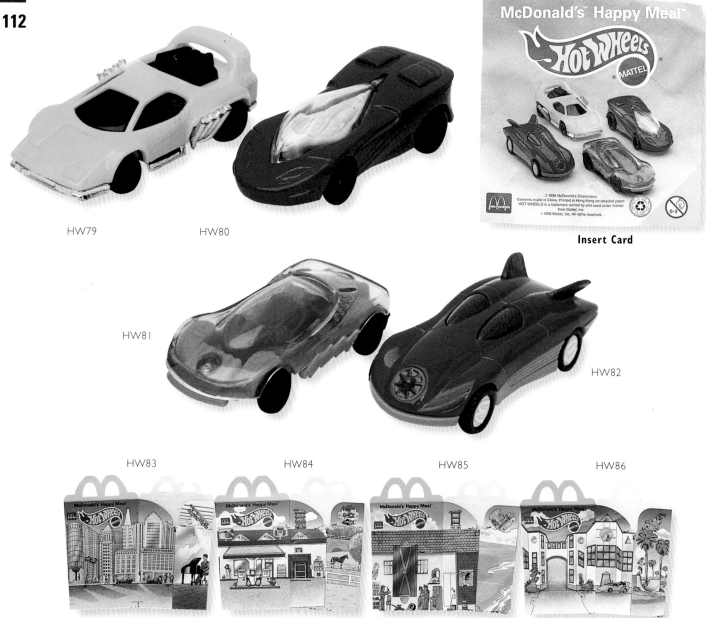

HW79   HW80

Insert Card

HW81

HW82

HW83   HW84   HW85   HW86

Dual Hot Wheels/Barbie Boxes

Hot Wheels- Attack Pack

USA

February 3 – March 2, 1995

Each premium is a hard plastic vehicle. Each vehicle has a lever or button that when opened reveals a mouth. The under-three premium is the same as the *Truck* in the set, but was packaged with the zebra stripe around the edge. Premiums marked: Hot Wheels ® © 1994 Mattel, Inc. China. There is no McDonald's identification on the premiums, only on the printed polybag. This promotion ran with Polly Pocket for girls. (See *Polly Pocket USA February 1995* page 196.) The *Attack Pack* promotion also ran in Canada at the same time (French and English language packaging).

Premiums

HW49   Truck [**A**]
HW50   Battle Bird [**A**]
HW51   Lunar Invader [**A**]
HW52   Sea Creature [**A**]
HW53   Truck (under-three) [**A**]

One dual bag was issued

HW54   Battle Bird Rescue bag [**A**]

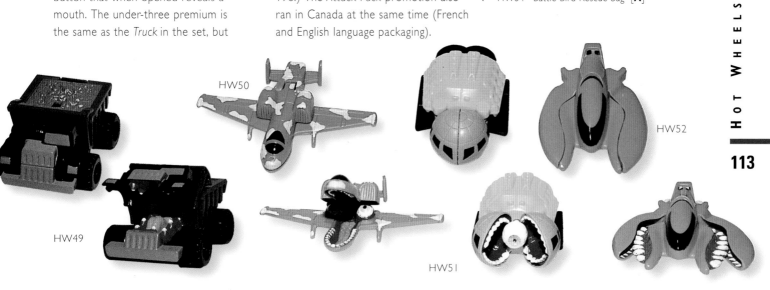

Hot Wheels-Attack Pack

UK

July 16 – August 12, 1993
Canada • Germany
1993

Each premium is a hard plastic vehicle, which opens at the front to reveal a mouth. Each premium came in a clear polybag with an insert card. Premiums marked: Hot Wheels ® Mattel © 1993 China. No McDonald's identification on premiums, only on insert card. This promotion was run with Barbie set 2 in July 1993.

Canada issued the same premiums but with four different Barbies (see *Barbie set 3 USA 1993* page 33), in dual languages on the packaging, French and English. Money-off vouchers were enclosed. Germany also issued the same premiums in October 93, as a Junior-Tüte (JT). No boxes were issued. Germany, Holland, and France also issued identical Attack-Packs with UK Barbie set 2. Japan ran it as a Test Market in 1994 with four Barbies from Barbie set 3 USA 1993.

Premiums UK

HW23   Slaughter Jaws [**A**]
HW24   Slash Cat [**A**]
HW25   Sand Stinger [**A**]
HW26   Taran Chewa [**A**]

Two boxes were issued in the UK

HW27   Space – Taran and Jaws [**A**]
HW28   Jungle – Cat and Stinger [**A**]

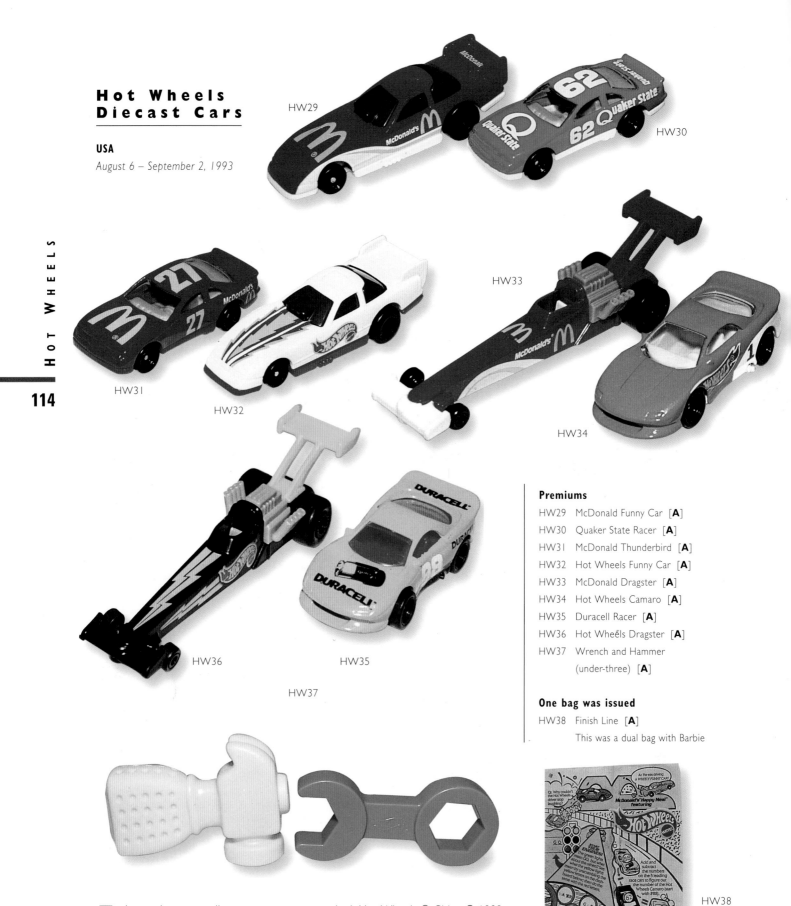

Hot Wheels Diecast Cars

USA

August 6 – September 2, 1993

HW29

HW30

HW31

HW32

HW33

HW34

HW36

HW35

HW37

Premiums

HW29   McDonald Funny Car [**A**]

HW30   Quaker State Racer [**A**]

HW31   McDonald Thunderbird [**A**]

HW32   Hot Wheels Funny Car [**A**]

HW33   McDonald Dragster [**A**]

HW34   Hot Wheels Camaro [**A**]

HW35   Duracell Racer [**A**]

HW36   Hot Wheels Dragster [**A**]

HW37   Wrench and Hammer
        (under-three) [**A**]

One bag was issued

HW38   Finish Line [**A**]
        This was a dual bag with Barbie

HW38

Each premium was a die-cast car. There were four styles of cars, *Funny Car, Racer, Camaro,* and *Dragster.* There was an under-three premium which ran with this promotion. It was a hollow plastic *Wrench and Hammer.* It was packaged with the familiar zebra stripe around the bag. Premiums marked: Hot Wheels ® China © 1993 Mattel Inc. Under-three HW37 Made for McDonalds © 1991 Mattel Inc. Made in China.

Promotion ran with Barbie (see *Barbie Set 3 USA August 1993* page 33).

Hot Wheels Mini Streex

USA

August 7 – September 3, 1992

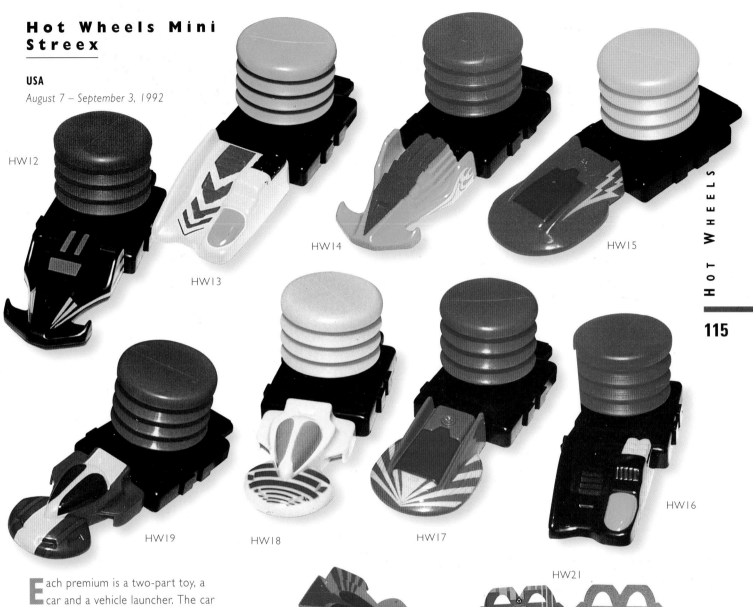

HW12

HW13

HW14

HW15

HW19

HW18

HW17

HW16

HW20

HW21

HW22

E ach premium is a two-part toy, a car and a vehicle launcher. The car connects to the launcher. When the bellows are pumped, the car was launched. Each vehicle is a hard molded plastic, futuristic type car, with matching bellows. Premiums came in a printed polybag. © 1991 McDonald's Corp Streex is a Registered Trademark of Mattel. Inc. Made in China.

This promotion was run with Barbie (See *Barbie Set 2 USA August 1992* page 31).

Premiums

HW12   Black Arrow Racer – Pink Pump   [**A**]

HW13   Blade Burner Racer –
            Turquoise Pump   [**A**]

HW14   Flame Out – Red Pump   [**A**]

HW15   Hot Shot Racer – Yellow Pump   [**A**]

HW16   Night Shadow – Mauve Pump   [**A**]

HW17   Quick Flash – Purple Pump   [**A**]

HW18   Race Tracer – Green Pump   [**A**]

HW19   Turbo Flyer – Dark Blue Pump   [**A**]

HW20   Orange Arrow (under-three)   [**B**]

Two boxes were issued

HW21   Daredevil Racers   [**B**]

HW22   Star Racers   [**B**]

World of Hot Wheels

USA • Canada
August 5 – September 2, 1994

116

HW39

HW40

HW41

HW42

HW43

HW44

HW47

HW45

HW46

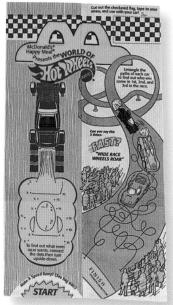

HW48

Each premium was a combined hard plastic and metal car. Premiums marked: © 1994 Mattel, Inc. Hot Wheels ®. The under-three premium was a Mini Streex vehicle. It came packaged with a zebra stripe around the package. All premiums came in a printed polybag. Premiums marked: © 1991 McDonald's Corp. Streex is a registered Trademark of Mattel, Inc.

This promotion ran with Barbie and Friends for girls. (See *Barbie and Friends USA August 1994* page 38.)

Japan also ran this promotion and issued all eight Hot Wheels and all eight Barbie and Friends in 1994.

Premiums

HW39	Bold Eagle	[A]
HW40	Black Cat	[A]
HW41	Flame Rider	[A]
HW42	Gas Hog © 1993	[A]
HW43	Turbine 4-2	[A]
HW44	2-Cool	[A]
HW45	Street Shocker © 1993	[A]
HW46	X21J Cruiser © 1993	[A]
HW47	Fast Forward (under-three)	[A]

One dual bag was issued

HW48	Race Track	[A]

The Hunchback of Notre Dame

UK
July 19 – August 15, 1996

HU02   HU03   HU04

HU01

**Photograph showing the three parts
to the Gargoyles HU05**

HU05

Premiums

HU01   Quasimodo [**A**]

HU02   Esmeralda [**A**]

HU03   Judge Frollo [**A**]

HU04   Phoebus [**A**]

HU05   Hugo/Laverne/Victor [**A**]

Five boxes were issued

HU06   Bell Tower [**A**]

HU07   Town Square [**A**]

HU08   Palace [**A**]

HU09   Street [**A**]

HU10   Notre Dame (see p. 118) [**A**]

This promotion coincided with the release of Walt Disney's 34th full-length animated film, *The Hunchback of Notre Dame,* at local theaters on July 19, 1996. With this promotion came a special meal called "Chicken Cordon Bleu" in a sesame seed bun with medium fries and drink, and ice cream "Blackcurrant Sundae" also in special pots, all in special packaging. Trayliners showed 100 family breaks to Disneyland Paris to be won, and a prize draw to see the new Notre Dame Carnival in November. A kids' coloring competition with a tie-breaker question offered a cuddly *Quasimodo* from the Disney Store and a free poster to every entrant.

All premiums are made from a hard plastic and are one-piece toys (except the *Gargoyles,* three-pieces) and measure between 3¼ inches (*Quasimodo*) to 5 inches (*Frollo*). Each

premium came in a polybag with an insert card. Each box can be made into a play scene or backdrop for each figure. Pull the *Quasimodo* string and watch him climb back up. *Esmeralda* has no moving parts and glows in the dark. *Frollo* comes with a cloth cape; press his arms down and then press his head down to release his arms. *Phoebus* is a solid figure with a movable head, waist, and arms. *Gargoyles* came with a cardboard backdrop; turning the mill knob at the front will revolve the *Gargoyles* from side to side.

Inspired by Victor Hugo's classic tale with an all star voice-cast: Demi Moore, Kevin Kline, and Academy Award nominee Tom Hulce. Gentle Quasimodo has been looked after by Judge Frollo (not by choice) since birth, locked away in the bell tower of Notre Dame, and told that everyone has rejected him because of his ugliness.

The gargoyles, Hugo, Laverne, and Victor (who only come alive for Quasimodo) persuaded him to go to the annual Festival of Fools. Quasimodo soon joined in the fun as everybody thought he was wearing a mask. Quasimodo was soon found out by the people and crowned the King of Fools. He was tied up and teased. Esmeralda, a gypsy girl who felt sorry for him, helped him escape. Frollo, who hated gypsies, ordered the girl's arrest. Phoebus, captain of the guard, was in love with Esmeralda. She claimed sanctuary in Notre Dame; for a time she was safe from Frollo. Esmeralda became fond of Quasimodo and told him he was not ugly like Frollo had said. Quasimodo helped the gypsy girl escape and when Frollo found out he sent his soldiers to find her, burning and destroying houses on the way. Phoebus turned against Frollo for his

HU06   HU07   HU08

HU09   HU10

Coloring competition

Some of the special packaging that was used

actions, so Frollo ordered his immediate arrest. Phoebus was struck by an arrow and left for dead by Frollo's men. He was saved by Esmeralda, who took him back to Notre Dame, where she begged Quasimodo to protect and hide him. Frollo arrived at Notre Dame and found Quasimodo in his room. Frollo knew that Quasimodo knew the whereabouts of the gypsies' hideout, "Court of Miracles," so Frollo lied to Quasimodo, saying he knew where the gypsy hideout was and would attack with a thousand men at dawn. Quasimodo, not realising this was a trap, told Phoebus and Esmeralda of Frollo's plan. Frollo followed Phoebus and Esmeralda to the gypsies' hideout where he arrested them and the other gypsies. Then he had Quasimodo chained up in Notre Dame. Phoebus was in prison and Esmeralda was to be tied to the stake and burned in the town's square. Quasimodo, with all his strength, broke free from his chains and saved the gypsy girl, who fainted and was carried back to the cathedral. Frollo attacked the cathedral. Quasimodo mistook Esmeralda for being dead and in his rage he attacked the soldiers from the balcony with pieces of wood and stone and then with a pot of molten lead tipped over the cathedral's wall. At this time, Phoebus freed himself and the gypsies from prison. They united to fight the soldiers. Frollo managed to enter the cathedral and found Quasimodo with Esmeralda, who was just waking up. A struggle broke out; they both slipped over the edge. Esmeralda caught hold of Quasimodo at the last minute; Frollo fell to his death. Esmeralda was losing her grip on Quasimodo; Phoebus arrived to save the day. Premiums *Esmeralda, Phoebus,* and *Frollo* marked: Made For McDonald's © Disney China. Quasimodo and Gargoyles marked: © Disney China.

Intergalactic Adventurer
Space Exploration Party

UK

February 24 – March 25, 1995

Japan

May – June, 1995

IA01

IA02

IA03

IA04

Each premium is a hard-plastic push-down action toy. Once they are pushed down, they spring back up, and race along on wheels. Premiums came in a polybag with an insert card.

Premiums and packaging marked: © 1995 McDonald's Corp. China.

This promotion was also released in Japan. The premiums are identical to the UK version, except the packaging was in Japanese and the promotion was called "Space Exploration Party." There are no boxes issued in Japan, as of yet;

only a plain white generic bag was issued like the one used on Peanuts Japan April/May 1995.

Intergalactic Adventurer was also issued in Europe May 1995; Germany in August 1995, Middle East and North Africa in May 1995.

Premiums

IA01	Space Shuttle with blue vehicle	[A]
IA02	Ronald with red vehicle	[A]
IA03	Grimace with green vehicle	[A]
IA04	Robot with yellow vehicle	[A]

Four UK boxes were issued

IA05	Space Station – Shuttle	[A]
IA06	Space City – Ronald	[A]
IA07	Moon-Planet – Grimace	[A]
IA08	Futuristic Planet – Robot	[A]

IA05

IA06

IA07

IA08

Island Holiday

UK
August 2–29, 1996

IS02

IS04

IS01

IS03

Photograph showing Birdie reeling in
a shark and Totem Pole extended

McDonaldland characters vacation on a desert island. This promotion was the first time McDonald's issued Fish Fingers in their Happy Meals for children. Each premium is a one-piece toy made from hard plastic. *Ronald* is taking it easy, stretched out on a hammock fixed between two palm trees. Press the palm tree down and *Ronald* swings to and fro. *Grimace* needs to be wound up; then let him dance the hula in a grass skirt. *Birdie* sits on the sand by the water's edge with her fishing rod cast out, and on the other end she has caught a shark. Turn the handle next to *Birdie* to reel

in her catch. The *Fry Guys* are hiding in a spring-loaded *Totem Pole*. Press the *Totem Pole* together to lock, then press the front top face of the *Totem Pole* and the *Fry Guys* will spring out.

Premiums came in a polybag with an insert card with instructions on the reverse. Premiums measure between 2¾ inches (*Birdie*) and 5½ (*Totem Pole* extended) inches tall. *Ronald* measures 5¾ inches long. There was also a competition trayliner issued.

Ronald, *Grimace*, and *Totem Pole* marked: © 1996 McD. Corp. China. *Birdie* marked: © 1996 McD. Corp. Thailand.

Premiums

IS01	Ronald	[**A**]
IS02	Grimace	[**A**]
IS03	Birdie	[**A**]
IS04	Fry Guys	[**A**]

Four boxes issued

IS05	Beach Scene	[**A**]
IS06	Grass Huts	[**A**]
IS07	Fishing Boats	[**A**]
IS08	Totem Pole	[**A**]

IS05

IS06

IS07

IS08

The Jungle Book

USA

July 6 – August 2, 1990

JB09

JB10

JB11

JB12

JB14

JB13

F irst released in 1967, this very popular Walt Disney animated film was one of the last to be supervised by Walt Disney himself and featured for the first time a totally new method for animation, where the cartoon characters are based on the people behind the voices. This promotion was issued to tie in with the re-release of the Disney film at theaters in America. It was the first time in the USA that wind-up toys were issued. All the premiums are made from a hard plastic, except the under-three premiums, which are a one-piece toy that rocks to and fro and is made from a solid plastic. *King Louie* is wound up by turning his arms around; watch him do somersaults. *Baloo* moves forward when wound up. *Kaa* and *Shere Khan* both move forward. *Kaa*'s head goes up and down and *Shere Khan* jumps as he goes along. These last two premiums were later used in a UK promotion and are identical. Each premium came in a printed polybag and the under-threes had a black and white zebra stripe around the polybag.

Premiums marked: © Disney China.

Polybags marked: © 1989 McDonald's Corporation, © The Walt Disney Company.

Premiums USA

JB09   Baloo [**B**]

JB10   King Louie [**B**]

JB11   Kaa [**B**]

JB12   Shere Khan [**B**]

JB13   Junior Elephant (under-three) [**C**]

JB14   Mowgli in Pot (under-three) [**C**]

Four boxes were issued

JB13   Baloo [**C**]

JB14   Hidden Animal [**C**]

JB15   Kaa [**C**]

JB16   King Louie [**C**]

JB13

JB13

JB14

JB15

JB16

The Jungle Book

UK
March 26, 1993

JB01   JB02   JB03

JB04

Inspired by Rudyard Kipling's *Mowgli* stories of a boy brought up by wolves in the jungle, who refuses to leave the jungle for the main village and ends up with two unwilling guardians, Bagheera the panther and Baloo the bear, who try to keep him out of trouble. This is not easy when you have King Louie, Kaa, and Shere Khan around looking for a quick and tasty meal.

This promotion was issued to tie in with the re-release of the Disney film at theaters in England. There were two premiums different from the American promotion in 1990: Mowgli replaced Baloo and King Louie had a banana. All four premiums are made from hard plastic. *Mowgli* is just a push-along toy; his head bobs in and out of the pot. The rest of the premiums are wind-up and all move forward. *King Louie*'s banana moves up to his mouth and down. *Kaa*'s head moves forward and back as he moves along and, finally, *Shere Khan* moves forward and jumps.

Premiums came in a clear polybag with an insert card, are marked: © Disney © 1993 McDonald's Corporation, Simon Marketing International GmbH D-6072 Dreieich.

Premiums marked: © Disney China. *Jungle Book* also ran in Belgium, Denmark, Sweden, Finland, Spain, France, Portugal, Greece, Norway, Italy, Holland, and Switzerland. (Switzerland in May 1993.)

The same premiums were issued in Germany in 1993, as a clean-up, and *not* as a Junior-Tüte (Happy Meal). The packaging was the same as the UK. No boxes were issued.

Premiums UK

JB01   King Louie (with banana)   [**B**]
JB02   Kaa   [**B**]
JB03   Mowgli   [**B**]
JB04   Shere Khan   [**B**]

Four UK boxes were issued

JB05   Ruins   [**B**]
JB06   Jungle Tree   [**B**]
JB07   Elephants   [**B**]
JB08   Shere Khan Chases Mowgli   [**B**]

JB05   JB07

JB06   JB08

122

Jurassic Park Cups

UK

October 22, 1993

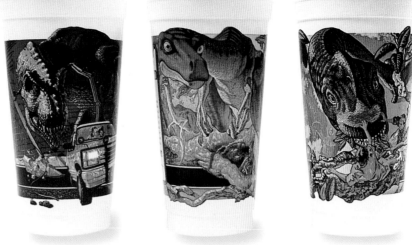

JP01   JP02   JP03

This promotion was released to coincide with the Steven Spielberg film *Jurassic Park* in theaters. An approximately 120-minutes-long film by Universal City Studios with the most spectacular computer-generated special effects to date, *Jurassic Park* is one of the top-grossing movies of all time. The original book was written by Michael Crichton. John Hammond, an obsessive billionaire, has a dream to build a park on an island for dinosaurs. Scientists were brought in to start a DNA program where the secret of cloning was held in prehistoric amber from fossilised animal remains. The six cups are made from plastic and are numbered one to six. Each was issued with a soft drink purchase. Each cup shows a scene from the film and has a little history on each dinosaur. Each cup has a McDonald's logo and Coca-Cola logo and marked: ™ and © 1992 Universal City Studios, Inc, and Amblin Entertainment, Inc. "The Collectibles ®" Made in Canada.

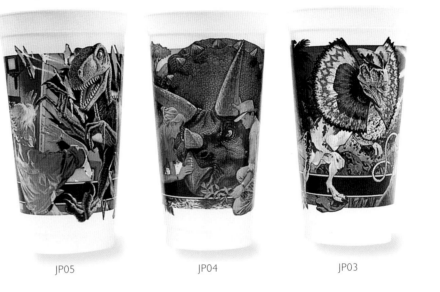

JP05   JP04   JP03

There were also four dinosaur cardboard glasses to wear. They were a free give-away, at the same time as the Jurassic cups. There was also another promotion run by McDonald's "The World of Dinosaurs." (See *World of Dinosaurs UK October 22, 1993* page 247.)

The cups were issued in Germany and America (larger cups USA). France issued the cups and fries cartons.

Purchases

JP01	Tyrannosaurus	[A]
JP02	Gallimimus	[A]
JP03	Dilophosaur	[A]
JP04	Triceratops	[A]
JP05	Velociraptor	[A]
JP06	Brachiosaur	[A]

Free give-aways

| JB07 | Four Cardboard Glasses | [B] |

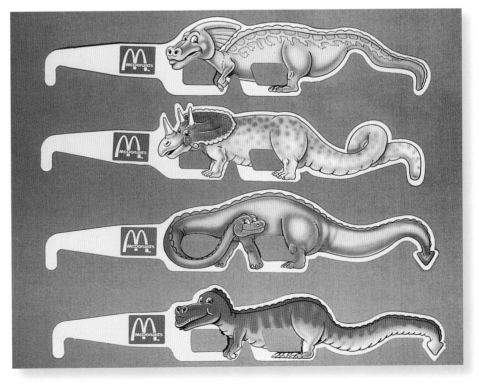

JP07 Free give-aways

Lego System

UK
September 9, 1994
Belgium • France • Holland
September, 1994

LS05

LS03

LS02

LS01

LS04

Each premium is a set of *Lego Bricks*, which can be constructed into a model using the instructions enclosed in the packet. The instructions also contain photographs of other models, which can be constructed by combining the other premiums together. Premiums marked: © 1989, 1994 Lego Group.

Because these premiums were suitable only for ages three to 12 years, an under-three premium was issued. This premium was advertised on the translite. This under-three premium was a set of *Duplo Bricks*. When constructed together they made an alligator. The packet of this premium did not contain any mention of McDonald's.

This *Lego System* set was part of a Happy Meal promotion that ran in America. It was called *Lego Motion* in America. It was released in 1989.

LS06

LS08

LS09

LS07

Premiums

LS01	Land Laser Vehicle	[**A**]
LS02	Wind Whirler Helicopter	[**A**]
LS03	Sea Eagle Airplane	[**A**]
LS04	Sea Skimmer Craft	[**A**]
LS05	Giddy the Gator (under-three)	[**A**]

Four boxes were issued

LS06	Moon Base	[**A**]
LS07	Space Runway	[**A**]
LS08	Helicopter Pad	[**A**]
LS09	Jungle Base	[**A**]

The Lion King

Panama
July, 1994

A plastic lunch kit from Central and South America was released in Mexico, Costa Rica, Guatemala, Venezuela, Argentina, and Chile in July 1994.

Premiums

LK14 Vinyl Lunch Bag *"Porta Equipo de Exploradores"* with Lion King graphics (not shown) **[A]**

LK15 *"Binoculares Exploradores"* – Fold-up binoculars (not shown) **[A]**

LK16 *"Portavianda Simba"* – Ronald plastic food container with pull-back lid (not shown) **[A]**

LK17 *"Cantimplora de la Jungla"* – Canteen (not shown) **[A]**

LK18 Plastic placemat with Nala and Simba (premiums and one carton of Spanish design) (not shown) **[A]**

LK19 One carton issued (not shown) **[A]**

125

The Lion King

UK
October 7, 1994

Each premium is a hard plastic action figure. *Simba* is spring-loaded; when pushed down and released he jumps in the air. *Zazu* and *Scar* are both wind-up toys, and finally *Pumbaa* is a push-along. When pushed along, the figure spins around on his back. This promotion was issued to tie in with the release of the Walt Disney film *The Lion King* in theaters. © Disney China. *The Lion King* was also released in Europe in November 1994, and in Germany in December 1994, as a Junior-Tüte (JT). Premiums were the same as the UK; no boxes were issued in Germany.

Premiums

LK01 Simba – Lion Cub **[A]**
LK02 Zazu – Bird **[A]**
LK03 Scar – Evil Brother **[A]**
LK04 Pumbaa – Wart Hog **[A]**

Four boxes were issued

LK05 Planes – Simba **[B]**
LK06 Pride Rock – Zazu **[B]**
LK07 Grave Yard – Scar **[B]**
LK08 Waterfall – Pumbaa **[B]**

LK02

LK01

LK03

LK04

LK08   LK05   LK06   LK07

The Lion King

Australia
October 6 – November 2, 1995

This Australian promotion was to coincide with the release of the Walt Disney video, *The Lion King*. All four premiums are made from a hard plastic and come in two pieces, top and base. Each premium has a rubber stamp underneath, and has a scene from the film, the same picture on both sides of the handle. Premiums measure 2¼ inches long and 2¼ inches high. Underneath each rubber stamp is an ink pad. Each premium has a different color ink. The bases clip on to protect the rubber stamp and ink pad. You roll the premium over a piece of paper, etc., and each premium produces a different mark. *The Lion King* prints out the words "The Lion King," in black. This comes with a blue base. *Simba and*

Photograph showing Stamp, Ink Pad, and Bases

Nala prints out cub footprints in green, and this comes with a brown base. *Scar* prints out a lion's foot showing claws, colored orange with a brown base. *Pumbaa and Timon* prints out a bug in purple, and this comes with a dark green base.

Premiums came in a clear polybag with brown printing on: The Lion King, "Yours to own on video," Walt Disney

Home Video. "M" logo, McDonald's Australia Ltd, © 1995, Contents made in China by Creata-Promotions © Disney. Premiums marked: © Disney, Made in China.

Issued with each Happy Meal was a FREE entry form for one child, between the ages of four and 15 years, to any participating Wildlife Parks and Zoos in Australia.

LK20 LK21 LK22 LK23

LK24 Front LK24 Back

Premiums
LK20   The Lion King [**A**]

LK21   Simba and Nala [**A**]

LK22   Scar [**A**]

LK23   Pumbaa and Timon [**A**]

One themed box was issued
LK24   The Lion King [**A**]

Zoo Ticket

The Little Mermaid

UK
November 2 – 29, 1990
USA
November 24 – December 21, 1989

These premiums are made from a hard plastic, except *Flounder* which is made from a soft rubber and is hollow. All these toys were made to be used with water. *Ariel* was a solid figure that floated in water, *Eric* sat in a yellow boat, *Flounder* was a water squirter, and finally *Ursula* was a solid figure with a suction pad, which could be stuck to a bath tub.

The British premiums are identical to the American set and both were released in conjunction with the animated Walt Disney film *The Little Mermaid* in each country. The film was based on the fairy tale by Hans Christian Andersen.

Premiums marked: © Disney China. No under-three was issued. Boxes and bags not shown. *The Little Mermaid* also ran in Belgium, Denmark, Finland, France, Italy, Holland, Norway, Spain, Sweden, and Switzerland in December 1990; Guatemala in 1989. Germany was called "Arielle" and ran in December 5–24, 1990, and only issued three premiums (no Ursula). No boxes were issued on this Junior-Tüte.

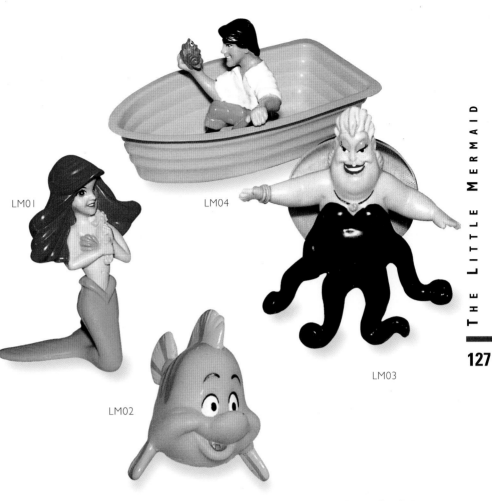

LM01

LM04

LM03

LM02

Premiums
LM01 Ariel [**B**]
LM02 Flounder [**B**]
LM03 Ursula (not shown) [**B**]
LM04 Eric [**B**]

Four UK boxes were issued (not shown)
LM05 Ariel's Garden [**C**]
LM06 Village Lagoon [**C**]
LM07 Sea Garden [**C**]
LM08 Ursula's Domain [**C**]

Four US boxes issued (not shown)
LM09 Ariel's Grotto [**C**]
LM10 Sea Garden [**C**]
LM11 Ursula's Domain [**C**]
LM12 Village Lagoon [**C**]

Two trial USA bags issued (not shown)
LM13 Ursula's Domain [**C**]
LM14 Village Lagoon [**C**]

Purchase
USA
December, 1989
LM15 Sebastian [**B**]
LM16 Flounder [**B**]

Sebastian and *Flounder* are both soft, plush toys, and were released over the Christmas period in America. Each plush ornament measures approximately 4¼ inches long and came in sealed polybags, inside boxes with the character's picture on them. Purchases marked: © The Walt Disney Company. "M®" logo. Simon Marketing, Inc, Los Angeles, CA. Made in China.

LM15

LM16

Littlest Pet Shop

USA • Canada
March 15 – April 11, 1996

LP01

LP02

LP03

LP04

LP05

Littlest Pet Shop is an animated TV series about a pet shop and its owner who collects and sells strange animals. All premiums are made from a hard plastic and they all have some form of hair, except the swan, and they measure from 2 to 2½ inches tall. Week one was the *Swan*. Move its head back and forward to make the wings flap. Week two, the *Unicorn,* has hair for its tail and its head can be moved up and down. Week three is the

Dragon. The tail turns to make his wings flap. Week four, the *Tiger*, has movable back legs and when you move his front legs this will make his tail wag. The packaging is a printed polybag in three languages: French, Spanish, and English, bags numbered one to four. Premiums marked: © 1996 Tonka Corp. China/Chine. Packaging marked: © 1995 McDonald's Corporation, Tonka, etc. The under-three is a one-piece premium in the shape of a yellow

drum with a wheel inside with a hamster running around it. The packaging is an orange and white zebra striped polybag. Each box would create your own Littlest Pet Shop fantasy storyland! Box one carried a $1.50-off coupon on a Littlest Pet Shop Fancy Curls carousel toy. Box two carried a $1.50-off coupon on the Littlest Pet Shop Video. Transformers were issued at the same time for boys (see *Transformers USA 1996* page 231).

LP06

LP07

Premiums

LP01   Swan [**A**]

LP02   Unicorn [**A**]

LP03   Dragon [**A**]

LP04   Tiger [**A**]

LP05   Hamster in Wheel (under-three) [**A**]

Two boxes were issued

LP06   What are a Cat's Favorite Jewels? [**A**]

LP07   Why Did The Littlest Pet Shop Friends
Stay at Home? [**A**]

Looney Tunes Clip-on Clothes

USA
November 8 – December 6, 1991
UK
December 17, 1993

LT03

LT01

LT02

Made of a hard plastic, each figure has a two-piece suit which snaps together, so that they turn into superheroes. *Bugs Bunny* becomes *Super Bugs, Tazmanian Devil* becomes *Taz-Flash, Petunia Pig* becomes *Wonder Pig,* and *Daffy Duck* becomes *Bat Duck.* Looney Tunes Clip-on Clothes (UK) are identical to the USA premiums, called Super Looney Tunes, released in 1991, except the American set had an under-three premium issued, *Daffy Duck in Bat Car:* ™ © 91 Warner Authorized Parody. China.

LT04

LT09

LT07

LT08

Looney Tunes was also released in Panama in January 1994; Germany in July 1994 (no boxes were issued on this Junior-Tüte); Guatemala in February 1994; Venezuela in March 1994; and Japan Test Market in September 1994.

Premiums		
LT01	Bugs Bunny	[**A**]
LT02	Tazmanian Devil	[**A**]
LT03	Petunia Pig	[**A**]
LT04	Daffy Duck	[**A**]

USA Premium		
LT09	Daffy Duck in Bat Car	[**B**]

Four UK boxes were issued		
LT05	Phone Box	Bugs	[**B**]
LT06	Bank	Duck	[**B**]
LT07	Cave	Taz	[**B**]
LT08	House	Petunia	[**B**]

USA bag was issued (not shown)		
LT10	Looney-Tune Maze	[**A**]

LT05

LT06

Looney Tunes Parade

UK
November 1–28, 1996

LT38

LT39

Leon Schlesinger produced the first Looney Tunes cartoon, *Sinkin' in the Bathtub*, in 1930. *Daffy Duck* was introduced in 1937, *Porky's Duck Hunt*, and in the same year Mel Blanc began the first of many character voices. *Bugs Bunny* was introduced in 1938, *Porky's Hare Hunt*, and said his first "What's Up Doc?" in *A Wild Hare*, 1940. *Tweety* first appeared in 1942, *A Tale of Two Kitties*. In 1944, Leon Schlesinger sold the cartoon rights to Warner Bros. In 1945, *Sylvester J. Pussycat* debuted in *Life with Feathers*; and *Road Runner* and *Wile E. Coyote* first appeared in *Fast and Furry-ous* in 1949. 1954 was the first appearance of *Tasmanian Devil* in *Devil May Hare*.

LT40

LT41

All premiums are made from a hard plastic and can be joined together to form a train of 14¼ inches long. Premiums stand between 3½ and 4 inches tall and when pulled along each toy moves, cymbals closing, *Taz* spinning within a collapsing crate, *Road Runner/Wile E. Coyote* moving forward and back, and poor *Sylvester* spinning in the washing machine. Premiums came in a clear sealed polybag with an insert card.

Premiums marked: © 1995 Warner Bros. China. (Bugs Bunny/Daffy Duck marked © 1994 Warner Bros. China). Insert card marked: © 1996 McDonald's Corporation.

Window poster

Premiums

LT38	Bugs Bunny and Daffy Duck	**[A]**
LT39	Taz	**[A]**
LT40	Wile E. Coyote and Road Runner	**[A]**
LT41	Sylvester and Tweety	**[A]**

Four boxes were issued

LT42	Parade	**[A]**
LT43	Cargo Ship	**[A]**
LT44	Railway Canyon	**[A]**
LT45	Wash Room	**[A]**

LT42   LT43

LT44   LT45

Looney Tunes Quack-up Cars

USA
April 9 – May 6, 1993
Costa Rica
1994

Each of these premiums are made from a hard plastic and are all push-along vehicles from the American TV Cartoon series *Looney Tunes* by Warner Bros. ™ and © '92 Warner Bros. China. *Bugs Bunny* has a red stretch limo, *Porky Ghost Catcher* is pushed along, and the Ghost moves up and down. *Taz* spins around when the back or front of the car is hit, and finally when *Daffy Duck*'s front bumper is knocked, the car falls in half.

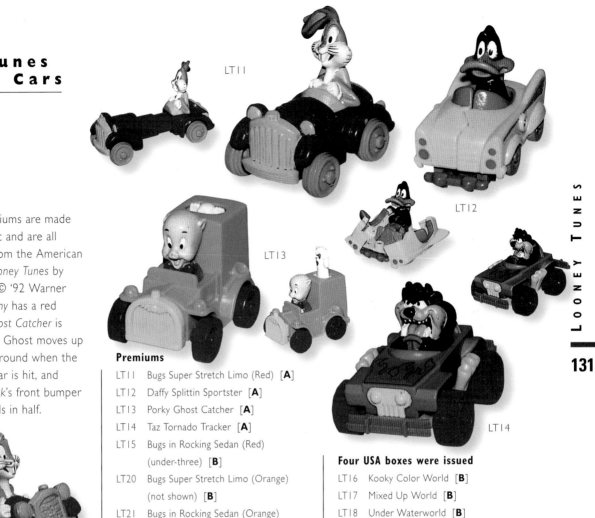

LT11

LT12

LT13

LT14

LT15

Premiums

LT11   Bugs Super Stretch Limo (Red) **[A]**
LT12   Daffy Splittin Sportster **[A]**
LT13   Porky Ghost Catcher **[A]**
LT14   Taz Tornado Tracker **[A]**
LT15   Bugs in Rocking Sedan (Red)
          (under-three) **[B]**
LT20   Bugs Super Stretch Limo (Orange)
          (not shown) **[B]**
LT21   Bugs in Rocking Sedan (Orange)
          (under-three) (not shown) **[B]**

Four USA boxes were issued

LT16   Kooky Color World **[B]**
LT17   Mixed Up World **[B]**
LT18   Under Waterworld **[B]**
LT19   Upside Down World **[B]**

Looney Tunes

Canada
1989

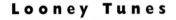

LT21

LT22

LT23

LT24

Each of the premiums are made of hard plastic, with a hard rubber character which comes with each vehicle. *Sylvester* and *Tweety* are in a blue plane, *Wile E. Coyote* and *Road Runner* are on a hand pump railway truck, *Bugs Bunny* is on a green and red scooter, and finally *Daffy Duck* sits in a yellow car with red wheels.

All the figures marked with Charan

Ind. © Warner Bros. Inc. 1989 and all the vehicles marked: © 1989 McDonald's China (except the blue plane, which had no markings on it at all). Each of these cartoon characters have their own TV series by Warner Bros. This set was released in Canada only and was called *What's Up Doc?* It was a Point of Purchase (P.O.P.) for 59 cents each.

Premiums

LT21   Sylvester and Tweety **[B]**
LT22   Wile E. Coyote and Road Runner **[B]**
LT23   Bugs Bunny **[B]**
LT24   Daffy Duck **[B]**

Looney Tunes NBA All-star Showdown

USA

April, 1995

Seven plastic tall cups came with this promotion, approximately 7 inches high and each one based on a famous American basketball player. Issued with each cup was also a fries carton with a photograph of the same star. Each cup and carton came free when you purchased any Extra Value Meal. "Try the McBacon DeLuxe, two beef patties, smoky bacon, lettuce, tomato, mayo, and cheese on a double decker bun with fries" was advertised on the trayliner. Also appearing with the famous basketball players are the famous Looney Tunes characters by Warner Bros.

Cup and cartons marked: © 1995 McDonald's Corporation, Looney Tunes ™ and © 1995 Warner Bros. © 1995 NBA Properties, Inc.

Fries cartons made in USA. Cup LT34 made by Packer Plastics, Cups LT29, LT30, LT32 and LT35 Made by Packaging Resources. (Cups LT31 and LT33 Made by "The Collectibles ®" Toronto in Canada.)

LT29

LT30

LT31

LT32

LT33   LT34   LT35

LT29

LT30

LT31

LT32   LT33   LT34   LT35

Trayliner

LT29   Michael Jordan – Bugs Bunny [**A**]
LT30   Larry Johnson – Wile E. Coyote [**A**]
LT31   Larry Bird – Sylvester [**A**]
LT32   Reggie Miller – Road Runner [**A**]
LT33   Patrick Ewing – Yosemite Sam [**A**]
LT34   Shawn Kemp – Daffy Duck [**A**]
LT35   Charles Barkley – Tasmanian Devil [**A**]
        (Cups plus fries cartons)

Mac Tonight

USA • 3rd Set Issue

September 7 – October 4, 1990

Mac Tonight was first released as a regional test promotion in California in 1988 with one box issued for all premiums (MT10). The *Surf Ski* (MT07) was issued without wheels and the *Airplane* had blue lenses in sunglasses (MT08).

It was re-released again in September 1989; same premiums but with a bag instead of a box. In the early part of 1990, Mac Tonight was re-released in parts of St. Louis, Missouri, where they used a Happy Meal bag (MT11) and in September in Chicago. Two premiums were different in this 1990 promotion. The *Surf Ski* had three white wheels underneath and the *Airplane* had black lenses in his sunglasses. All premiums came polybagged with an insert card. © 1988 McDonald's China.

Mac Tonight also ran in New Zealand in September 1990, Venezuela in June 1991.

Mac Tonight

Australia

1993

This consisted of four plastic premiums. The *Pencil* had a Mac Tonight head on it. The *Mask* was 2¾ inches in size and the *Photo Frame* was 1¾ inches.

Premiums (not shown)

MT12 Plastic Cup [**A**]
MT13 Pencil [**A**]
(premiums and box not shown)
MT14 Mask [**A**]
MT15 Photo Frame [**A**]

One box was issued (not shown)

MT16 Mac Tonight Skyline Box [**A**]

MT01

MT02

MT03

MT05

MT04

MT06

MT08

MT09

Premiums

MT01 Jeep Green [**A**]
MT02 Sports Car Red Porsche [**A**]
MT03 Surf Ski (yellow lens in sunglasses) [**A**]
MT04 Scooter Black [**A**]
MT05 Motor Cycle Red [**A**]
MT06 Airplane (black lens in sunglasses) [**A**]
MT07 Surf Ski (no wheels, not shown) [**B**]
MT08 Airplane (blue lens in sunglasses) [**B**]
MT09 Mac/Skateboard (under-three) [**B**]

MT10 Box issued – On the Road 1988
       (not shown) [**B**]
MT11 Bag issued – Mac/Vehicles 1989,
       1990 (not shown) [**B**]

Magic School Bus

USA • Canada
September 9 – October 6, 1994

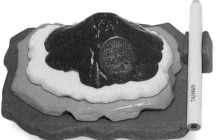

MH03

MH01

MH04

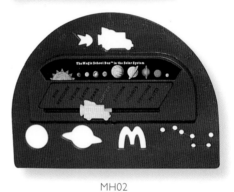

MH02

MH06

This national promotion is based on an American TV series of the same name (Scholastic's The Magic School Bus) and McDonald's is just one of several sponsors to encourage a more interesting way for kids to learn science. Books were also available from your local library. A 13-part series, shown on PBS-TV, featured field trips made on a School Bus. The monthly magazine produced by McDonald's for kids, called "Fun Time" (FT, for short) dedicated a complete month's issue (issue 5, October 1994) to the Magic School Bus.

Premiums came in a printed polybag, and each premium is made from a hard plastic. The *Collector Card Kit* is a yellow bus. Inside is a sheet of stickers and 10 double-sided picture cards, with useful information, i.e., Ocean, Desert, Planet Earth, Sound, Dinosaurs, Food, and the Human Body. The *Space Tracer* shows the planets in the solar system, on a sliding scale. This can also be used

as a protractor, stencil, or ruler. The *Undersea Adventure Game* is a maze game, showing you different sea creatures on the way. This is also used as a clipboard. The *Geo Fossil* Finder is a five-piece premium, including the pencil, which can be clipped together. Each section represents a layer of the Earth starting from the volcano (red), then Limestone (yellow), Shale (aqua), Sandstone (blue). The Sandstone can be used as a stencil. The Shale and Limestone can be used as rub and draw templates of animal fossils. The under-three is the same as the Undersea Adventure Game, except that the under-threes does not have the yellow clipboard on the end.

Premiums marked: © 1994 Scholastic Inc. – China/Chine.

Packaging marked: © 1994 Scholastic Inc. – © 1994 McDonald's Corporation.

Premiums

MH01 Collector Card Kit **[A]**
MH02 Space Tracer-Ruler **[A]**
MH03 Geo Fossil Finder **[A]**
MH04 Undersea Adventure Gamej **[A]**
MH05 Undersea Adventure Game
       (under-three) (not shown) **[A]**

One bag was issued

MH06 Magic School Bus **[A]**

Makin' Movies

USA • Canada

January 7 – February 3, 1994

MA01

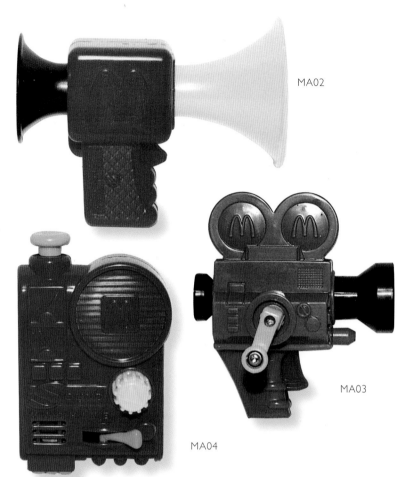

MA02

MA03

MA04

MA06   MA07

his national promotion had the theme of making your own movies. Each premium is made from a hard plastic (except the Chalk). The *Clapboard* is used at the beginning of each scene before filming, to tell the Editor where this scene goes in the film, and also helps the sound to be synchronised with the talking. This *Clapboard* was later used in another UK promotion called "McFilms," November 1994, except that the UK version only had McDonald's printed on the front of the board. The *Director's Megaphone* was also used in the UK promotion "McFilms" and was identical. The *Movie Camera* has a viewer to look through, a red button that you can press, and a yellow handle which you can turn. When you look through the viewer, it gives the impression of the film frames flicking through the *Camera*. The *Camera* also had a Warning on it: "Do Not Look into The Sun." The under-three is identical to the *Sounds Effects Machine* (MA04).

All premiums came in printed polybags and marked: © 1993 McDonald's Corp. China. *Makin' Movies* ran in Puerto Rico in January 1994; Panama (Spanish box) in March 1994; Japan Test Market in June 1994.

MA08   MA09

Premiums

MA01 Clapboard with Chalk [**A**]
MA02 Director's Megaphone [**A**]
MA03 Makin' Movies Camera [**A**]
MA04 Sound Effects Machine [**A**]
MA05 Sound Effects Machine (under-three)
      (not shown) [**A**]

Four boxes were issued

MA06 Makin Prints [**B**]
MA07 Popcorn [**B**]
MA08 Scoreboard [**B**]
MA09 Tickets [**B**]

Marvel Super Heroes

USA • Canada
May 17 – June 13, 1996

SH01

SH02

SH03

SH04

SH05

SH06

SH07

SH08

SH10

This promotion from the USA are all Super Heroes that originated in the Marvel Comics and are now showing in most countries as an animated cartoon called *Marvel Hour*. It is shown in the UK on a children's program called *Saturday Aardvark* shown on BBC 1 on Saturday mornings. Each character/vehicle is made from a hard plastic and stand between 4¼ inches tall (the *Hulk* being the tallest) and 1½ inches tall (*Wolverine* being the smallest). *Spider Man* and *The Incredible Hulk* each have their own comic series. *Storm, Wolverine,* and *Jubilee* come from the *X-Men* series; and *Invisible Woman,* the *Blue-Eyed Thing,* and *Human Torch* come from the *Fantastic Four* series. Press *Spider Man* down and he will cast his net. Push *Storm* along and watch

her spin with the clouds lighting up. Slide the levers on the back of *Wolverine*'s ship to expose the weapons. When pushed along *Jubilee* will keep changing the color on her disc. *Invisible Woman* will change color when dipped in icy cold water. Press down the exhaust on his vehicle and *Thing* will spin around inside his vehicle and knock down the sides. *Hulk* has a moving head and arms and a spring-loaded torso when pushed down. *Human Torch* has movable arms and waist. All premiums came in printed polybags written in French, Spanish, and English. One bag was issued with a coupon to send away for two free issues of Spider Man Magazine. Premiums marked: © 1996 Marvel China/Chine.

Premiums

SH01 Spider Man™ Vehicle [**A**]
SH02 Storm™ Vehicle [**A**]
SH03 Wolverine™ Vehicle [**A**]
SH04 Jubilee™ Vehicle [**A**]
SH05 Invisible Woman™ [**A**]
SH06 Thing™ Vehicle [**A**]
SH07 Hulk™ Figurine [**A**]
SH08 Human Torch™ Figurine [**A**]
SH09 Spider Man Ball (under-three) [**A**]

One bag was issued

SH10 Marvel Super Heroes [**A**]

Masterpiece Collection

WALT DISNEY

USA • Canada
April 19 – May 16, 1996

DW02

DW09 (under-three)

DW01

DW03

DW04

Walt Disney Masterpiece Collection celebrates these timeless classics which have been released on home video in America and in most other countries. Each premium came in a box in the shape of a video case, 5¼ inches high x 4 inches wide x 1¾ inches deep. Each box came in a cellophane wrapper. Each figurine is a one-piece toy, except *Pocahontas* and *Alice in Wonderland*, which are two-piece premiums. They each came with a comb/stand. *Merlin* stands the tallest at 4 inches and the shortest are the *Aristocats*, at 3¼ inches. All have movable heads and arms and some have movable waists. *Merlin* (beard), *Cinderella, Pocahontas, Snow White*, and *Alice* have real hair and *Robin Hood* has a fur-covered tail. *Scat Cat (Aristocats)* comes with a plush tummy; the rest of the toy is made from a hard plastic. Premiums marked: © Disney China/Chine.

DW10

Premiums

DW01   Cinderella
DW02   Robin Hood
DW03   Pocahontas
DW04   The Return of Jafar
DW05   Snow White
DW06   The Sword in the Stone
DW07   Alice in Wonderland
DW08   The Aristocats
DW09   Dumbo (under-three)

One bag was issued

DW10   Masterpiece Collection

DW06

DW05

DW07

DW08

Premium Boxes

McBoo Bags

USA

October 11–31, 1991

Released for Halloween in 1991. All bags were glow-in-the-dark treat bags made of vinyl. In some regions, to meet the demands, the bags were replaced with Halloween Pails, which came out in 1990 (the handles were re-designed to look like a McDonald's "M" or like rabbit ears). Each handle had a safety sticker, stating that "handles are not to be used as hats; they may cause discomfort." There were no bags or boxes issued with this promotion as the food was taken away in the actual McBoo Bag.

McBoo Bags: "Safety tested for children of all ages. Recommended for children age one and over."

© 1990 McDonald's Corporation. Made and printed in Taiwan.

Panama issued *McBoo Bags*, but only two of them, *Witch* and *Ghost*, in 1992.

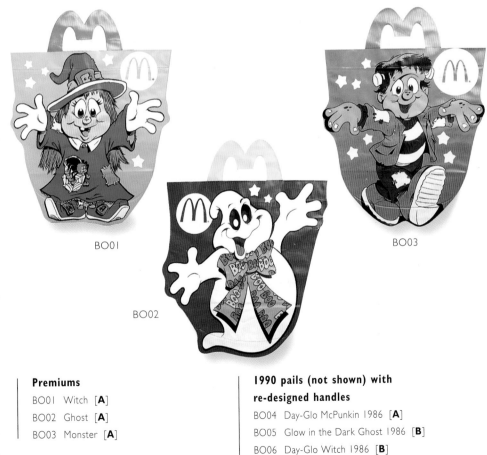

BO01

BO02

BO03

Premiums

BO01 Witch [**A**]

BO02 Ghost [**A**]

BO03 Monster [**A**]

1990 pails (not shown) with re-designed handles

BO04 Day-Glo McPunkin 1986 [**A**]

BO05 Glow in the Dark Ghost 1986 [**B**]

BO06 Day-Glo Witch 1986 [**B**]

McCharacters on Bikes
(McDonaldland on Wheels)

USA
August 29 – September 6, 1991
New Zealand • Europe

OB01

OB02

OB03

OB04

This regional promotion was brought in as a fill-in, when certain McDonald's restaurants in the USA became short on supplies of the previous promotion, "Barbie and Hot Wheels." There were no boxes issued in the USA, but four themed boxes were issued in Europe. All premiums, USA and Europe, came in clear polybags with insert cards, and each McDonaldland figure came in its own sealed polybag, within the main packaging. The insert cards in the USA are all the same, and show all four bikes on one color picture, and on the bottom right of the insert card is a photo of all the bikes joined together. "Happy Meal" is printed on each insert card. The European insert card is different with each of the premiums. Each has a drawing of a bike, and one drawing with all of them joined together. Each card was printed in a

different color, i.e., pink, mauve, green, or red. Printed on the insert card is "McDonaldland on Wheels Happy Meal." Each premium is made from a hard plastic, and comes in four sections: front wheel, frame, back wheels, and character. Each premium measures about 3¾ inches long when the bike is assembled, and when all the bikes are joined together, this measures 8½ inches long. These bikes were also used in the USA 1989 Muppet Kids Happy Meal. Bikes marked: © 1989 McDonald's Corp. © 1989 Simon Mkt. Figures marked: © 1990 McDonald's Corp. China. *McDonaldland on Wheels* also ran in Belgium, Denmark, France, Italy, Holland, Norway, Spain, Sweden, and Switzerland in March–April 1991. Malaysia ran it as a self-liquidator with a food purchase in April–May 1991, called "McWheels."

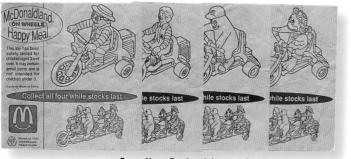

Four New Zealand Insert Cards

Premiums

OB01	Birdie	[**B**]
OB02	Grimace	[**B**]
OB03	Hamburglar	[**B**]
OB04	Ronald	[**B**]

Four European boxes were issued (not shown)

OB05	Themed
OB06	Themed
OB07	Themed
OB08	Themed

McDino Changeables

USA

May 24 – June 20, 1991

DC10   DC12

Each of these premiums was a food, or a food packaging that transformed into a dinosaur. Two were issued each week. In some of the polybags there was a 12-cent bonus savings coupon book on some well-known products. A variation on one under-three, in some states, was *Small Fry-Ceratops* with the red arches on the front. Premiums came in a clear polybag with an insert card. The USA premiums differ slightly to the UK premiums; the USA premiums marked: ® (Registered); unlike the UK set, marked: ™ (Trade Mark). © 1990 McDonald's Corp. China.

Premiums

DC01 Happy Meal-o-Don [**A**]

DC02 Quarter Pounder With Cheese-o-Saurus [**A**]

DC03 Hot Cakes-o-Dactyl [**A**]

DC04 McNuggets-o-Saurus [**A**]

DC05 Big Mac-o-Saurus Rex [**A**]

DC06 Fry-Ceratops [**A**]

DC07 McDino Cone [**A**]

DC08 Tri-Shake-Atops [**A**]

One bag was issued

DC11 Two McDinos [**A**]

DC09 Bronto CheeseBurger (under-three) [**B**]

DC10 Small Fry-Ceratops (under-three) (yellow arches) [**B**]

DC12 Small Fry-Ceratops (under-three) (red arches) [**B**]

DC09

DC01

DC02

DC03

DC04

DC05

DC06

DC07

DC08

McDinosaurs
(McDinos)

UK
April 3, 1992
Germany
January 9 – February 2, 1992

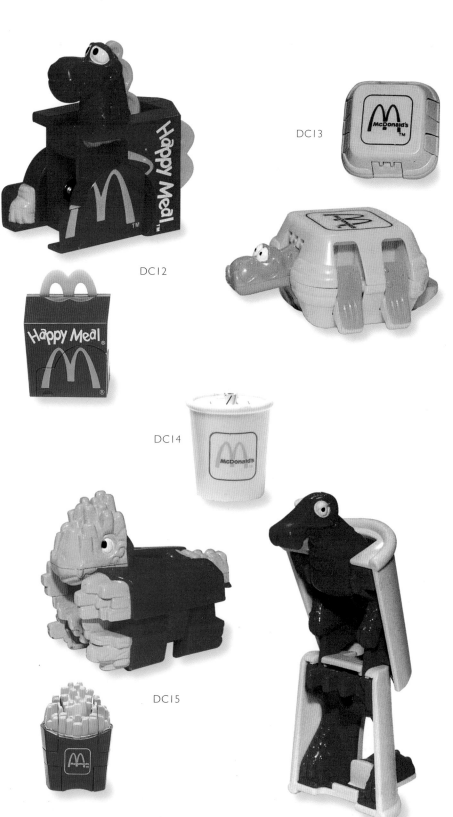

DC13

DC12

DC14

DC15

These four premiums were first issued in the USA, called McDino Changeables (see *McDino Changeables USA 1991* page 141). All premiums are made from a hard plastic and relate to food packaging that changes into dinosaurs. Each premium stands about 2½ inches high. Four related boxes were issued with this set. They could be punched out and built into slopes and caves for the McDinos to play in.

The UK set marked: ™ (Trade Mark) whereas the USA set (which contained eight premiums) marked: ® (Registered). © 1990 McDonald's Corp ™. China.

McDino also ran in Switzerland, Belgium, Sweden, Denmark, Spain, Finland, Portugal, France, Norway, Greece, and Italy on January 2, 1992; China on April 5, 1994; Singapore and Puerto Rico in June 1991. Taiwan, Malaysia and Panama in July 1991; New Zealand in August 1991. Japan (Test Market May 1991) ran the promotion on August 8, 1992.

Germany only issued three premiums; French Fries (DC15), Sandwich (DC13), and Drink (DC14). Once again all these premiums marked: ® and not with ™. No boxes issued on this Junior-Tüte (Happy Meal).

DC19   DC17

Premiums
DC12 Happy Meal-o-Don [**B**]
DC13 McNuggets-o-Saurus [**B**]
DC14 Tri-Shake-Atops [**B**]
DC15 Fry-Ceratops [**B**]

Four UK boxes were issued
DC16 Purple Egg (not shown) [**B**]
DC17 Surf Board [**B**]
DC18 Dinosaurs (not shown) [**B**]
DC19 Volcano [**B**]

McDonaldland Figurines

Canada *1985*

FI01

FI02

FI03

FI04

Each character is made from solid rubber and stands about 2½ to 3 inches high. This set is quite old going by the date stamped on each premium. They were made in Canada.

Premiums marked: McDonald's ® 1985 Made in Canada.

Canada *1990*

These stand between 2 and 2¼ inches high and are made from solid rubber. *Ronald* and *Birdie* have a maple leaf under the "M," but *Hamburglar* and *Grimace* do not. There are no dates or McDonald's name marked on any premium. All premiums marked: Made in China (only).

Canada *1992*

Four premiums are made from solid soft rubber and stand 2 inches high. Premiums marked: © 1992 McDonald's Corp. Taiwan.

McDonaldland Figurines

Odd

These odd figurines are made from solid rubber. There is a slight difference in each, compared to the above figurines: *Big Mac* has his arms out, plus he has a yellow "M" on his belt and hat and has black shoes. *Grimace* is the same as above except that it is marked with McDonald's 1985 only, and the other two premiums marked: McDonald's 1985 made in China.

Hamburglar has a longer nose, yellow

FI10

shoes, and orange inside his cape, and we know that he was issued in Germany as a clean-up in 1991. He was accompanied by *Ronald*, *Grimace*, and *Mayor McCheese* (not shown). These last four premiums mentioned may not have been unique to Germany.

FI11

FI12

Ronald McDonald Flyers

UK

From August 16, 1980

FY01   FY02

T hese Ronald McDonald Flyers were free give-aways with any purchase to any child under the age of 12. This promotion started from August 16, while stocks lasted. Made from a flexible plastic, each measures about 6 inches in diameter.

Free give-aways

FY01   Ronald (Red) [**A**]
FY02   Ronald (Blue) [**A**]
FY03   Ronald (Yellow) (not shown) [**A**]

McDonaldland Flyers

UK

1990

FY05

FY04

FY07

FY06

E ach Flyer was made from a flexible plastic and measured about 6 inches in diameter. Each Flyer had the character's name embossed on it. These Flyers were given away with any food or drink purchase.

Note: This *Ronald* has wider arms and legs, compared to the earlier UK Flyers. Flyers are not dated or marked, except for the character's name on the front.

Free give-aways

FY04   Ronald (Red) [**A**]
FY05   Grimace (Purple) [**A**]
FY06   Hamburglar (Orange) [**A**]
FY07   Officer Big Mac (Yellow) - [**A**]

Flying Rings

USA

(not dated)

O nce again very much like the UK, a set of three flyers with *Ronald McDonald* standing with his arms not outstretched; still only about 6 inches in diameter and made from a flexible plastic. Flyers are marked on the back: "Safety Tested for Children 3 and Over." Printed on the front is Ronald McDonald®, plus the McDonald's "M" logo. Flyers are not dated.

There is another set of three USA Flyers, same size and colors: Red, Yellow, Blue, but they have *Ronald McDonald* with his arms and legs outstretched like the UK ones.

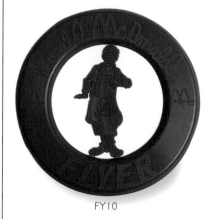

FY10

Free give-aways

FY08   Ronald McDonald (Red) (not shown) [**A**]
FY09   Ronald McDonald (Yellow) (not shown) [**A**]
FY10   Ronald McDonald (Blue) [**A**]

McDonaldland Magic

New Zealand
March 4, 1992

This is an unusual set. There are four premiums to this promotion and they all do a magic trick. Each premium is made from a hard plastic and they stand between 2½ and 3 inches high. *Ronald* is a two-piece premium. He comes with a piece of string. *Ronald* has a hole in the top of his hat which leads down into a hollow stomach where there sits a loose marble. The hole in *Ronald's* hat is too small for the marble to escape. We think the trick is to thread the string into the hole, turn *Ronald* upside down, pull the string gently out so that the marble will lock the string in place, and *Ronald* can hang from the string. If this is not right please let us know. Thank you. *Birdie* is also a two-piece premium. The famous disappearing coin trick is in *Birdie's* case the disappearing burgers. Pull out the plastic tray on her back and in the middle of the tray is a picture of a burger. Rotate the tray 180° and place the tray back into the slot on *Birdie's* back. Say a few magic words, remove the tray, and the burgers have disappeared. Repeat the moves and the burgers will reappear. *Grimace* is the famous disappearing egg trick, but in this case *Grimace* has a milkshake instead. *Grimace* comes in three pieces. Join *Grimace* together; lift off the first top section to show the milkshake. Replace the top section over the milkshake, say a few magic words and then remove the first two sections together to reveal the milkshake has gone. *Fry-Guy*: four friends of *Ronald* appear and disappear in a box. Each premium marked: © 1991 McDonald's Corp. China. Japan (Test Market October 1991) ran on October 1992; Malaysia, Taiwan on March 4, 1992; Panama in May 1992; Mexico in April 1993; Argentina in May 1993.

MG01
MG02
MG03

Premiums

MG01 Ronald [**A**]
MG02 Birdie [**A**]
MG03 Grimace [**A**]
MG04 Fry-Guy (not shown) [**A**]

One box was issued

MG04 (not shown)

McDonaldland Maze Game

Australia
December 10, 1993 – January 8, 1994

This McDonaldland character promotion from Australia is a set of four pinball-type games made from a hard plastic. Each stands 3¼ inches high with a width of 2 inches. Each shows a McDonaldland character with a food theme: *Ronald* with Big Mac, *Grimace* with Milkshake, *Birdie* with French Fries, and *Hamburglar* with a Hamburger. Each premium has a different color all inside.

Premiums marked: © 1993 McDonald's Aust Ltd China.

Packaging is a clear polybag, with printed writing on: "M" ™ (logo) © 1995 McDonald's Australia Ltd. Contents made in China by Creata Promotion. "Safety tested for children aged 3 and over. Caution: Not Intended for children under 3."

Australia may have issued this promotion in December, 1993, with a variation.

MG01
MG04
MG02
MG03

Premiums

MG01 Ronald [**A**]
MG02 Grimace [**A**]
MG03 Birdie [**A**]
MG04 Hamburglar [**A**]

One box was issued

MG05 Generic Box (not shown) [**A**]

McFarm

UK
June 2 – July 2, 1995

MC03

MC01

MC04

MC02

In this promotion the McDonaldland characters are down on the farm. Each premium is made from a hard plastic and they are all push-along toys on wheels. *Ronald* is in his tractor. When he is pushed along, *Ronald* and the brown exhaust pipe will bob up and down. *Hamburglar* is driving a combine harvester. When he is pushed along the front yellow harvester blade revolves around and acts like a screw thread, which sends some lose corn from one end to the other. *Birdie* is working in the barn, pushing a wheelbarrow with three hens in it. The hens bob up and down when pushed

along. *Birdie*'s arms can also be moved. *Grimace* sits in an orange van and is driving to the village with corn on the cob in the back of the van. When pushed along the van's storage compartment's floor will vibrate, sending the corn up in the air.

All premiums came in polybags with insert cards.

The premiums with vehicles marked: © 1995 McDonald's Corp. China.

Birdie marked: © 1995 McDonald's Corp Macau SN.

McFarm also ran in Germany in May 1995, with the same packaging, but in German instead.

Premiums

MC01   Ronald   [**A**]
MC02   Hamburglar   [**A**]
MC03   Birdie   [**A**]
MC04   Grimace   [**A**]

Four UK boxes were issued

MC05   Farm House   [**A**]
MC06   The Fields   [**A**]
MC07   The Barn   [**A**]
MC08   The Village   [**A**]

MC05   MC06   MC07   MC08

McFilms

MF02

MF03

MF01

This UK set is actually a variation of three different USA sets, except that there is a slight difference in each premium. The *Applause Paws* was marked Nickelodeon and the *Clapper Board* had Director, Take, and Title stenciled on the front. The *Film Wheel* was first issued in *Behind the Scenes* in the USA, September 1992. The *Loud Mouth Mike* and *Applause Paws* were first issued in Nickelodeon USA, June 1993. The *Clapper Board* was first issued in *Makin' Movies* in the USA, January 1994. © McDonald's Corp. ™ China.

McFilms also ran in Holland in March 1994, France in April 1994.

Premiums

MF01   Film Wheel © 1992 [**A**]
MF02   Loud Mouth Mic © 1993 [**A**]
MF03   Clapper Board and Chalk © 1993 [**A**]
MF04   Applause Paws © 1993 [**A**]

Four boxes were issued

MF05   Art and Editing Room [**A**]
MF06   Wild West Movie Set [**A**]
MF07   Pirate Boat Scene – with Grimace [**A**]
MF08   Magic Show with Ronald [**A**]

MF04

MF08   MF05   MF06   MF07

McMusic

UK *August 12, 1994*
Germany *April, 1992*

MM02   MM04

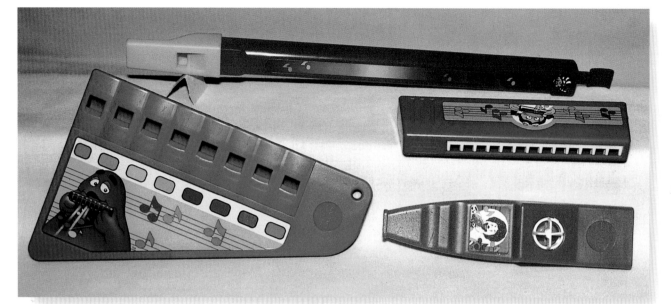

MM01   MM03

E ach UK premium was a hard plastic musical instrument. All are wind instruments. They were made by Bontempi in Italy. Premiums came in clear polybags with insert cards. *McMusic* also ran in Europe in May 1994; Germany February 1995.

In 1992, Germany, Bontempi, and McDonald's introduced three musical premiums. Two of them are the same design as the UK promotion, *Flute* and *Harmonica*. With these premiums the stickers are of the same theme, i.e. Ronald McDonald conducting with baton, with the music score behind him, and all three premiums are one color, blue. This promotion was called *Musikinstrumente*. Each premium came in polybag with an insert card.

UK Premiums

MM01 Grimace Pan Pipes [**A**]
MM02 Hamburglar Magic Flute [**A**]
MM03 Ronald Kazoo [**A**]
MM04 Birdie Harmonica [**A**]

German Premiums (not shown)

MM09 Maraca [**A**]
MM10 Harmonica [**A**]
MM11 Flute [**A**]

Four UK boxes were issued

MM05 Theatre (Grimace) [**A**]
MM06 Music Class (Hamburglar) [**A**]
MM07 Bandstand (Ronald) [**A**]
MM08 Barn Dance (Birdie) [**A**]

MM08   MM06   MM07   MM05

McNugget Buddies

USA
December 30, 1988 – January 26, 1989

MB01

MB02

MB03

MB04

MB05

MB07

MB08

MB09

MB10

MB11

MB12

The McNugget Buddies were part of the McDonald's commercials which were shown on Saturday morning TV. Each of the 10 characters was made from a semi-hard plastic and came with three interchangeable pieces: body, hair or hat, and belt. The under-threes had no moving parts. The *Corny* character came with either a red or beige popcorn belt. Some stores issued a sheet of stickers, facial features and clothing, etc., which could be placed onto McNugget body outlines. Premiums marked: © 1988 McDonald's China.

A combination of four premiums from the eight was used in Hong Kong and Singapore, as a self-liquidator. A self-liquidator is where McDonald's restaurants just sell them off, no purchase necessary. Hong Kong ran this promotion in March–April 1989 and used: *Corny, Snorkel, Drummer,* and *Rocker*. Singapore ran in July–August 1989 and used: *Corny, Snorkel, Rocker,* and *Boomerang*.

Premiums

MB01	Cowpoke	[A]
MB02	First-Class	[A]
MB03	Sarge	[A]
MB04	Drummer	[A]
MB05	Corny (red popcorn belt)	[B]
MB06	Corny (beige popcorn belt, not shown)	[A]
MB07	Sparky	[A]
MB08	Boomerang	[A]
MB09	Volley	[A]
MB10	Snorkel	[A]
MB11	Rocker	[A]
MB12	Daisy (under-three)	[C]
MB13	Slugger (under-three) (not shown)	[C]
MB14	Dress-up McNuggets sheet (not shown)	[B]

Four boxes were issued (not shown)

MB15	Apartments	[C]
MB16	Beauty Store	[C]
MB17	Gardens	[C]
MB18	Post Office	[C]

KR01

KR02

KR03

McRings

Round Top • Test I
USA
1977

KR05

KR06

T he *Rings* and *Wrist Wallets* were issued at the same time. Being one of the very first concepts for a "Happy Meal" in the USA, called "Round Top," unlike the traditional Happy Meal box with a slanted top, these three boxes were of a curved design, hence the name. *McWrist Wallets* were in the form of a watch strap (the clock face lifted to reveal the wallet), made from a transparent colored plastic.

Premiums Rings

KR01   Big Mac (Yellow/Blue)
KR02   Captain (Orange/Black)
KR03   Hamburglar (Yellow/Black)
KR04   Grimace (Purple/Red) (not shown)
KR05   Ronald (White/Red)
KR06   Hamburglar

Three boxes were issued (not shown)

KR15   Riddle–What's Wrong Here?
KR16   Lion–Ronald–Big Mac
KR17   Giraffe–Ronald–Mayor–Big Mac–
           Hamburglar

McWrist Wallets (not shown)

KR11   Big Mac (Blue)
KR12   Captain (Green)
KR13   Hamburglar (Yellow)
KR14   Ronald (Red)

150

McRobots

UK
April – May, 1990

MR03   MR02   MR04   MR01

E ach premium was a food or food packet, and was made of hard plastic. All the premiums transformed into robots. This set originated from an American promotion called "New Food Changeables" which was released in 1989. This American set contained eight premiums. © 1987 McDonald's Corp. Made in China.

   McRobots also ran in Guatemala and Germany from February 21 – March 17, 1991 and Belgium, Denmark, Finland, France, Holland, Italy, Norway, Spain, Sweden, and Switzerland in November 1989.

Premiums

MR01   Fry Force – Large Fries [**B**]
MR02   Macro Mac – Big Mac [**B**]
MR03   Gallacta Burger – Quarter-Pounder
           with Cheese [**B**]
MR04   Krypto Cup – Soft Drink [**B**]

Four UK boxes were issued

MR05   Large Fries [**C**]
MR06   Big Mac (not shown) [**C**]
MR07   Quarter-Pounder with Cheese [**C**]
MR08   Soft Drink [**C**]

McRockin Foods

UK
November 27, 1992

RK03

RK01

RK02

RK04

Each premium was a McDonald's food or carton with facial features. They were all made from a hard plastic, except for the milkshake which was made from soft rubber. All the premiums are wind-up toys. The Cheese Burger has feet. When wound up it will jump up and down; at the same time the top half of the bun is hinged and will act as a clapper. The *Fries* walks forward as the fries on top move from side to side. *The Milkshake* will revolve around and dance. Finally *The Filet-o-Fish* will move round in a circle with its fins revolving. Premiums marked: © 1991 McDonald's Corp. Made in China.

McRockin Foods also ran in: Switzerland, Sweden, Spain, Belgium, Denmark, Finland, Portugal, Norway, Holland, France, Greece, and Italy in April–May 1992; Germany ran this promotion from February 9–29, 1993. Japan Market Tested this promotion in December 1991, then ran December 1992–January 1993; Taiwan in July 1992; Singapore in June 1992. Panama called this promotion "Rockomida Divertida" with a generic bag in a Spanish design.

Premiums

RK01	Cheese Burger	[**A**]
RK02	Fries	[**A**]
RK03	Milkshake	[**A**]
RK04	Filet-o-Fish	[**A**]

Two boxes were issued

RK05	On Stage	[**B**]
RK06	On Tour	[**B**]

FK05

RK06

McRodeo

RD02

RD04

RD01

RD03

Each premium is made from a hard plastic, and stands about 2 to 2½ inches high. All are wind-up toys. *Ronald* is in a yellow barrel and comes with a sticker of a bulls-eye for the barrel. Once wound up, *Ronald* will revolve in the barrel with his head popping up and down. *Grimace* is on a bucking bronco horse; when wound up the horse starts to buck. *Birdie* is a two-piece premium; a rope that fits around *Birdie* spins like a lasso when she is wound up. *Hamburglar* is a rodeo cowboy and walks forward and his head rocks from side to side when wound up. Each premium comes in a clear polybag with an insert paper and marked: © 1995 McD Corp. China.

McRodeo was also released in Japan in November 1994, as a Test Market; Mexico in March–April 1995; New Zealand and Panama in May 1995. The packaging and box/bag may vary in design from country to country.

McRodeo is the very first Official Happy Meal to be released in Hong Kong, in December 1995. The previous promotions have either been a Point of Purchase (P.O.P.) or a Test Market.

Premiums

RD01   Ronald   [**A**]
RD02   Grimace   [**A**]
RD03   Birdie   [**A**]
RD04   Hamburglar   [**A**]

Four UK boxes were issued

RD05   Rodeo Arena   [**A**]
RD06   Camp Site   [**A**]
RD07   Saloon   [**A**]
RD08   Western Town   [**A**]

RD05   RD06   RD07   RD08

McDonald's Shades

UK

July – August 1991

A set of three hard plastic sunglasses, each with a different color arm. All had black rims. Each has McDonald's ™ stenciled on the outside of the right arm and Taiwan embossed on the inside of the right arm. All premiums came in a clear polybag with a black and yellow insert card. Insert cards marked: "Be Cool with your Hot Neon Shades, safety tested for children age 3 and over. Not intended for children under 3." Premiums marked: CE Simon Marketing Int. Gmbh D-6072 Dreieich © 1991 McDonald's Corporation.

Germany also issued identical shades in April–May 1991 as a self-liquidator.

Purchases

PS01   Pink Shades [**A**]
PS02   Yellow Shades [**A**]
PS03   Blue Shades [**A**]

PS01

PS02

PS03

McDonald's Skimmers

UK

1989

These skimmers are made from a semi-hard plastic and are approximately 8 inches in diameter. Both skimmers are slightly transparent in color and have a large McDonald's "M" logo on the front of them.

Both purchases marked: McDonald's Corporation. Made in West Germany by Wedo Promotion.

Purchases

PS07   Red Skimmer [**A**]
PS08   Yellow Skimmer [**A**]

PS07

PS08

McDonald Sports

Australia

June 9 – July, 2 1995

A sports theme with McDonaldland characters. *Ronald* is playing football, *Birdie* is playing tennis, *Grimace* is playing baseball, and *Hamburglar* is lifting weights. Each character is made from a solid hard plastic and stands between 2¼ and 3¾ inches high. The premiums themselves are not dated.

The packaging is a clear polybag with black writing on it. Premiums marked: "M" logo, © 1994 McDonald's Australia Ltd. Contents made in China by Creata Promotion. "Caution: Not intended for children under three."

DP01

DP02

DP03

DP04

DP05 Front

DP05 Back

Premiums

DP01   Ronald [**A**]

DP02   Birdie [**A**]

DP03   Grimace [**A**]

DP04   Hamburglar [**A**]

One box was issued

DP05   Generic Box [**A**]

McSpy

(Mission Undercover)

Europe

June, 1993

Premiums

MS07   Blue Lunch Box © 1988 [**A**]

MS08   Phone/Periscope © 1991 [**A**]

MS09   Decoder Wheel © 1992 [**A**]

MS10   Spy-Noculars © 1992 [**A**]

(Premiums not shown)

These premiums were also known as "Agent 008" in Hong Kong, Macau, and China in August 1994 and "Mystery II" in Puerto Rico in December 1993; "McSpy" in Japan in December 1993 and in Europe, "Mission Undercover" in June 1993. The *Blue Lunch Box* was originally issued in the USA, but in red and green with *Ronald McDonald* and *Grimace* with a bulletin board. This could be used as a surveillance case to hold all the gadgets. *Phone/Periscope* is identical to the one issued in "Mystery of the Lost Arches" (USA, January 1992). *Decoder Wheel* was yellow and red, with the alphabet around the yellow outside, and around the inner red disc. Two pens, one yellow, and one white with a blue pen-holder was a part of the Decoder. This made a five-piece premium. *Spy-Noculars* are identical to the ones issued in "M Squad" USA January 1991.

Europe issued a Mystery activities and games bag. Hong Kong issued four generic boxes with McDonaldland characters on them.

McDonaldland Straws

Australia

January, 1993

DS01   DS02   DS03   DS04

Premiums

DS01   Ronald   [**A**]

DS02   Birdie   [**A**]

DS03   Grimace   [**A**]

DS04   Hamburglar   [**A**]

One box was issued

DS05   Generic Box (not shown)

Four crazy McDonaldland character straws featured in this promotion. Each premium is a two-piece item, where the McDonaldland character is detachable, and can be placed anywhere along the straw. Each straw is shaped differently and is a different color. Both character and straw are made from a hard plastic and measure: straw, 9½–10½ inches long, and characters, 2¼–2½ inches high. The McDonaldland characters are in their own sealed polybags, within the main packaging. The main packaging is a clear polybag, with black writing on it. Premiums marked: "M" ™ logo, © 1993 McDonald's Australia Ltd. Contents made in China by Creata Promotion. "Caution: Not intended for children under three."

155

McDonald's Travel

Japan

October, 1995

TV01   TV02   TV03   TV04

McDonaldland characters in turbo racing cars. Each vehicle is push-down-and-go. Premiums are made from a hard plastic and measure about 3 inches long.

Each premium comes in a clear polybag with an insert card, accompanied by a set of stickers.

Premiums marked: © 1995 McDonald's Corp. China.

Premiums

TV01   Ronald   [**A**]

TV02   Hamburglar   [**A**]

TV03   Birdie   [**A**]

TV04   Grimace   [**A**]

One generic bag issued (not shown)

TV05   Ronald   [**A**]

McDonald's Waist Pouch

UK

July – August, 1991

Once again this promotion followed the Shades (see page 153). These came in the same colors: red, yellow, and blue. They also came in clear polybags with black and yellow insert cards. Insert cards marked: "Be Cool With Your Hot Neon Waist Pouch, safety tested age 3 and over etc." CE Simon Marketing Int. Gmbh D-6072 Dreieich.

Purchases marked: © 1991 McDonald's Corporation. Contents made in China.

Each waist pouch is made from nylon fabric and is all black with black adjustable straps, except the zipper lid is a different color. Each has a "McDonald's™" printed in small letters on the front.

PS05

PS0457

PS06

Purchases

PS04 Pink Waist Pouch [**A**]

PS05 Yellow Waist Pouch [**A**]

PS06 Blue Waist Pouch [**A**]

(Ronald) McDonald's Watch

UK

1986

Two battery-operated LCD watches were on offer at McDonald's restaurants. Each one is made from a soft plastic (except the buckle), and measured 7½ inches long, with a picture of *Ronald* on the face. Both watches cost £2.40 each; £1 was donated to the Ronald McDonald House at Guy's Hospital, London. There are three functions to each watch: time, date, and seconds.

The back of the watch reads: © 1984 McDonald's Corp. "Not intended for use by children under 3." Made in Hong Kong.

PS28

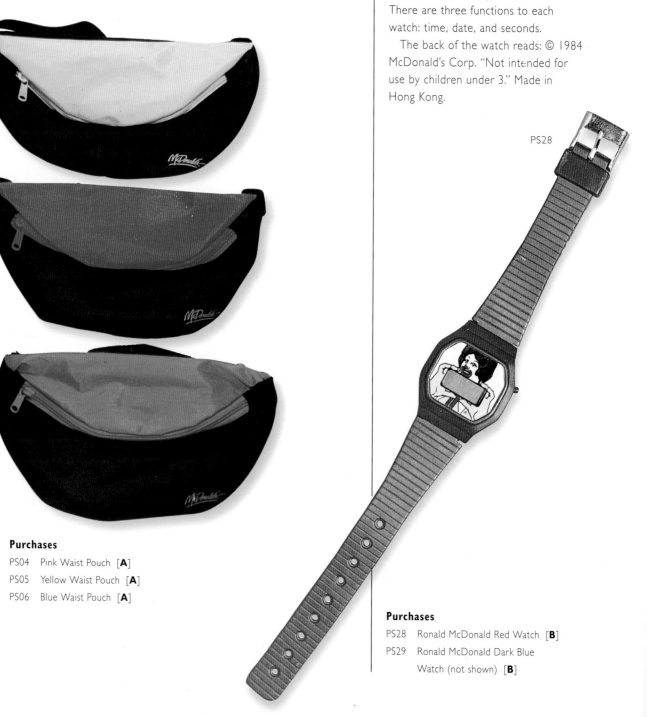

Purchases

PS28 Ronald McDonald Red Watch [**B**]

PS29 Ronald McDonald Dark Blue
Watch (not shown) [**B**]

The McWeatherman Kit

Japan
April – May, 1993

WM01

WM02

WM04

These are quite large premiums, and are weather-themed using McDonaldland characters. Each premium measures approximately 4½ inches high and ranges between 2½ and 5¼ inches long. Each premium also comes in two parts that just clip together. Premiums came in a clear polybag with an insert card in Japanese and English, complete with assembly instructions. *Ronald, Grimace,* and *Birdie* are stand-free, or wall-hanging premiums. *Hamburglar* is a wind gauge. Hold him up to the wind to show wind direction and speed. *Birdie* is a rain gauge; it will catch the falling rain. *Birdie* will start to float, and show the rain level. *Grimace Thermometer* will of course show the temperature. *Ronald* is a weather recorder with three sliding scales for temperature, wind speed, and precipitation. The wheel on top can be turned for the appropriate weather condition.

Premiums marked: © 1992 McDonald's Corp. China.

Weatherman also ran in Denmark, Belgium, Finland, France, Holland, Italy, Norway, Portugal, Spain, Sweden, and Switzerland in October–November 1993; Hong Kong (Test Market) in May 1992.

Insert Card

WM03

Premiums

WM01 Wind Gauge [**A**]
WM02 Rain Gauge [**A**]
WM03 Thermometer [**A**]
WM04 Weather Recorder [**A**]

One bag was issued

WM05 Generic Bag

WM05

Mickey's Merry Band

Australia
December, 1995

ML22

ML23

ML20

ML21

This is one fantastic Disney promotion, from McDonald's Australia, featuring the four most famous Disney characters: *Mickey* and *Minnie Mouse* with *Goofy* and *Donald Duck*. Each is dressed in traditional majorette costume. This was a Christmas purchase, one available per week for $7.99 each. What makes this a very good purchase is the free audio tape with each doll, featuring well-known Disney songs. Each toy has a hollow molded PVC head, and the rest is made from a soft plush material. All premiums stand between 11 and 14 inches tall, *Goofy* being the tallest, and *Minnie Mouse* the shortest premium.

Purchases marked: (with character's name) Mickey © Disney Creata Promotion (Australia) Pty Ltd. Made in China.

The audio cassettes have four Disney film songs to each tape. The cassette tapes are made in Hong Kong by Creata Promotion.

All purchases came in a printed polybag marked: "M" logo © 1995 McDonald's Australia Ltd. printed on the back.

Photograph showing front and back of the audio tapes

Dolls came in four printed polybags

Purchases

ML20   Act 1, Mickey Mouse plus tape [**D**]

ML21   Act 2, Minnie Mouse plus tape [**D**]

ML22   Act 3, Goofy plus tape [**D**]

ML23   Act 4, Donald Duck plus tape [**D**]

Mickey's Birthdayland

USA

March 17 – April 20, 1988

ML02

ML01

ML03

ML05

ML04

ML11

Each premium is a motorized vehicle. When pulled back and let go, each toy runs and spins around. Premiums marked: © Disney China.

The under-three toys were imported from Sweden. They were made by Viking Toys. Four under-three premiums were issued with this promotion. Two premiums came in two separate colors making six premiums altogether.

This was the first time McDonald's promoted the major Disney characters. *Mickey's Birthdayland* was based on the attraction at Walt Disney World in Orlando, Florida.

This promotion was also called *Disney Racers* in Japan in May 1989 and in Taiwan in July 1990.

Premiums

ML01   Donald Duck in Green Train Engine [**B**]

ML02   Minnie Mouse in Pink Convertible [**B**]

ML03   Goofy in Blue Jalopy [**B**]

ML04   Pluto in Purple Car [**B**]

ML05   Mickey Mouse in Red Roaster [**B**]

Four under-three premiums were issued

ML06   Donald Duck, Jeepster (blue) [**C**]

ML07   Donald Duck, Jeepster (green) [**C**]

ML08   Goofy, Sedan (blue) [**C**]

ML09   Goofy, Sedan (green) [**C**]

ML10   Mickey, Roadster (red) [**B**]

ML11   Minnie, Convertible (pink) [**B**]

(under-threes not shown except Minnie Convertible)

Five boxes were issued (not shown)

ML12   Barn [**C**]

ML13   Mickey's House [**C**]

ML14   Minnie's Dress Store [**C**]

ML15   Theater [**C**]

ML16   Train Station [**C**]

EP01

EP03

Mickey and
Friends Epcot 94

USA
Canada
July 8 – August 4, 1994

EP05   EP06   EP07

EP04

EP02

160

EP08

EP10

Each premium is a hard PVC Disney animated figure sized 3–4 inches tall. Each character is dressed in a national costume from one of the countries featured at the Epcot Center, Florida. Premiums marked: © Disney. China.

The under-three premium in this promotion was *Mickey in America*, the same but with a zebra stripe around the packet.

In the Canadian promotion, *Dale in Morocco* was replaced by *Dale in Canada*. He was dressed as a Mountie. The box was not changed. It remained the same as the USA box, *Dale in Morocco*. Ontario issued both *Dale in Canada* and *Dale in Morocco*. Puerto Rico also released *Mickey and Friends* in July 1994.

Premiums

EP01	Chip in China	[**A**]
EP02	Daisy in Germany	[**A**]
EP03	Dale in Morocco	[**A**]
EP04	Donald in Mexico	[**A**]
EP05	Goofy in Norway	[**A**]
EP06	Mickey in USA	[**A**]
EP07	Minnie in Japan	[**A**]
EP08	Pluto in France	[**A**]
EP09	Mickey in USA (under-three) (not shown)	[**B**]
EP10	Dale in Canada	[**B**]

Four boxes were issued

EP11	Chip China – Dale Morroco	[**B**]
EP12	Donald Mexico – Daisy Germany	[**B**]
EP13	Mickey USA – Minnie Japan	[**B**]
EP14	Pluto France – Goofy Norway	[**B**]

EP12   EP11   EP13   EP14

Mickey's Toontown

Australia
October, 1994

Each premium is made from a hollow soft rubber with no moving parts and stands about 2¾ to 3 inches high. This is a very colorful Disney set. All premiums have a hole at their base and are used as finger puppets very much like Oliver and Company, issued in America in 1988. There were two boxes issued. Each side of the box shows a different house, one for each character, and each of the boxes can be opened up and joined together to create a puppet theater, Toontown. Both boxes are approximately 10½ inches long and 5¾ inches high when the boxes are laid flat. Each premium is packed in a clear polybag with black print: "M"™ logo, © 1994 McDonald's Australia Ltd. Contents made in China by Creata Promotion, "safety tested for children aged 3 and over, etc." Premiums marked: © Disney Made in China.

Mickey's Toontown also ran in Guatemala in December 1993; Europe in 1994; Taiwan in March 1994; Singapore in November 1994.

MT01

MT02

MT03

MT04

Premiums

MT01   Mickey Mouse [**A**]
MT02   Minnie Mouse [**A**]
MT03   Donald Duck [**A**]
MT04   Goofy [**A**]

Two boxes were issued

MT05   Mickey's and Minnie's House [**A**]
MT06   Goofy's and Donald Duck's House [**A**]

MT05 Front

MT06 Front

MT05 Back

MT06 Back

Mighty Minis 4 x 4

UK
February 26 – March 25, 1993
USA
March 8 – April 12, 1991

Each premium is a hard molded plastic car with rubber wheels. All these premiums are wind-up toys.

This promotion was issued in the USA. All the premiums were the same.

The UK packaging was marked 1993. No date was marked on the premiums. Germany premiums are identical, called "Starke Minis," Junior Tüte (JT), Happy Meal. No boxes were issued.

Premiums

MI01   Pocket Pick-Up [**A**]
MI02   Li'l Classic (57 T-Bird) [**A**]
MI03   Cargo Climber (Sport Van) [**A**]
MI04   Dune Buster (Baja Bug) [**A**]

Four UK boxes were issued

MI05   Desert Scene [**B**]
MI06   City Highway [**B**]
MI07   Snow Scene [**B**]
MI08   Long Camp – Canyon [**B**]

MI01

MI02

MI03

MI04

MI08

MI05

MI07

MI06

MI09

The American premiums were issued in a different order, *Dune Buster, Li'l Classic, Cargo Climber,* and *Pocket Pick-Up.* This set was first released March 8–April 12, 1991, as a regional promotion in California, Washington, Pennsylvania, and parts of New England, with one box for all premiums, then re-released in several areas February 7–March 6, 1992, when they replaced the box with a bag.

One under-three premium was issued. It is a hollow rubber premium with no moving parts. The USA packaging was marked 1990. No date was marked on the premiums. © McDonald's Corp. Made in China.

Mighty Minis also ran in Mexico (one carton called Riddle and Games) in November 1991.

Mighty Minis was also re-released January 31–March 5 1992 (premiums were the same as 1991, including the under-three; one bag was issued, Go for Gold); in Chicago and Minneapolis they were called Mighty Minis II.

Mighty Minis also ran in Germany in May 1993; Belgium, Denmark, Finland, France, Greece, Italy, Norway, Portugal, Spain, Sweden, Switzerland, and Hong Kong in January 1993. Japan ran a Test Market in July 1991 and ran the promotion in March 1992.

MI11

USA Premiums

MI09   Pocket Pick-Up (under-three) [**B**]
MI10   Four Minis Box (not shown) [**A**]
MI11   Mighty Mini Bag [**A**]

Mighty Morphin Power Rangers

USA

July 1 – 28, 1995

PR02

PR03

PR01

PR05

PR04

PR06

USA Trayliner

This promotion is one of the best-selling toys by McDonald's to date and was soon snapped up by children and collectors alike. These particular premiums were used as a self-liquidator.

Power Rangers first appeared on TV as a series. When this proved to be very popular with the children, a full-length movie was produced by Twentieth Century Fox Film Corporation and Saban Entertainment, Inc. Hence the release of these premiums to coincide with the movie at theaters in America. The figures are made from a solid rubber and stand about 4 inches tall. Each have movable head, arms, and legs. The vehicles are made from a hard plastic and are push-along, and run on small wheels. Each vehicle measures about 5 to 6 inches long, except the *Red Rangers* vehicle, which stands 4 inches high. Vehicles and figures marked: ™ and © 1995 TCFFC ™ and © 1995 Saban China KH Chine.

The packaging was a large clear polybag, sectioned off in three parts. Part 1 contained the insert card. Part 2 contained the figure and part 3 the vehicle. The polybag and insert card displayed a warning for suffocation and to keep away from children, etc.

Insert card marked: © 1994 McDonald's Corporation, Oak Brook, IL, plus McDonald's "M" logo. ™ and © 1995 TCFFC, Saban Entertainment Inc.

Purchases

PR01	White Ranger with Falcon Ninjazord	**[B]**
PR02	Red Ranger with Ape Ninjazord	**[B]**
PR03	Black Ranger with Frog Ninjazord	**[B]**
PR04	Blue Ranger with Wolf Ninjazord	**[B]**
PR05	Yellow Ranger with Bear Ninjazord	**[B]**
PR06	Pink Ranger with Crane Ninjazord	**[B]**

PR07

PR08

PR09

PR10

PR11 (under-three)

PR12

PR13

This promotion ran at the same time as the Power Ranger purchases. The premiums are accessories used by the Power Rangers. All are made from a hard plastic (except watch strap and under-three) and come in numbered, printed polybags. The under-three is a soft, squeaky rubber toy, measuring 4¼ inches high, which came in a yellow-orange zebra stripe edging (packaging for under-three marked: © 1995 McDonald's Corp.). Packaging marked for premiums: © 1994 McDonald's Corporation. ™ and © 1995 Twentieth Century Fox Film Corporation. ™ and © 1995 Saban Entertainment, Inc. and Saban International N.V.

The *Power Com* is a watch the Power Rangers can use to call back to the command center, for help or information. The watch has three pictures on it. Each will appear when you tilt the watch and catch the light. The *Alien Detector* is used to tell the Rangers if there are any bad guys near by. This also has three pictures on it, Lord Zedd, Rita Repulsa, and Ivon Ooze. The *Powermorpher Buckle*

contains three gold power coins, a different Zord on each side of the power coin. Each Power Ranger will have a power coin with his animal (Zord) symbol on it, the animal he can call on to aid him, i.e., Blue Ranger-Wolf, Pink Ranger-Crane. The *Power Siren* is used by the White Ranger to call his Zord (Falcon) to aid him in battle. You blow into it, to make it whistle. Each premium measures between 2¾ and 3½ inches long (not including watch strap). Premiums marked: ™ © 1995 TCFFC. ™ and © 1995 Saban China SV Chine.

Premiums

PR07   Power Com™ [**A**]
PR08   Powermorpher™ Buckle [**A**]
PR09   Power Siren [**A**]
PR10   Alien Detector™ [**A**]

One under-three was issued

PR11   Power Flute [**A**]

Two bags were issued

PR12   Find Power Coins [**A**]
PR13   Planet Phaedos [**A**]

Mix 'em up Monsters

UK
May 10 – June 6, 1991
USA
January and October 1989–90

MU01

MU04

MU03

MU02

Each premium is a hard rubber monster, with three interchangeable body parts: head, body, and tail. By interchanging the parts 64 different monsters could be made. USA premiums came in printed polybags. UK premiums came in a polybag with an insert card. This promotion was first released in the USA as a regional Happy Meal in January and October 1989 and re-released in Northern California, St. Louis, and Missouri September 7–October 4, 1990. Premiums marked: © Current Inc. China.

Mix 'em up Monsters also ran in Belgium, Denmark, Finland, France, Greece, Italy, Holland, Norway, Portugal, Spain, Sweden, and Switzerland in March 1992; Germany ran this promotion (one white bag with *Ronald* and Balloons), Junior Tüte, in May 1990. Austria tested this promotion in March 1989.

MU09 Front

MU09 Back

Premiums

MU01 Corkle [**B**]
MU02 Gropple [**B**]
MU03 Thugger [**B**]
MU04 Blibble [**B**]

Four UK boxes were issued

MU05 Corkle [**C**]
MU06 Gropple [**C**]
MU07 Thugger [**C**]
MU08 Blibble [**C**]
(UK boxes not shown)

One USA box was issued

MU09 Monsters on the Moon [**A**]

UK Translite

Movables

USA
Regional 1988

These premiums were released as a regional promotion in St. Louis, Missouri, in Spring of 1988. Each character is made of a semi-hard rubber and you can bend each one, but the small premiums move little due to their size. The *Professor, Ronald,* and the *Captain* are approximately 4 inches tall and *Birdie, Fry Girl,* and *Hamburglar* are approximately 2 inches high. Each figure came in a printed polybag stating: "Safety tested for children age three and over," and a caution, "May contain small parts not intended for children under three."

© 1988 MCDS Corp. Made in China.

MV01

MV02

MV03

MV04

MV05

MV06

Premiums
MV01 Birdie [**C**]
MV02 Captain [**C**]
MV03 Fry Girl [**C**]
MV04 Hamburglar [**C**]
MV05 Professor [**C**]
MV06 Ronald [**C**]

One box was issued
MV07 Ship (not shown) [**B**]

M-Squad

(Secret Agent Toy)

USA

January 8 – February 4, 1993

MS01

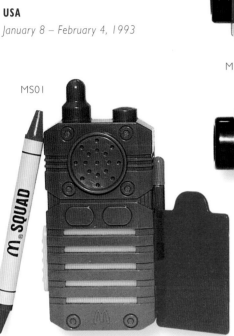

MS02

MS03

MS04

This national promotion, as you can see, is for the adventurous ones of you out there who want to be secret agents. All premiums came in a clear polybag with an insert card. The insert card opens up to reveal puzzles that can be solved by using each of the premiums. On the reverse side of the insert card is a McDonaldland character instructing you on how to use the premium. The *Spycoder* is hinged on one side, and opens up in half to reveal inside the M-Squad crayon and red plastic filter. There is a warning on a slip of paper with the crayon: "This toy uses non-toxic ink that may stain certain surfaces and fabrics, parental supervision is strongly recommended." Write your message with the blue end of the crayon on a piece of paper, then by using the red end of the crayon, obscure your message by scribbling over it. Then use the red plastic filter by passing it over the scribbling to reveal the message. On the side of the *Spycoder* is a yellow button. When moved up and down, the front will flash yellow to send Morse code. *Hamburglar* shows you how to use the *Spy-Noculars*. In the disguise of

a movie camera, this acts like a telescope. Looking through one end makes things bigger, looking through the other end makes things smaller. The purple handle folds out from the red camera's handle to form *Binoculars*. The *Binoculars* have a warning embossed on them: "Do not look into the sun." *Grimace* describes how to use the *Spystamper*. In the disguise of a calculator, this acts as a stamp pad. The yellow button on the side, when pushed down, will reveal a stamp pad behind the number display. Remove the top of the calculator to reveal a rubber stamp (revolve the rubber stamp for a choice of four stamps). When the pad gets dry, use only water on the stamp pad. At the back of the *Spystamper* is a secret compartment. The final premium is *Ronald* showing you the *Spytracker*, which is a wristwatch. Open the clock face to reveal a compass underneath. The *Wristwatch* came double-bagged in the packaging. The under-three is a *Wristwatch* that does not open, and has zebra stripes around the edge of the packaging.

Premiums marked: © 1992 McDonald's Corp. China.

Premiums

MS01   Spycoder [**A**]

MS02   Spy-Noculars [**A**]

MS03   Spystamper [**A**]

MS04   Spytracker Watch [**A**]

MS05   Spytracker Watch (under-three) [**A**]
          (not shown)

One bag was issued

MS06   Top Secret [**A**]

MS06

Muppet Babies

USA
June 5 – July 9, 1986
Canada
1986

MP04

MP01

MP02

MP03

MP05

MP06

MP11

The Muppet Babies were created by Jim Henson, and first appeared in the 1984 movie *The Muppets Take Manhattan*, then shortly after a cartoon series started on CBS Saturday morning TV. Each figure is made of a solid rubber and they all came with a hard plastic molded vehicle with wheels. The under-three premiums issued were one-piece premiums made of hard rubber. All came polybagged with insert cards.

The Canadian premiums were identical to the American ones, except there was an additional character called "Animal," making five figures to the set. *Animal* is in a pull-along red truck with a yellow handle. All Canadian premiums came with a maple leaf printed under the McDonald's "M," on the inserts. Each was a Point of Purchase (P.O.P.) for 49 cents each.

© 1986 McDonald's China (accessories only).

© 1986 HA I China (figures only) (Henson Associates Inc).

Muppet Babies also ran in Guatemala in 1987 and 1989; Australia in April– May 1988; Belgium, Finland, France, Italy, Holland, Norway, Spain, Sweden, and Switzerland in 1988. Hong Kong ran it as a self-liquidator in 1988. Germany ran it on March 25–April 17, 1988 and repeated November 25– December 13, 1988, as a self-liquidator.

Premiums

MP01 Gonzo on Trike [**A**]
MP02 Fozzie on Rocking Horse [**A**]
MP03 Miss Piggy in Pink Car [**A**]
MP04 Kermit on Red Skateboard [**A**]

MP05 Kermit on Skates (under-three) [**B**]
MP06 Miss Piggy on Skates (under-three) [**B**]
MP11 Animal (Canadian premium)

Four boxes were issued (not shown)

MP07 Gonzo [**C**]
MP08 Fozzie [**C**]
MP09 Miss Piggy [**C**]
MP10 Kermit [**C**]

Muppet Babies

USA

March 8 – April 12, 1991 and February, 1992

Canada

Guatemala

March – April, 1993

Once again these premiums were created by Jim Henson. This promotion was released in the Chicago region March 8–April 12, 1991, and again in February 1992 during some clean-up weeks. Each premium was made from a solid rubber and the vehicles were made from a hard plastic. The premiums could be hooked together to form a train. The premiums came packaged in clear polybags with a card insert.

The Canadian set was called *Muppet Connectibles*, they were identical to the American ones, except that the packaging was different, the inserts were written in English and French, they also had a maple leaf sign printed under the "M." Point of Purchase (P.O.P.) 59 cents each.

© 1990 McDonald's Corp. China (accessories only).

© 1990 HA I China (figures only).

Muppet Babies also ran in Guatemala in September 1991; Mexico in July 1991. Muppet Babies on vehicles were identical to the vehicles used on the UK promotion "Rev-ups" 1993 and "Yo Yogi Bear" USA 1992 promotion. All premiums are made from a hard plastic and are all pull-back-and-go vehicles. *Miss Piggy* on a three-wheeled moped, *Kermit* on a three-wheeled jet ski, *Fozzie* in a race car, *Gonzo* on a motorized skateboard.

Muppet Babies also ran in Puerto Rico, Costa Rica, and Venezuela in April 1993; Mexico and Panama in March 1993.

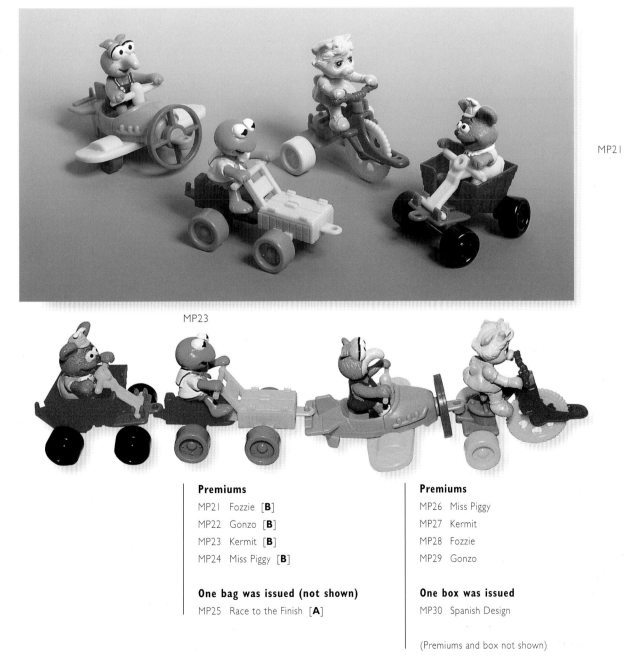

MP22

MP24

MP21

MP23

Premiums

MP21 Fozzie [**B**]

MP22 Gonzo [**B**]

MP23 Kermit [**B**]

MP24 Miss Piggy [**B**]

One bag was issued (not shown)

MP25 Race to the Finish [**A**]

Premiums

MP26 Miss Piggy

MP27 Kermit

MP28 Fozzie

MP29 Gonzo

One box was issued

MP30 Spanish Design

(Premiums and box not shown)

Muppet Treasure Island

USA • Canada

February 16 – March 14, 1996

MP31

MP32

MP33

MP34

MP35

Muppet Treasure Island promotion tied in with the release of the movie of the same name at local theaters, starring Jim Henson's flamboyant characters The Muppets, and also starring Tim Curry and Billy Connolly. Inspired by the classic novel by Robert Louis Stevenson, the story is told through the eyes of a young lad, Jim Hawkins, who finds himself on a sea voyage with the most dangerous fictional pirates of the eighteenth century, on a boat captained by one of the most notorious pirates ever created, Long John Silver. A tale of colorful islands, mutiny on the high seas, and the greed for treasure.

Each premium is made from a hard plastic, except the under-three toy and *Kermit* which is made from a soft pliable plastic or rubber. Each is a one-piece premium except *Kermit* which has a detachable sail. All toys are designed for use in the bath. Premiums measure approximately 4 inches long (except *Fozzie*) and can stand up to 3½ inches tall. All came in a printed polybag in French, English, and Spanish, numbered one to four.

Week 1, *Miss Piggy*, is a color-change toy activated by warm water. Week 2, *Kermit*, is a hollow rubber boat that can be used as a water squirter; squeeze the toy and immerse it under water, then release the toy to draw in water. Squeeze the toy when out of the water to fire out of the cannon. Week 3, *Gonzo*: push down the yellow treasure chest on top of the boat, which in turn will wind up the paddle at the rear of the boat. Place onto water and watch it go along. Week 4, *Fozzie*: push from the bottom of the barrel to reveal *Fozzie's* head. *Gonzo* and *Fozzie* each came with a $5 saving on Muppet Treasure Island CD-ROM for interactive learning from ActiVison ®. The under-three is a two-page bath book showing *Kermit* looking through an eyeglass, finding a treasure chest, then opening the chest to find *Gonzo* inside. The under-three marked: China/Chine © 1995 Henson. © 1995 McDonald's Corp, and came in white/purple zebra striped packaging.

Premiums marked: © 1995 Henson China/Chine, only.

Premiums

MP31   Miss Piggy ™ [**A**]

MP32   Kermit ™ [**A**]

MP33   Gonzo ™ [**A**]

MP34   Fozzie ™ [**A**]

MP35   Book for Bath (under-three) [**A**]

One bag was issued

MP36   Muppet Treasure Island ™ [**A**]

MP36

Muppet
Workshop

USA

January 6 – February 2, 1995

MP14

MP15

MP12

MP13

Premiums

MP12   Bird [**A**]

MP13   Dog [**A**]

MP14   Monster [**A**]

MP15   What-Not [**A**]

MP16   What-Not (under-three)
          (not shown) [**A**]

Four boxes were issued

MP17   Make a Bird Puppet [**B**]

MP18   Make a Dog Puppet [**B**]

MP19   Make a Monster Puppet [**B**]

MP20   Make a What-Not Puppet [**B**]

These colorful characters are a creation of Jim Henson. The premiums are made of a molded hard plastic. Each premium came in a printed polybag, with coupons for discounts on certain products enclosed. It stated on the packet "Figurine and 2 Accessories" but there are really four parts to each premium: a head, body, and two accessories. The accessories could be changed with one another to create different characters. Each head clips onto the body and is a flip top. *What-Not* was used as the under-three premium and came

packaged with the zebra stripe around the packet. It was safety tested for children of all ages. "Recommended for children age one and over."

Packaging marked: © 1994 McDonald's Corporation. Premiums marked: © Jim Henson Productions Inc. China/China CL. The premiums themselves are not dated.

Muppet Workshop also ran in Canada (French-English language) at the same time: Argentina, Chile, Costa Rica, Mexico, Panama, Uruguay and Venezuela in March 1995.

MP19   MP20   MP17   MP18

Mystery of the Lost Arches

USA

January 3–31, 1992

LA01

LA02

LA03

LA04

LA05 (under-three)

172

This promotion reminds us very much of "M-Squad," 1993, USA, in that the premiums are not what they seem, they turn into something else, and they come packed the same way, in clear polybags with insert cards. The insert cards open up and each one has a puzzle to help solve the *Mystery of the Lost Arches*. The reverse side of the insert card shows you how to use the toy. All premiums are made from a hard plastic and measure from the smallest premium (*Cassette/Magnifier*, not extended), 2½ inches long, to the largest premium (*Phone/Periscope*, not extended), 4½ inches tall. The *Magic Camera* has a special-effects lens which gives you hundreds of the same image. The *Micro-Cassette* contains a *Magnifying Glass*, ideal for reading maps. The *Phone* can be extended by pulling it out, and the black ear and mouth pieces can be opened by sliding to reveal a 45-degree mirror behind. To use your *Periscope*, you place the

mouth piece mirror to your eye to help you see over walls, etc. The *Flashlight* can be extended to make a telescope. The under-three was also the *Magic Camera*, except that the search team label on the under-three was a white label and the other premiums have a silver one. The under-three was also polybagged with an insert card with zebra stripes around the edge.

The *Magic Camera* and the *Magic Camera* under-three were both withdrawn within the first week of release due to children catching their fingers in the hole at the back of the camera. All premiums carried a warning: "Do not look into the sun." Premiums marked: © 1991 McDonald's Corp. China.

Premiums were called "McDetectives" in Guatemala in 1992. Japan tested in March 1993 as *Mystery of the Lost Arches*. Both countries only issued three lots; they did not issue the *Magic Lens Camera*.

Premiums

LA01   Magic Lens Camera [**B**]

LA02   Micro-Cassette, Magnifier [**A**]

LA03   Phone, Periscope [**A**]

LA04   Flashlight, Telescope [**A**]

One under-three was issued

LA05   Magic Lens Camera (white label) [**B**]

One bag was issued

LA06   Lost Arches [**A**]

LA06 bag

NBA Cups

USA

1994

A set of six 32-oz, 6¾-inch-tall drinking cups and six fry cartons, featuring famous American basketball players. Each cup has details of each player's MVP statistics (Most Valuable Player) and details of their most incredible shots from their careers. Each fry carton contains more information on each player, i.e. points, team, year, birthdate, height, weight, and college.

Each cup was free when you bought a Super-Size Extra Value Meal, or with a purchase of any soft drink while supplies lasted. Each cup is numbered from one to six. There may have been two sizes of paper cups issued also. (See *Looney Tunes NBA All-Star Show Down June 95* page 132.) Base of cup marked: The Collectibles® Made in Toronto Canada.

Side of cup marked: © 1993 McDonald's Corporation. © 1994 NBA Properties, Inc.

NB01

NB02

NB03

NB04

NB05

NB06

NB07

NB01

NB02

NB03

NB04

NB04

NB05

NB06

Purchases

NB01   Michael Jordan   [**A**]

NB02   Julius Erving   [**A**]

NB03   Larry Bird   [**A**]

NB04   Moses Malone   [**A**]

NB05   Charles Barkley   [**A**]

NB06   Bill Walton   [**A**]

NB07   NBA Paper Cup
        (there may be two sizes)

New Food Changeables

USA
May 19 – June 15, 1989

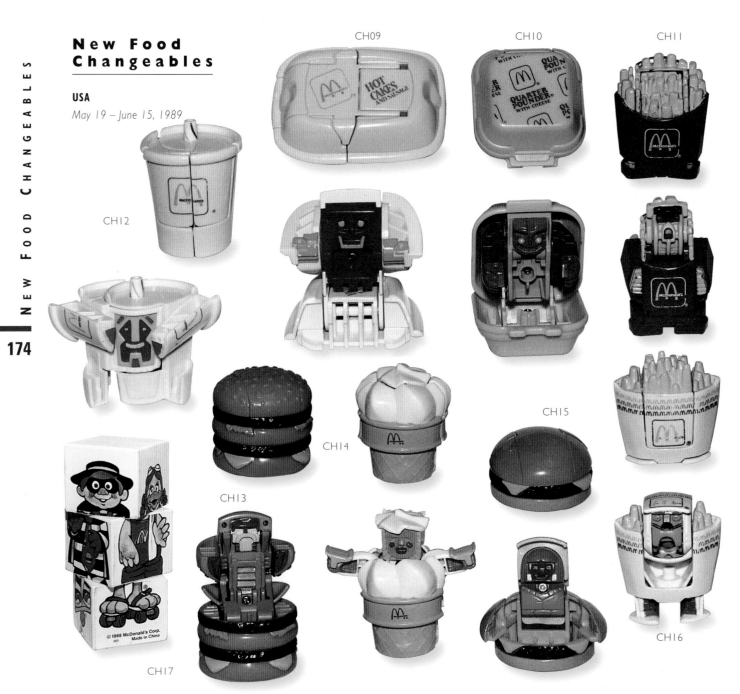

CH09 CH10 CH11

CH12

CH15

CH14

CH13

CH17

CH16

These premiums are the third version from the same theme where food items change into robots. The first two versions were released in 1987 and were called *Changeables*. Only two premiums from the original set were re-issued, *Large Fries* and *Quarter Pounder with Cheese*. The other six premiums are of a new design and unlike the 1987 *Changeables* these *New Food Changeables* have painted hands. Two a week were issued in polybags with insert cards except the under-three, *Pals Changeable Cube*, which came in a printed polybag. The *Pals Changeable Cube* is three cubes joined on top of each other and had four

characters printed on each side, *Birdie*, *Grimace*, *CosMc*, and *Hamburglar*; each cube twisted to give each other different heads, bodies, and feet.

Premiums marked: © 1987 McDonald's Corporation. Made in China (Large Fries and Big Mac only). The other premiums marked: © 1988 McDonald's Corporation, China.

Germany called this promotion "McRobots," four premiums only were issued, *Big Mac, Turbo Cone, Cheese Burger, Small Fries*; Junior Tüte February – March 1991.

Premiums

CH09   RoBocakes – Hot Cakes and Sausage [**B**]

CH10   Gallacta Burger – Quarter Pounder [**B**]

CH11   Fry Force – Large Fries [**B**]

CH12   Krypto Cup – Shake [**B**]

CH13   Macro Mac – Big Mac [**B**]

CH14   Turbo Cone – Cone [**B**]

CH15   C² Cheese Burger – Cheese Burger [**B**]

CH16   Fry Bot – Small Fries [**B**]

CH17   Pals Changeable Cube (under-three) [**C**]

Four boxes were issued (not shown)

CH18   Lost in Space [**B**]

CH19   Jeepers Peepers [**B**]

CH20   Tongue Tippers [**B**]

CH21   Who's That? [**B**]

Nickelodeon Game Gadgets

USA

June 11 – July 8, 1993

This national promotion came from the TV station called "Nickelodeon." Each premium is made from a hard plastic and each has Nickelodeon printed on them. Press the *Applause Paws* trigger and the hands will clap. This toy was later used in a UK promotion called *McFilms 1994*, but with a slight variation. *Blimp Game* is also a whistle. When blown, two wheels will spin; one wheel will give you a letter from the alphabet and the other will stop at a category, i.e.: Food, I See ..., Songs, Cartons, or Animals. The *Gotcha Gusher* is also a whistle and a water squirter. Pull the orange handle when under water; remove from the water and push the handle to squirt water. *Loud-Mouth Mike* amplifies your voice when you sing or talk into it. Each premium was packed in a printed polybag. One under-three was issued and one Happy Meal Bag.

Premiums marked: Nickelodeon™ © 1992 McDonald's Corp. © 1992 Nickelodeon China. Nickelodeon also ran in Latin America in 1993 and in certain countries it has been known to be called "Sounds of McDonaldland."

NI06

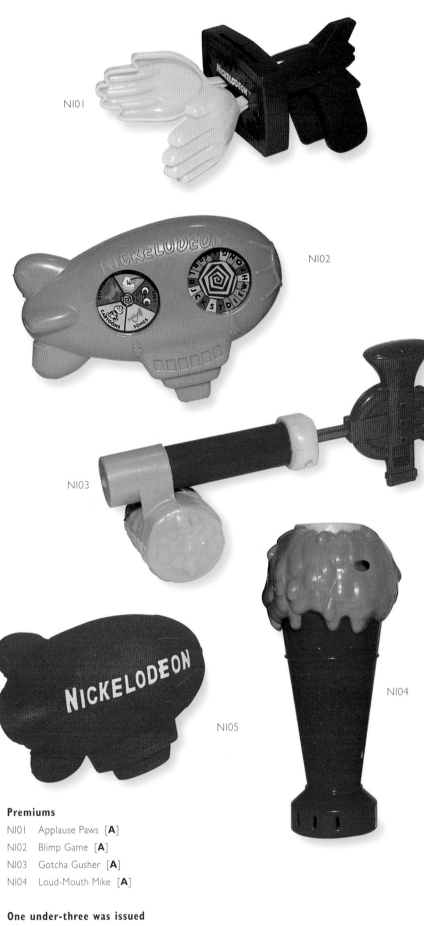

NI01

NI02

NI03

NI04

NI05

Premiums

NI01   Applause Paws [**A**]

NI02   Blimp Game [**A**]

NI03   Gotcha Gusher [**A**]

NI04   Loud-Mouth Mike [**A**]

One under-three was issued

NI05   Blimp Red Blimp Rubber [**A**]

One bag was issued

NI06   Nickelodeon Game Gadgets [**A**]

Oliver and Company

USA
November 22 – December 29, 1988

The release of these premiums coincided with the release of the Walt Disney movie, *Oliver and Company*, from a Charles Dickens story called *Oliver Twist*. They were released in the vacation season of 1988. Each premium was polybagged with a card insert. Each toy is made from a soft rubber, exclusively for McDonald's and is designed to be used as a finger puppet. Premiums marked: © Disney China.

Oliver and Company also ran in Belgium, Finland, France, Italy, Holland, Norway, Spain, Sweden. Switzerland ran this promotion in December 1989.

OC02

OC01

OC03

OC04

Premiums
OC01 Oliver – Kitten [B]
OC02 Francis – Bulldog [B]
OC03 Georgette – Poodle [B]
OC04 Dodger – Dog [B]

Four boxes were issued (not shown)
OC05 Funny Bones [C]
OC06 Noisy Neighborhood [C]
OC07 Shadow Scramble [C]
OC08 Tricky Trike [C]

Oliver and Company Musical Toys

USA
December, 1988

OC09

OC10

These soft toys were also available over the Christmas period. Each is a 3½-inch-tall character, and they both play Christmas tunes. Just press the button in their chest. Dodger plays "When Santa Claus Comes to Town" and Oliver plays "Jingle Bells." Each purchase came in a clear polybag, inside a box showing the character

Toys marked: © 1988 The Walt Disney Company. "M®" logo Simon Marketing Inc. Los Angeles, CA. Made in China.

Germany's promotion was called "Oliver and Co," and is identical to the USA; and coincided with the release of the movie in Europe. No boxes were issued with this self-liquidator, November–December 1989.

Purchases
OC09 Oliver [B]
OC10 Dodger [B]
(Box not shown for Oliver)

Olympic Time

Australia
February – March, 1996

McDonaldland characters with an Olympic theme. *Ronald* is swimming, *Hamburglar* is cycling, *Birdie* is an artistic gymnast, and *Grimace* is a track runner. Each cup stands approximately 7¼ inches tall (straw not included in measurement) and is a three-piece premium made from plastic: straw, cup, and lid. (Also see *"Winnie the Pooh" cups Australia, May 1995* page 243.) Like the Winnie the Pooh cups these cups also have "M's" embossed around the lid.

Lid colors are orange, blue, pink, and aqua. **Note**: when we received this set the lids and straws were mixed, so the illustration may not be as cups were issued. McDonald's was the official sponsor of the Australian Olympic team. Two themed boxes were issued with the Australian flag and Olympic rings pictured on them.

Cups marked along the side with: © 1996 McDonald's Australia Limited.

Cups marked on the bottom with: The Collectibles ® Made in Toronto Canada.

Premiums
OL01   Ronald [**A**]
OL02   Hamburglar [**A**]
OL03   Birdie [**A**]
OL04   Grimace [**A**]

Two themed boxes were issued
OL05   McD Characters on Bikes [**A**]
OL06   McD Characters with Medals [**A**]

OL01   OL02

OL03   OL04

OL05   OL06

Out For Fun

USA

May 7 – June 10, 1993

OF01

OF02

OF04

OF03

OF06

Premiums

OF01   Ronald's Balloon Ball   [**A**]

OF02   Ronald's Bubble Shoe Wand   [**A**]

OF03   Ronald's Fun Pail   [**A**]

OF04   McDonaldland Sunglasses   [**A**]

OF05   Ronald's Fun Pail (under-three)   [**A**]

One bag was issued

OF06   Out For Fun   [**A**]

Beach time fun for kids is the theme for this promotion, in association with the American Red Cross. Each premium, except *Pail*, came in a clear polybag with a folded insert card, with safety reminders and fun games inside, and a special offer on the back: "Save 25 cents on Curad for Kids™, different kinds of first aid kits available for children, featuring McDonaldland characters." The *Balloon Ball* is an inflatable beach ball, with a blow-up *Ronald* inside, pictured in an air balloon. The ball measures 6½ inches when inflated and carries a caution: "Not To Be Used As Flotation Device." The *Bubble Show Wand* is a two-piece

premium made from hard plastic and measures 9 inches long. The *Fun Pail* stands 5¼ inches high and is made from hard plastic with a yellow handle and features McDonaldland characters on the beach. This was also used as the under-three premium. *McDonaldland Sunglasses* had pink and green arms and a blue frame, with an "M" molded on the two top corners of the frame. All premiums plus insert cards are marked: © 1992 McDonald's Corporation. *Balloon Ball* made in China. *Bubble Shoe Wand* made in the Philippines. *Fun Pail* made in the USA. *Sunglasses* made in Taiwan.

A *Fun Pail* has been found with the same design picture. The pail is of the same size; as with *Out for Fun*, it also has a yellow handle. The picture is smaller on this pail, because the pail base is a castle molded design. This pail has © 1986 on it, and made in the USA. It may have been from an earlier promotion.

101 Dalmatians

USA
July 5 – August 1, 1991
UK
April 7 – May 4, 1995
Europe
1995

DA01

DA02

DA03

DA04

*1*01 *Dalmatians* was first released in 1961, and was the first animated Walt Disney film to be set in modern times. New animation techniques allowed the animators to overcome some big difficulties.

Each premium is a molded figure with movable limbs, made from a hard plastic. This promotion was issued in England and America to tie in with the re-release of the film *101 Dalmatians* in theaters.

USA and UK premiums are identical, and marked: © Disney CHINA, except the UK *Lucky Pup* which was made in Macau and is marked on the base with "Macau SN © Disney."

101 Dalmatians were also issued in Mexico and in Holland.

Premiums

DA01   Pongo, large dalmatian [**A**]
DA02   Cruella de Vil, the villainess [**A**]
DA03   Lucky, dalmatian pup [**A**]
DA04   The Colonel and Sgt. Tibbs, the absent-minded sheepdog and scruffy cat [**A**]

Four UK boxes were issued

DA05   The Park [**B**]
DA06   Cruella's Hideaway [**B**]
DA07   Pongo's Home [**B**]
DA08   The Barn [**B**]

Four USA boxes were issued

(New size USA box that measured approximately 10 inches in length and approximately 8 inches high.)

DA09   Barn
DA10   Dog Leashes
DA11   Piano
DA12   Staircase

DA09

DA10

DA11

DA12

DA05

DA06

DA07

DA08

101 Dalmatians

Australia

March 24 – April 20, 1995

DA13

DA14

DA16

DA15

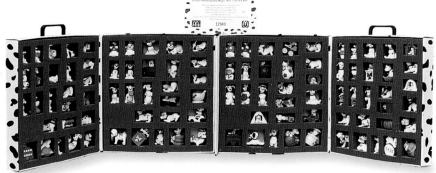

DA17 Front

Once again this very popular animated Walt Disney film was the theme in Australia in April 1995. This was also to tie in with the re-release of the film in theaters over there. *101 Dalmatians* was first released by Walt Disney in 1961 and is 79 minutes of pure delight. It has the evil villainess, Cruella De Vil, who kidnaps all the puppies from the city, including 15 belonging to *Pongo* and *Perdita*, so *Pongo* and *Perdita* with a few friends go in search for them.

These premiums are made from a hard plastic with no moving parts. The packaging is clear polybags with a printed "M" logo plus © 1995 McDonald's Australia Ltd. Contents made in China by Creata Promotion. "Safety tested for children aged three and over. Caution: Not intended for children under three." One box was issued, approximate size, length 6¼ inches, width 4 inches, height 5¼ inches. Boxes in Australia and New Zealand are a lot smaller than European and American ones. Premiums marked: © Disney China.

Premiums

DA13　Pongo [**A**]

DA14　Cruella De Vil　[**A**]

DA15　Lucky Pup　[**A**]

DA16　Colonel and Sgt. Tibbs　[**A**]

One box was issued

DA17　101 Dalmatians　[**A**]

101 Dalmatians

USA

November 27, 1996 – January 2, 1997

UK

December 13, 1996 – January 3, 1997

One Happy Meal™ bag was used with a puzzle and coupons-off, *101 Dalmatians* books, soft toys and Disney CD Roms, booklet attached. Free paper hats were issued and five different wall posters given out, one side showing all the 101 Dalmatians premiums and on the other side real live puppies. A special purchase of Cinnamon Graham cookies in the shape of 101 Dalmatians was available as well as McDonald's gift certificates: a book of five for $5.00, or $1.00 for individual certificates.

In America only, there was a chance to order a complete 101 Dalmatians Happy Meal® Collector box set for $101.00 each (excluding postage) with Certificate of Authenticity. *The 101 Dalmatians Collector Box* measures 17 inches long, 17¼ inches high by 9¾ inches wide, when packed in its attractive spotted 101 Dalmatians color carrying case. Complete with two handles for lifting, the collector box is secured together by velcro strips with the 101 Dalmatians placed in foam cut-out compartments. When the collector box is opened out and displayed, it measures 69 inches long.

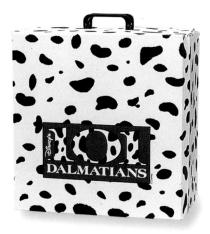

101 Dalmations Happy Meal Collector Box Plus Certificate

This is the most ambitious promotion to date from McDonald's with 101 different premiums. This was to celebrate the release of the live action film *Disney's 101 Dalmatians* on December 13, 1996, in the UK. This set was released all around the world in opaque packaging, although markings on packets and Happy Meal™ packaging may vary.

UK Trayliner

01	Puppy wrapped in gold bow [B]
02	Puppy standing with orange collar [B]
03	Puppy in truck [B]
04	Puppy sitting with bowler hat on [B]
05	Puppy with soldier in mouth [B]
06	Puppy with blue collar [B]
07	Puppy with Christmas wreath on rear [B]
08	Puppy begging with flower on rear [B]
09	Puppy with pink collar [B]
10	Puppy sitting with cowboy hat [B]
11	Puppy in pink teapot [B]
12	Puppy carrying a blue glove [B]
13	Puppy carrying newspaper [B]
14	Puppy in green and yellow scarf [B]
15	Puppy with brown bucket on rear [B]
16	Puppy carrying bone with green Christmas hat on [B]
17	Puppy sitting with green collar on [B]
18	Puppy in pink pram [B]
19	Puppy in newspaper [B]
20	Puppy in red and yellow scarf [B]
21	Puppy with Christmas lights [B]
22	Puppy sitting on drum [C]
23	Puppy standing with yellow collar [B]
24	Puppy with blue collar [B]
25	Puppy in red Christmas present [B]
26	Puppy with candy cane [B]
27	Puppy laying down with red book [B]
28	Puppy in yellow pot [B]
29	Puppy holding brown shoe [B]
30	Puppy in yellow present [B]
31	Puppy holding bone with candy cane [B]
32	Puppy sitting with blue collar on [B]
33	Puppy sitting in red Christmas stocking, bone in mouth [B]
34	Puppy in hat with red collar [B]
35	Puppy standing with purple collar [B]
36	Puppy sitting with bird on head [B]
37	Puppy in blue and purple scarf [B]
38	Puppy in black and white car [B]
39	Puppy begging with purple collar [B]
40	Puppy sitting in Christmas wreath with red hat on [B]
41	Puppy sitting holding cookie [B]
42	Puppy with trainer in mouth [B]
43	Puppy sitting on red bauble [C]
44	Puppy begging with brown hat [B]
45	Puppy with candle in mouth [B]
46	Puppy wrapped in green bow [B]
47	Puppy holding yellow teddy bear [B]
48	Puppy in green bus [B]
49	Puppy wrapped in silver bow [B]
50	Puppy in purple book [B]
51	Puppy with Mickey Mouse ears on [C]
52	Puppy in blue pram [B]
53	Puppy with blue/purple sweater on [B]
54	Puppy in Christmas wreath holding candy cane [B]
55	Puppy with policeman's hat on [B]
56	Puppy with purple/gold crown on [C]
57	Puppy in red bus [B]
58	Puppy sitting in policeman's hat [B]
59	Puppy holding yellow bell [B]
60	Puppy wearing red/green sweater [B]
61	Puppy in blue present with bone [B]
62	Puppy with lead [B]
63	Puppy in paint pot [B]
64	Puppy holding two bones [B]
65	Puppy sitting on football [B]
66	Puppy sitting with red collar on [B]
67	Puppy laying with red bowl in mouth [B]
68	Puppy sitting with frog on head [B]
69	Puppy standing with blue hat on rear [B]
70	Puppy sitting with butterfly on head [B]
71	Puppy with red flower on nose [B]
72	Puppy sitting with can of dog food [B]
73	Puppy with red present on rear [B]
74	Puppy sitting hold red bowl [B]
75	Puppy sitting with log in mouth [B]
76	Puppy in dog kennel [B]
77	Puppy holding purple present [B]
78	Puppy sitting in green Christmas stocking with candy cane [B]
79	Puppy wearing bearskin hat [B]
80	Puppy standing holding blue lead [B]
81	Puppy holding green bell [B]
82	Puppy with purple flower on head [C]
83	Puppy in brown barrel [B]
84	Puppy sitting in umbrella [E]
85	Puppy wearing court wig [B]
86	Puppy sitting on tortoise [B]
87	Puppy playing with football [B]
88	Puppy with red bauble on nose [B]
89	Puppy with orange leaf on head [B]
90	Puppy begging with green Christmas stocking on rear [B]
91	Puppy sitting wearing purple flat cap [B]
92	Puppy sitting on car tire [B]
93	Puppy begging wearing blue cap [B]
94	Puppy with gold present [B]
95	Puppy standing with wreath on nose [B]
96	Puppy sitting on grasshopper head [B]
97	Puppy with pink present on rear [B]
98	Puppy holding brown purse [B]
99	Puppy with red hat [B]
100	Puppy wearing deerstalker hat [B]
101	Puppy in red/black car [B]

01 02 03 04 05

06 07 08 09 10 11 12

13 14 15 16 17 18 19

20 21 22 23 24 25 26 27

28 29 30 31 32 33 34 35

36 37 38 39 40 41 42 43

44 45 46 47 48 49 50

51

52

53

54

55

56

57

58

59

60

61

62

63

64

65

66

67

68

69

70

71

72

73

74

75

76

77

78

79

80

81

82

84

83

85

86

87

88

89

90

91

92

93

94

95

96

97

98

99

100

IOI

101 Dalmatians Snow Domes

USA

November 27, 1996 – January 2, 1997

DA21

DA22

DA20

DA24 Front

DA24 Back

Snow Dome boxes

McDonald's celebrated Walt Disney's *101 Dalmatians* in a big way over the Christmas period in 1996 with the release of an all-live action movie in the theaters. This all-live action version is a very close re-make of the original animated *101 Dalmatians* released in 1961. The original 1961 film was the start of new technical developments in animation presenting the artist's with an immense challenge to keep all those spots in the correct place throughout the film. The new live action version is no exception with over 200 6–8 week old pups used; this was a real challenge for the film crew and trainers: there were four or five stand-in pups for each of the 15 main character pups, each of these pups had make-up to remove spots to keep them identical throughout filming. The pups grew so quickly that each one was used for only two weeks before they became too big. As well as live pups there were mechanical robot models made and computer generated graphics created for the more tricky scenes.

One snow dome was issued per week and was $1.99 each with a purchase or $2.99 without purchase. Snow domes are made from a hard plastic and sealed in a clear polybag in an attractive box. Premiums marked: © Disney Made for McDonald's ® China/Chine.

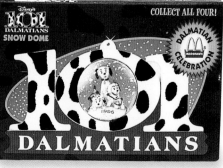

Purchases

DA20 Snowman's Best Friend
(4 inches tall) [**C**]

DA21 Snow Furries (3¼ inches tall) [**C**]

DA22 Dog Sledding (4 inches tall) [**C**]

DA23 Dalmation Celebration
(5 inches long) [**C**]

One bag was issued

DA24 101 Dalmatians [**A**]

Peanuts

USA

March 30 – April 26, 1990

PN05

PN01

PN02

PN03

PN04

Peanuts down on the farm is the setting for this promotion. This set was released to celebrate the fortieth anniversary of the comic strip cartoon series by Charles Schultz. Each premium comes in three parts and their accessories are interchangeable. The premiums are made from soft hollow rubber and the accessories are made from a hard plastic. *Snoopy* pulls a hay hauler, *Charlie Brown* pushes a seed bag and tiller, *Lucy* pushes an apple cart, and *Linus* pushes a milk churn trolley. The under-threes are one-piece premiums of soft rubber. They were issued in printed polybags.

Premiums marked: © 1952 1966 United Feat Synd. China.

Premiums

PN01   Snoopy [**B**]

PN02   Charlie Brown [**B**]

PN03   Lucy [**B**]

PN04   Linus [**B**]

PN05   Charlie Brown's Egg Basket
           (under-three) [**B**]

PN06   Snoopy Potato Sack (under-three) [**B**]

Four boxes were issued

PN07   County Fair [**B**]

PN08   E-I-E-I-O! [**B**]

PN09   Field Day [**B**]

PN10   Hoe Down [**B**]

PN06

PN07   PN08   PN09   PN10

Peanuts

Japan
April, 1995

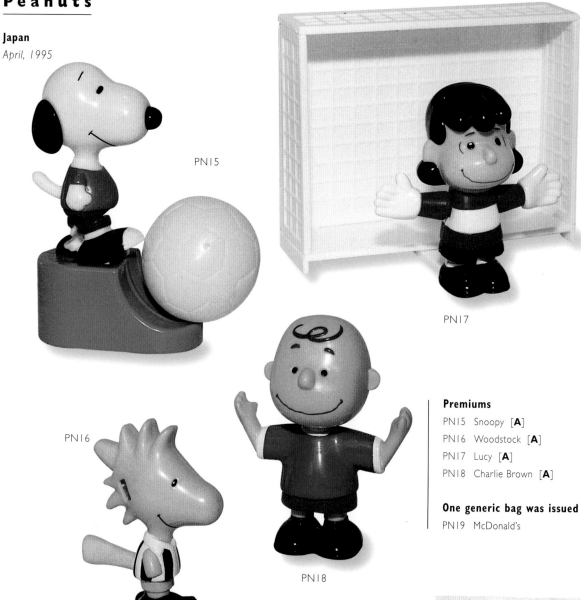

PN15

PN17

PN16

PN18

Premiums

PN15 Snoopy [**A**]
PN16 Woodstock [**A**]
PN17 Lucy [**A**]
PN18 Charlie Brown [**A**]

One generic bag was issued
PN19 McDonald's

This Japanese promotion features Peanuts playing soccer. All premiums are made from a hard plastic. *Snoopy* is a two-piece premium. Push *Snoopy's* foot down and place the soccer ball in front of him, then press his tail down and watch him kick the ball. The soccer ball has no markings at all. *Woodstock* is a one-piece premium with no moving parts. He acts as a whistle; blow into the back of his head. *Lucy* plays the goal keeper. Her arms move up and down slightly and the goal is in six pieces that join together. One of the goal pieces fits on the base of the goal and can pivot from side to side. *Lucy* fits on one end, and the other end is behind the goal, so you can move *Lucy* from behind the goal to save goals. *Charlie Brown* is a one-piece premium. His head can be turned around. You press him down and he springs back up.

Premiums are packed in clear polybags with insert cards with the writing and instructions on the reverse of the inserts in Japanese. McDonald's "M" logo is on the front of the inserts. There was no themed packaging issued in Japan at this time; only generic bags were used. Premiums marked: Peanuts © United Feature Syndicate. Inc. China.

— 街の美化にご協力を —

McDonald's

— お早目にお召し上がり下さい —

PN19

Peanuts Popmobiles

Canada
July 11 – August 11, 1989

Purchases
PN11 Lucy in Fire Truck [**B**]
PN12 Charlie Brown in Train [**B**]
PN13 Woodstock in Car [**B**]
PN14 Snoopy in Flying Dog Kennel [**B**]

Once again the famous Peanuts characters from the popular TV cartoon series. Each premium is made of a hard plastic and is a push-down-and-go toy. When the character is pushed down, the vehicle whizzes along. They sold for 69 cents each. Also see McDonaldland Headstarters Hong Kong 1992.
© 1952 1966 UFS. Inc. China *(Lucy)*
© 1950 1966 UFS. Inc. China *(Charlie)*
© 1965 1972 UFS. Inc. China *(Woodstock)*
© 1958 1966 UFS. Inc. China *(Snoopy)*.

Peanuts also ran in Germany July 11–August 11, 1991 as a self-liquidator, no boxes; Japan in February 1991; Malaysia on November 12, 1992. It was called "Peanuts Headstarters" in Latin America. It ran in Guatemala in June 1991; Panama and Venezuela in April 1991; Mexico (called "Snoopy and Friends") and Puerto Rico ran this promotion in March 1991; and Costa Rica in June 1991.

PN11   PN12   PN13   PN14

Peanuts Soft Toys

Japan
November, 1993 – December, 1994

Charlie Brown and Lucy both have hollow soft PVC heads, and are wearing shoes made out of vinyl. Each shoe has fixed laces. Both dolls stand 10½ inches tall. *Charlie Brown* comes with a red Santa's hat and *Lucy* has a furry muff. *Woodstock* and *Snoopy* are both soft material toys and stand 6¼ and 6½ inches tall. *Woodstock* has a knitted hat and *Snoopy* has a knitted scarf. Purchases came in a clear sealed polybag. Each toy carries a tag with the character's name on it, for example: *Charlie Brown* © 1950, 1966 United Feature Syndicate, Inc. Made exclusively by McDonald's Company (Japan) Ltd. Made in China. *Lucy* © 1952, 1966. *Woodstock* © 1965, 1972. *Snoopy* © 1958, 1966.

Peanuts Soft Toys were issued in Mexico in December 1991 and New Zealand in December 1994.

Purchases
PN20 Charlie Brown [**D**]
PN21 Lucy [**D**]
PN22 Woodstock [**C**]
PN23 Snoopy [**C**]

PN24 Generic bag

PN20   PN21   PN22

PN23

Polybags in Japanese

Peanuts Snoopys

Japan

July – August, 1996

This promotion features *Snoopy* (from the famous Peanut comic strip) playing four different roles. All premiums are made from a hard plastic and have moving parts: head, arms, and legs. *Snoopy's Joe Cool:* placing him somewhere cold, the refrigerator or under cold water, will reveal black glasses and the name Joe Cool on the front of his T-shirt. *Snoopy's Typewriter* note reads: "It was a dark and stormy night . . . I left, leaving my wife with 'Great Reluctance' – our St. Bernard." *Snoopy's Biggles* has goggles which can be pivoted at the ears so the goggles will slide over his eyes and hat. *Snoopy's Scout* is carrying a backpack which can open up to reveal a picture of a hamburger, fries, and milkshake.

The premiums came in a printed polybag numbered from one to four, all written in Japanese. Each was between 2¾ and 3½ inches tall.

Premiums marked: Peanuts © United Feature Syndicate, Inc. China.

Trayliner that was issued

Joe Cool when he has been placed in a cold area

Premiums

PN25 Snoopy's Joe Cool [**A**]
PN26 Snoopy with Typewriter [**A**]
PN27 Snoopy's Biggles [**A**]
PN28 Snoopy's Scout [**A**]

One bag was issued

PN29 Ronald Generic [**A**]

PN27

PN25

PN26

PN28

Packaging that came with premiums

PN29

Penfriends (The Ronald McDonald's)

UK
1983
UK
1989

One pen was available each week, with any purchase. Each pen was made from a hard plastic and measured approximately 5¼ inches high. Each character was detachable from the pen. Each premium came in a clear sealed polybag with the "M" logo and McDonald's written in black print on the front of the bag. Premiums marked: © 1980 or © 1981 McDonald's Corp.

Purchases

PE01   Ronald [**C**]
PE02   Officer Big Mac [**C**]
PE03   Hamburglar [**C**]
PE04   Mayor McCheese [**C**]

This was similar to the previous promotion, except that the pens have 12 inch string cords, so you can hang them around your neck. There are also some slight variations to some of the characters. *Hamburglar* has less of an evil looking face in this set and *Officer Big Mac* in the first promotion looked like he was holding a gun, but in the second set, he looks like he is holding a whistle. Premiums are the same size and made from the same material as the 1983 models, they are also packed the same. One pen was issued each week with any purchase. Due to the variations over the years, the © may differ from pen to pen: *Grimace, Hamburglar, Ronald* © 1980; *Officer Big Mac*, are found with © 1981 Korea and another Officer © 1983 Hong Kong. *Mayor McCheese* © 1982. Translite dated May 1985.

PE04   PE03   PE01   PE02

Purchases

PE05   Ronald [**B**]
PE06   Hamburglar [**B**]
PE07   Officer Big Mac [**B**]
PE08   Mayor McCheese [**B**]
PE09   Grimace [**B**]

Translite

Play-Doh (set one)

UK
1989

PLAY-DOH

190

This promotion was released in England in 1989, and each Play-Doh came in yellow pots with colored lids. This promotion did NOT have a picture of Ronald McDonald on the sides of the pots, unlike the UK 1994 Play-Doh promotion. The four boxes issued with this set are identical to the USA Play-Doh promotion issued in 1986.

Premiums (not shown)

PD01   Red Lid [**C**]
PD02   Blue Lid [**C**]
PD03   Yellow Lid [**C**]
PD04   White Lid [**C**]

Four boxes were issued (not shown)

PD05   Circus Animals [**E**]
PD06   Farm Animals [**E**]
PD07   House Pets [**E**]
PD08   Yesterday's Animals [**E**]

History of the USA Play-Doh (no premiums shown)

Play-Doh first appeared in a Happy Meal promotion in the USA in May of 1983 in parts of Boston and New England. It came in two-ounce cans and was made from a non-toxic material which first appeared on the market in 1955 in Cincinnati, where it was developed and marketed by Kenner Products in cardboard containers with a bottom made from tin. Four colors issued: *Blue, Red, White, and Yellow.* © 1981 no McDonald's markings.

The same promotion as in 1983 was re-released in Wichita (March 23 to April 22), and Nebraska (March 2 to April 1), 1984. For hygiene reasons the Play-Doh was not placed with the food in the boxes. © 1981.

Two colors were added to the 1983 and 1984 promotions to make the 1985 six-premium promotion. The two additional colors are *Pink* and *Green*, both still made from cardboard containers with bottoms made from tin. One box issued: *Play-Doh Place* © 1985, which contained money-off coupons for a Count Creepyhead and Friends playset.

Regional: Kansas, Missouri, Arkansas, Alabama, Illinois, Tennessee, Oklahoma, Texas, and Indiana February 15 to March 29.

A National promotion ran from July 7 to August 3, 1986. The containers in this promotion were completely redesigned and made out of plastic, but still only held two ounces of Play-Doh. This promotion had eight premiums, two per week. Colors are: *Pink, Blue, Purple, Red, Green, Yellow, Orange,* and *White,* © 1984. There are no McDonald's markings on the premiums. Four boxes issued: *Circus Animals, Farm Animals, House Pets,* and *Yesterday's Animals,* © 1986.

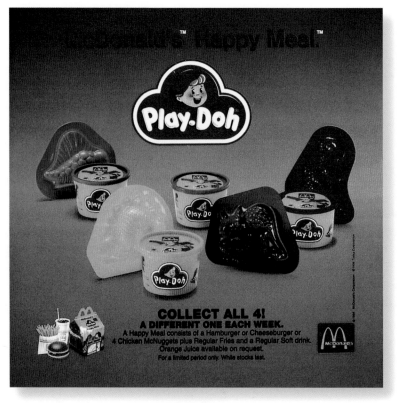

Translite

Play-Doh Dinosaurs
(set two)

UK
May 6, 1994
Germany
November, 1994

PD12   PD10   PD09   PD11

This promotion featured Play-Doh, with bright plastic molds in the form of dinosaurs. Each Play-Doh pot has the McDonald's logo on it and a picture of Ronald McDonald waving. Each pot has a different color lid to match the plastic molds. Each lid, under the Play-Doh instructions, was engraved with the face of *Ronald* or *Hamburglar*. Marked on each Play-Doh pot is MB Waterford Ireland, Made in Ireland.

Each Play-doh instruction book marked: © All Rights Reserved Tonka Corporation 1993. In the instruction leaflet are other products from Play-Doh and a £1 cash-back coupon on any Play-Doh playset. All the plastic dinosaur molds are marked with CE McDonald's™.

Germany issued the same premiums but in different packaging, written in German, as a Junior Tüte. No boxes were issued.

Premiums

PD09	Yellow Mold	[**A**]
PD10	Green Mold	[**A**]
PD11	Red Mold	[**A**]
PD12	Blue Mold	[**A**]

Four UK boxes were issued

PD13	Elephant House	[**B**]
PD14	Panda Park	[**B**]
PD15	Pets Corner	[**B**]
PD16	Snacks	[**B**]

PD15   PD13

PD16   PD14

Pocahontas

UK

September – October, 1995

PO01   PO02   PO03   PO04   PO05

This is the very first time McDonald's UK issued five premiums in one promotion, not to be confused with the UK's "Lego System" September 1994, where five premiums were issued, but one was an under-three. Each premium stands approximately 2½ to 4½ inches high and is made from a hard plastic. *Pocahontas* is a push-along toy. She twists from the waist to paddle. *John Smith* is a three-piece premium, with detachable armor. His head and waist can be turned and his arms can move. *John Ratcliff* twists at the waist, which in turn makes Percy the pug dog nod his head. *Grandmother Willow* has a button you press in to make her face disappear, to be replaced with tree bark. *Meeko the raccoon* is a two-piece premium and is what they call an *Insider*. This is where the premium is inside something and can spring out. See also *Disneyland Adventures Japan August 1995* page 75. Meeko is spring loaded. He folds up inside the barrel;

press the side of the barrel and Meeko pops out like a jack-in-the-box.

With this promotion came free give-aways: two Pocahontas cardboard hats and four flags with scenes from the film on one side and colored red on the other side with a large yellow "M." There was also a competition, a free prize draw to win 200 Sega Pico Systems, "Computer-based, interactive early learning systems," and a £5 off on any Sega Pico Pocahontas storyware at Toys'R'Us.

Premiums came in polybags with insert cards. Insert cards marked: © Disney © 1995 McDonald's Corporation. Premiums marked: © Disney.

Pocahontas and *Meeko* were made in Macau. *Grandmother Willow* was made in The Philippines and Indonesia. *John Smith* and *John Ratcliff* were made in China.

Apart from the free give-aways, flags, hats, etc., there was a special meal introduced in many restaurants and this was called "McChief."

Premiums

PO01 Pocahontas [**A**]

PO02 John Smith [**A**]

PO03 John Ratcliff and Percy [**A**]

PO04 Grandmother Willow [**A**]

PO05 Meeko the Raccoon (insider) [**A**]

Five UK boxes were issued

PO06 John Smith by Waterfall [**B**]

PO07 Shoreline with Ship Anchored [**B**]

PO08 Governor's Log Fortress [**B**]

PO09 Pocahontas on Riverbank [**B**]

PO10 Indian Village [**B**]

PO06   PO07   PO08   PO09   PO10

Free give-aways

Pocahontas

Australia

September 8 – October 5, 1995

PO12

PO13

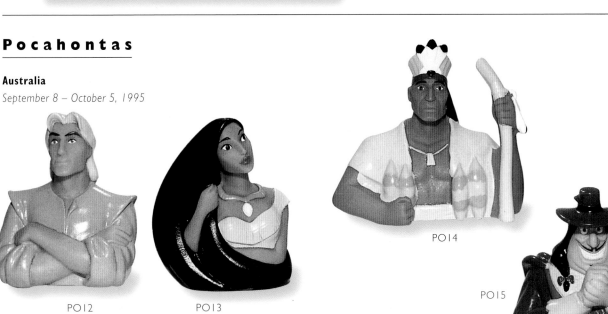

PO14

PO15

Pocahontas in Australia was released to coincide with the Walt Disney film of the same name at local theaters. Each premium is a one-piece toy, made from a molded soft rubber, standing about 2¾ inches tall, and each one has a hole in its base, so they can be used as finger puppets.

Premiums came in a clear polybag, with a printed green picture of Pocahontas and John Smith, followed by the "M" logo, © 1995 McDonald's Australia Ltd. Contents made in China by Creata Promotions.

Premiums marked: © Disney. Made in China.

PO16 Front

PO16 Back

Premiums

PO12 John Smith **[A]**

PO13 Pocahontas **[A]**

PO14 Chief Powhatan **[A]**

PO15 John Ratcliff **[A]**

One themed box was issued

PO16 Pocahontas **[A]**

Polly Pocket

USA

February 3 – March 2, 1995

PP01

PP03

USA till topper

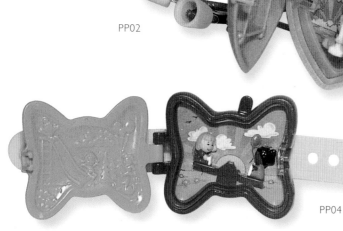

PP02

PP06

PP04

These premiums are made from a hard plastic. The *Ring* shows Polly Pocket dressed like a ballerina standing in the middle of a flower whose petals rotate. The *Locket* opens up to reveal Polly Pocket on a swing and opposite the swing on the locket lid is a place to put a small photograph. There is a warning attached to the cord: "Not intended for infants. String may cause entanglement or strangulation." The *Watch*: turn the winder and the hands go around. This was also used as the under-three premium with the zebra stripe around the edge of the packet. Safety tested – recommended for children aged one and over. The last premium issued in this set was the *Bracelet* which opens up to reveal two Polly Pockets on a see-saw; to make the see-saw move there is a handle on top of the *bracelet* which moves from side to side. All premiums came in a printed polybag numbered one to four on the outside of the packets. This set also ran with Attack Pack for boys. There was also one bag used for both promotions with coupons for retail discounts on toy lines.

Mattel ® © 1994 Bluebird Toys China. *Polly Pocket* also ran in Canada at the same time (French and English language packaging).

Premiums

PP01 Ring [**A**]
PP02 Locket [**A**]
PP03 Watch [**A**]
PP04 Bracelet [**A**]
PP05 Watch (under-three) (not shown) [**A**]

One bag was issued

PP06 Polly Pocket [**A**]

Raggedy Ann and Andy

USA

September 1–28, 1989
September 7 – October 4, 1990

RA01

RA02

RA05

RA03

RA04

The Adventures of Raggedy Ann and Andy have been around for over 70 years and she was one of the original characters to have a licensed patent. This is an animated cartoon made for TV and was shown on a Saturday morning CBS show in America. A regional promotion ran in San Francisco, Portland, Las Vegas, Southern Pennsylvania, Nevada, and Hawaii. This regional promotion was re-released in other areas in 1990 from September 7 to October 4. Raggedy Ann and Andy was a promotion that managers could order if they wished to. This type of promotion is known as an open window. Each premium came in a clear polybag with insert cards. On the reverse side of each insert was a short tale about the character. Accessories were made exclusively for McDonald's. The under-three is a camel identical to the one used with the see-saw but with zebra stripes around the packaging. One test box was issued with premiums. Each premium is made from hard plastic in three sections.

Premiums marked: © 1988 MacMillan Inc. China.

Accessories marked: © 1989 Simon Marketing, Inc. Made in China.

Premiums

RA01   Raggedy Andy [**B**]
RA02   Raggedy Ann [**B**]
RA03   Grouchy Bear [**B**]
RA04   Camel [**B**]

One under-three was issued

RA05   Camel with the Wrinkled Knees [**C**]

One box was issued (not shown)

RA06   School House [**A**]

Rev-Ups

UK
May 7, 1993
Japan
1994

Japanese Trayliner

UK Counter Display

RV01

RV02

RV03

RV04

These McDonaldland characters are made from solid rubber and sit on hard plastic vehicles. Each vehicle runs on wheels and is a pull-back-and-let-go premium. The vehicles used in this promotion first appeared in America on February 7, 1992 in *Yo Yogi,* but in different colors. Premiums marked: © 1992 McDonald's Corp. China.

This promotion was also released in Japan in 1994, called the "Great Charity Chase." The premiums are identical. Packaging and food boxes/bags may differ.

Rev-ups also ran in Denmark as "Vroomers," and Finland, Belgium, France, Greece, Italy, Holland, Norway, Portugal, Spain, Sweden, Switzerland, Guatemala, Mexico, Panama, and Venezuela in February 1993; Taiwan in February 1994; Costa Rica in January 1993. Puerto Rico and Singapore used RV04, RV03, RV02 only in April–May 1993. Germany used it as a clean-up, in UK packaging in 1994. Hong Kong ran "McRacers," Macau, China in December 1994 as a self-liquidator; Israel ran it in 1993.

Premiums

RV01   Ronald – Race Car [**A**]

RV02   Hamburglar – Wave Jumper [**A**]

RV03   Grimace – Skateboard [**A**]

RV04   Birdie – Scooter [**A**]

Four UK boxes were issued

RV05   Country – Ronald [**B**]

RV06   Town Square – Birdie [**B**]

RV07   Skateboard Arena – Grimace [**B**]

RV08   Beach – Hamburglar [**B**]

RV08

RV05

RV06

RV07

Richard Scarry
(The Busy World of)

USA

September 1 – 28, 1995

RS04   RS01   RS02

Richard Scarry is an American author well known for teaching children with the help of illustrations of animals. Each premium is made from a hard plastic (except the under-three) and comes in three pieces: 1) Vehicle, 2) Building, 3) Picture card backdrop. The Vehicle and Picture card backdrop came in their own sealed polybag inside the main printed polybag. Each main polybag was numbered one to four. The vehicles measure between 2 and 2½ inches long and are push-along toys. The buildings measure approximately 3 inches wide by 3¼ inches high and each one comes with a double-sided picture card that slots in the top of the building. The packaging is marked: © 1995, but all the premiums are marked: © 1994 R.Scarry 11/™ Paramount Pictures. China/Chine. The under-three is a one-piece toy of *Lowly Worm*, made from hollow soft PVC and came in a polybag with blue and white zebra stripes. All

RS06

packaging was in three languages, English, French, and Spanish. One bag was issued from which you could make a play mat for your buildings and vehicles.

Premiums

RS01 Lowly Worm and Post Office [**A**]

RS02 Huckle Cat and School [**A**]

RS03 Mr. Frumble and Fire Station
   (not shown) [**A**]

RS04 Bananas Gorilla and Grocery
   Store [**A**]

RS05 Lowly Worm (under-three) [**A**]

One bag was issued

RS06 The Busy World of Richard Scarry [**A**]

RS05

Rip Racers

Australia

November 17 – December 14, 1995

McDonaldland pull-through cars from Australia. Each premium is in three parts: A) Vehicle, B) Rip Cord (7¼ inches long), C) Stickers. Each premium came in a clear sealed polybag with instructions on it in black writing. *Instructions:* 1) Place stickers onto vehicle. 2) Insert rip cord (teeth of rip cord facing front of vehicle) into slot on top of the vehicle. 3) Pull rip cord, place vehicle onto a flat surface. *Racing Tips* 1) Experiment on different surfaces. 2) The faster the rev-up, the better the performance. Polybag was also marked: "M™" logo © 1995 McDonald's Australia Ltd. Contents made in China by Creata Promotions.

Each premium is made from a hard plastic and contains a large heavy metal wheel protruding from beneath the vehicle, where the rip cord engages. Vehicles measure approximately 2½ inches long and marked: © 1995 McDonald's Made in China.

RI02

RI03

RI04

RI01

Stickers, Ronald, Birdie, Grimace and Hamburglar

Ronald in red car with yellow rip cord, Birdie in yellow car with pink rip cord, Grimace in purple car with aqua green rip cord, Hamburglar in green car with orange rip cord.

Polybag

Premiums

RI01 Ronald [**A**]

RI02 Birdie [**A**]

RI03 Grimace [**A**]

RI04 Hamburglar [**A**]

One box was issued

RI05 Generic [**A**]

Ronald McDonald Mug and Bowl

UK
1988

"Sit down to breakfast with Ronald McDonald" with a *Mug* and *Bowl*, each only 63 pence with any purchase. Both are made out of ceramic and feature Ronald McDonald sitting with crossed legs with his hands held up in front of him. The *Bowl* is just under

6½ inches in diameter and is unmarked on the base. The *Mug* marked: Kiln Craft Staffordshire England.

Purchases

PS09   Mug [**B**]

PS10   Bowl [**B**]

PS09   PS10

Runaway Robots

USA
February 6 – March 22, 1987

RR01   RR02   RR03   RR04   RR05   RR06

This was an early regional promotion in St. Louis, USA, and parts of New England, Tennessee, MI, ME, MA, and northern AL. Each premium is made from a hard plastic, and measures approximately 2 inches high. All are pull-back and let-go Robots and came polybagged with no McDonald's identification on premiums or packaging.

Premiums marked: © '85 S. Colburn Made in China.

Premiums

RR01   Beak [**C**]

RR02   Bolt [**C**]

RR03   Coil [**C**]

RR04   Flame [**C**]

RR05   Jab [**C**]

RR06   Skull [**C**]

One box was issued

RR07   Six Runaway Robots (not shown) [**B**]

School Kit
(First Issue)

UK

1983

Another purchase promotion by McDonald's aimed at the school classroom, for only 33 pence each with any purchase. The plastic *slip wallet case* came with a popper at one end, and *Ronald McDonald* standing in front of a blackboard. One *pencil sharpener* was issued, of the head and shoulders of *Ronald,* and one *Eraser* showing the top half of *Ronald.* One white plastic *ruler* was issued with red writing and with different shapes cut out. Two *pencils* were issued, both white with *Ronald McDonald's* name in yellow and an eraser on the end. Germany issued an identical School Kit called, "Schülerset," except that the ruler had a picture of *Ronald and the Arches* at either end. It was sold as a set only for 1.95 DM as a self-liquidator in April–May 1986.

Purchases were marked: McDonald's Corp. © 1983 Taiwan.

Purchases

PS11   Clear Plastic Case [**B**]

PS12   Pencil Sharpener [**B**]

PS13   Eraser [**B**]

PS14   Ruler [**B**]

PS15   2X Pencil [**B**]

School Kit
(Second Issue)
(Back to School)

UK

August, 1990

PS22   PS17   PS20

PS21

This promotion was available for 65 pence with any purchase. It contains the same items as School Kit 1, except that School Kit 2 premiums are of a different style and are displayed in McDonaldland colors. Also included is a notebook of plain paper. The plastic wallet *case* measures approximately 4½ inches wide and approximately 7 inches long. Premiums are not dated.

PS16   PS18

Purchases

PS16   Case with Red and Yellow Diagonal Stripes [**A**]

PS17   Pencil Sharpener Red [**A**]

PS18   Note Pad with Red and Yellow Diagonal Stripes [**A**]

PS19   Information Card and Timetable (not shown) [**A**]

PS20   Ruler Red [**A**]

PS21   Pencil Red with "McDonald's makes your day" [**A**]

PS22   Eraser Yellow with Red "M" [**A**]

Sea World of Ohio

USA

Spring 1988

This was a regional promotion from the southeast of Cleveland in Ohio. Each premium is made from solid hard rubber and stands approximately 3 inches high. They came polybagged with safety instructions printed on the bag. Premiums marked on their base with: © Made in China 1987, Sea World Inc. Made in China.

These premiums are also available in the gift stores in Sea World and are marked the same, except that the markings are printed on their bellies instead of their bases.

SE02

SE01

SE03

Premiums

SE01   Dolly the Dolphin [**E**]

SE02   Perry the Penguin [**E**]

SE03   Shamu the Whale [**E**]

One box was issued (not shown)

SE04   Whale with Three Kids [**C**]

Sea World of Texas

USA

Summer 1988

Summer 1989

This regional promotion was released in the summer of 1988 in San Antonio, Texas. Each premium was a soft stuffed toy, approximately 6 inches long. Labels marked: © 1988 Sea World Inc. Korea.

The regional promotion in San Antonio, in 1989, *The Dolphin* and *Whale* were re-issued from the 1988 Sea World Texas set. Soft stuffed animals and two hard plastic sunglasses were issued. The box was the same as 1988 but with a cut-out coupon on the back.

Premiums (not shown)

SE05   Dolphin, Gray and White with Black Eyes [**D**]

SE06   Penguin, Black and White with Orange Feet and Beak [**D**]

SE07   Walrus, Brown with White Face and Tusks [**D**]

SE08   Whale, Black and White [**D**]

One box was issued (not shown)

SE09   Ronald in Yellow Sub. © 1988

Premiums (not shown)

SE10   Dolphin [**D**]

SE11   Whale [**D**]

SE12   Sea Otter, Brown [**D**]

SE13   Penguin, White Sunglasses [**D**]

SE14   Whale, White, Black, and Blue Sunglasses [**D**]

One box was issued (not shown)

SE14   Ronald in Yellow Sub, Coupon on Back [**D**] © 1989

Shoe Ties
(Knotenbeisser)

Germany
March 4 – 28, 1993

ST01   ST02   ST03

There were only three premiums to this promotion. As the name suggests these are used to decorate your shoes with colorful McDonaldland characters. Just thread your laces through the holes and tie into a bow. Each premium is made from a hard plastic and came in a clear polybag, the end of the polybag just folded over and held with a small strip of cellotape. Insert cards came with the premiums. The premiums have no markings on them, except for the characters' names on the front.

Insert cards marked: © 1992 McDonald's Corporation. Made in China Wedo Promotions W-5000 Koln, Germany.

Premiums

ST01 Ronald [**A**]
ST02 Birdie [**A**]
ST03 Hamburglar [**A**]

One box was issued (not shown)

ST04 Bag

Snow Domes
"Schneekugeln"

Germany
November 4 – 28, 1993

Three plastic snow domes from Germany, each with a Christmas scene. Each measure 2¾ inches long, and 2¼ inches high. Packaging is a clear polybag with black writing, in German. There is a warning on the packaging: "Not intended for children under three."

Premiums and packaging marked: © 1993 McDonald's Corp. Wedo Promotions GmbH D-50829 Koln. Made in China.

Premiums

SD01 Ronald Skating [**B**]

SD02 Ronald with Snowman [**B**]

SD03 Snowman outside a McDonald's [**B**]

SD01

SD02

SD03

SW01

SW07

Snow White

USA

July 9 – August 5, 1993

SW05

SW08

SW10

SW06

SW04

SW03

SW02

This promotion ran with the re-release of the animated classic Walt Disney film. This was the first full-length animated film, approximately 80 minutes long, first released by Walt Disney in 1937 at Christmas time after four years in the making. Each premium is made from a hard plastic. The first premium was *Bashful* who hides in a mine truck full of diamonds. When pushed along, *Bashful* pops up. *Doc* is pushing a wheelbarrow full of diamonds with one very large blue diamond that sits on top and spins when the barrow is pushed. *Dopey and Sneezy*: *Dopey* stands on *Sneezy's* shoulders wearing a long blue coat that spins on a red mat. *Dopey and Sneezy* was also used as the under-three with the packaging marked with the zebra

stripes around the edge. *Happy and Grumpy* are both on a railroad push car; when pushed along they go up and down like on a see-saw. The *Prince* comes with a white horse. The horse's tail moves and the horse has no identification markings. The *Prince* has movable arms, legs, and head. The *Prince* came in two versions, one with a green base and one without. The evil *Queen/Witch* is a three-piece premium very much like Belle in the Beauty and the Beast UK set of 1992, except that the *Queen/Witch* has only one dress. *Sleepy*: when you move his arms up he yawns and his eyes close. The final premium was *Snow White* which came with a green wishing well and her arms and head moved. © Disney China.

Premiums

SW01 Bashful [**A**]

SW02 Doc [**A**]

SW03 Dopey-Sneezy [**A**]

SW04 Happy-Grumpy [**A**]

SW05 Prince and Horse [**A**]

SW06 Queen/Witch [**A**]

SW07 Sleepy [**A**]

SW08 Snow White [**A**]

SW09 Dopey-Sneezy (under-three)
(not shown [**B**]

SW10 Prince and Horse with green base [**B**]

Four boxes were issued

SW11 Dwarfs in Diamond Mine [**B**]

SW12 Dwarf's Cottage [**B**]

SW13 Snow White and Bashful at Castle [**B**]

SW14 Snow White with Prince and

SW13

SW11

SW14

SW12

Smurfs

Germany

September – October, 1996

Holland

September – October, 1996

SF01 SF02 SF03 SF04 SF05

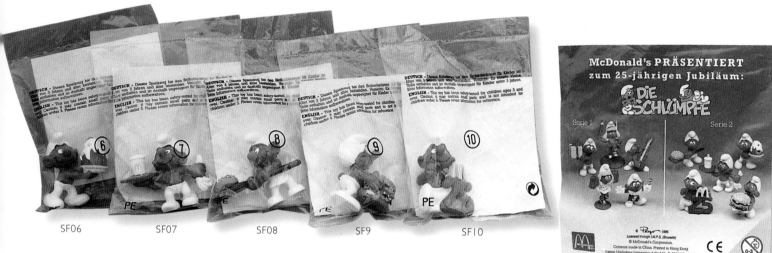

SF06 SF07 SF08 SF9 SF10

McDonald's PRÄSENTIERT
zum 25-jährigen Jubiläum:

Die SCHLÜMPFE

Serie 1   Serie 2

Insert Card

This promotion was celebrating 25 years of the Smurfs. In Germany the promotion was called "Die Schlümpfe" and in Holland it was called "Smurfen Happy Meal™." Ten characters in all, the last five are McDonald's-related (Series 2). Each is holding a food-related item except the last one; he is holding the number 25 with a yellow "M" on top. This is a very attractive set and a very difficult one to obtain because all 10 Smurfs were issued within four weeks. The Smurfs, being very popular in Europe, have had many spin-offs and have popped up throughout the years in other promotions by major companies. The TV cartoon series was also very popular and only this year there was a new song released called "I've Got A Little Puppy"

(Smurfs EMI TV) that reached the top 10 in the UK in September. "The Smurf Song" (Decca) by Father Abraham and the Smurfs was the first to be released in the UK on June 3, 1978 and reached number two. This was followed by "Dippety Day" and "Christmas in Smurfland" (both on Decca).

Each Smurf is made from solid rubber and is a one-piece toy. Each measures approximately 2 to 2½ inches tall and came in a sealed polybag with an insert card. On the back each polybag is numbered from one to 10.

Packaging marked: © Peyo 1996 Licensed through I.M.P.S. (Brussels) © McDonald's Corporation Simon Marketing International GmbH. D-63268 Dreieich. Contents made in China. Premiums marked: © Peyo 96.

Premiums

Series 1

SF01	Smurf with Guitar	**[B]**
SF02	Cheerleader	**[B]**
SF03	Majorette	**[B]**
SF04	Smurf Clown	**[B]**
SF05	Smurf with Parcel	**[B]**

Series 2

SF06	Smurf with Plate of Jello	**[B]**
SF07	Smurf with Milkshake	**[B]**
SF08	Smurf with Sesame Seed Bun	**[B]**
SF09	Smurf with Big Mac	**[B]**
SF10	25th Anniversary "M" Smurf	**[B]**

One bag was issued

SF11	Smurf's face (not shown)

Sonic 3 The Hedgehog

USA
February 4 – March 3, 1994
Canada
December, 1994

This national promotion was based on the SEGA computer game of the same name. Each premium is made from a hard plastic. The evil *Dr. Robotnik* is a one-piece toy which winds up and will move around in a large circle. *Knuckles* is also a one-piece toy which, when pushed along, will spin around. *Sonic* is a two-piece premium and is spring-loaded. When pushed together, press the button and *Sonic* will shoot forward. *Tails* is also a two-piece toy but with a string pull. When pulled, Tails will spin off. This premium has a CAUTION marked on the launcher, "Do Not Aim Or Launch At Faces." *Tails* was recalled in the last week of this promotion, due to a string pull problem. One under-three was issued, a soft yellow ball with *Sonic* on it. Each premium comes in a printed polybag. Premiums were marked: ™ and © 1993 SEGA China. (*Tails* has no date printed on it.)

The *Sonic 3* promotion also ran in Puerto Rico in 1994.

SO02

SO01

SO03

SO04

SO05

SO06

Premiums

SO01   Miles Tails Power [**A**]

SO02   Dr. Ivo Robotnik [**A**]

SO03   Sonic [**A**]

SO04   Knuckles [**A**]

SO05   Sonic Ball (under-three) [**B**]

One bag was issued

SO06   Sonic 3 the Hedgehog [**A**]

Translite

Sonic The Hedgehog

UK • Europe
January 27 – February 24, 1995
New Zealand
June, 1995
Japan
June, 1995

SO07

SO08

SO09

SO10

Sonic the Hedgehog is taken from the mega-popular SEGA Computer game and has now been made into a cartoon series and is shown on Saturday morning TV. Now five computer games have been released on this colorful character. Each premium comes in a polybag with an insert card. *Sonic*, *Dr. Robotnic*, and *Knuckles* are identical to the USA premiums, but *Tails* was re-designed for safety reasons. *Tails* is a two-piece toy made from a hard plastic. Once the pull-through is pulled, Tails will spin. Sonic was released in Canada in December 1994.

Premiums marked: ™ and © 1993 SEGA China. Sonic was also released in New Zealand in June. Identical premiums issued in Germany as a JT (Junior Tüte), no boxes, March 1995. Belgium ran it in 1995.

Only three premiums were issued in the Japanese promotion of Sonic. The premiums all work in the same way as the American and UK toys. The other difference with this promotion is that there is a variation on *Dr. Ivo Robotnik*. The vehicle he is in is almost identical to the other promotions, except that the wind-up knob is square shaped on the Japanese set, compared to being round on the USA and UK sets. The character of *Dr. Ivo Robotnik* is totally different. His arms are out-stretched over his vehicle and the color of his mustache and eyes and the shape of his head are different.

Each premium came in a clear polybag with an insert card (written in Japanese) with "M"® logo and © Sega on. Premiums marked: ™ and © 1993 SEGA China.

Premiums

SO07   Sonic   [**A**]
SO08   Dr. Robotnic   [**A**]
SO09   Knuckles   [**A**]
SO10   Tails Miles Power   [**A**]

Four UK boxes were issued

SO11   Angel Island   [**A**]
SO12   Launch Base   [**A**]
SO13   Ice Cap Zone   [**A**]
SO14   Marble Zone   [**A**]

Translite

SO17

SO15

SO16

Japan Premiums

SO15   Sonic   [**A**]
SO16   Knuckles   [**A**]
SO17   Dr. Ivo Robotnik   [**A**]
SO18   Generic bag Grimace   [**A**]
           (see *Disneyland 40 years Japan 1995* page 75)

Insert Card

Spaceship

UK
1984

Spaceship was the very first Happy Meal promotion in the UK, and was first issued in 1984. Each premium is made from a thin vacuformed plastic, and comes in three parts: 1) top, 2) base, and 3) stickers. The Spaceships had a sheet of stickers, each with McDonaldland characters and UK markings to fit the molded windows on the Spaceships. The Spaceships measure 7¾ inches in diameter and can be thrown like frisbees.

© McDonald's Corp. China.

Premiums

SS01	Yellow Spaceship	[D]
SS02	Green Spaceship	[D]
SS03	Red Spaceship	[D]
SS04	Blue Spaceship	[D]

SS01   SS02   SS03   S304

Space Launchers

UK
August 13 – September 9, 1993

This McDonaldland character promotion was on the theme of astronauts and each premium is made from a hard plastic. *Birdie's* blue propeller is wound up, then press the button on the front of her suit and watch the spinner fly. *Grimace* has a string pull on his back. Pulling his back pack sends the spinner flying. *Ronald* has a plastic pull-through which sets his spinner off and the *Fry Girl* also has a plastic pull-through, but no spinner. She just spins around by herself.

© 1992 McDonald's Corp. China.

Space Launchers also ran in France and as "McCopters" in Belgium, Denmark, Finland, Greece, Holland, Norway, Portugal, Spain, Sweden, and Switzerland November 5 – December 16, 1992; Argentina in August–September 1993; Hong Kong (Test Market) in December 1992; Singapore in August 1993; New Zealand in October 1993; Guatemala in 1994. Germany ran it in May 1994, called "Astro Mäcs," no boxes; Korea in April 1994. Japan ran a "McSpace Launchers" Test Market in April 1993. Mexico ran it in February 1994; Indonesia in September 1994; Chile and Venezuela in June 1993. There have been two variations found on this promotion: a pink *Birdie*; and on the top of the *Fry-Girl's* spaceship, there are yellow squares going around, inside the yellow round ones. Both variations have been found in Japan.

SL02

SL01

SL03

SL04

Birdie Variation

Premiums

SL01	Birdie	[A]
SL02	Fry Girl	[A]
SL03	Ronald	[A]
SL04	Grimace	[A]

Four UK boxes were issued (not shown)

SL05	Space Craft	[B]
SL06	Docking Bay	[B]
SL07	Blast Off	[B]
SL08	Moon Buggy	[B]

Speedies

Germany
November, 1987
Australia
1992

SE02   SE01   SE03   SE04

This is a very baffling promotion. It first came out in Germany in 1987 on blister packs, as a self-liquidator at a cost of 1 DM each. According to the back of the blister pack, these vehicles are all pull-back-and-let-go, with motors inside. Made by Wedo Promotion (Germany) © McDonald's Corp. In the Australian promotion of 1992, called Burger Buggy, the vehicles are just push-along. Premiums marked: © 1992 McDonald's Aust Ltd. China.

On the blister pack there was a sticker, placed on the back of the packet, with the McDonald's "M," and an outline of Australia underneath with a warning to children, "small parts and not intended for children under three." The blister pack read: © 1987 Corporation, made by Creata Promotions (Australia). Burger Buggies have also been issued in clear polybags with black printing.

Premiums

SE01 Big Mac [**B**]
SE02 Ronald [**B**]
SE03 Hamburglar [**B**]
SE04 Grimace [**B**]

Speedsters

UK
December 15 – January 12, 1996

SE06   SE07

SE08

SE09

McDonaldland characters were in vehicles in this promotion. Each premium is a two-piece toy, made from hard plastic. All the vehicles are on free-running wheels, and can be pushed along. Each vehicle comes with a garage that is 4 inches long, and inside each garage is a spring-loaded mechanism with a release button on top of the garage. When the vehicle is placed into the garage and the release button is pressed, the vehicle will be

propelled out at great speed. *Ronald* comes in a blue boat with a red garage. *Grimace* is on a green go-kart with a blue garage. *Birdie* is driving a pink car with a purple garage, and finally *Hamburglar* is on a red bike, with a yellow garage. All premiums came in a polybag with an insert card. Each Happy Meal box can be made into a play scene. Premiums and accessories marked: © 1995 McDonald's Corp. China.

Premiums

SE06 Ronald [**A**]
SE07 Grimace [**A**]
SE08 Birdie [**A**]
SE09 Hamburglar [**A**]

Four boxes were issued (not shown)

SE10 Lake [**A**]
SE11 Race track [**A**]
SE12 McDonald's drive-thru [**A**]
SE13 Obstacle course [**A**]

Spider-Man

USA • Canada
May 1–28, 1995

SM03

SM02

SM04

SM01

SM06

SM05

SM08

SM07

SM10

T his national promotion, which was based on the character in Marvel Comics, runs along the same lines as Batman the Animated series in June 1992. Four figures and four push-along vehicles, each packed in a printed polybag and each bag numbered one to eight. Each premium is made from a hard plastic. *Spider-Man* was also used as the under-three but in zebra stripe packaging. His head, waist, and arm joints can be turned. When *Scorpion Stingstriker* is pushed along the green tail will bob up and down. *Dr. Octopus*, like *Spider-Man*, has a moving head, waist, and arms, also his tentacles can be turned. When *Spider-Man Webrunner* is pushed along, the spider legs move from side to side. *Mary Jane Watson* has no moving parts but she comes with two accessory dresses with a hand case. *Venom Transport* vehicle's mouth opens and closes when pushed

along. *Spider-Sense Peter Parker*: lifting his right arm will turn his head to show a face without a mask. *Hobgoblin Landglider* vehicle's wings will flap when pushed along. Premiums marked: © 1995 Marvel China/Chine. Packaging marked: © 1994 McDonald's Corporation ™ and © 1995 Marvel. Canada issued a dual language bag in French/English.

Premiums

SM01 Spider-Man™ [**A**]
SM02 Scorpion™ Stingstriker [**A**]
SM03 Dr. Octopus® [**A**]
SM04 Spider-Man® Webrunner [**A**]
SM05 Mary Jane Watson™ [**A**]
SM06 Venom™ Transport [**A**]
SM07 Spider-Sense Peter Parker™ [**A**]
SM08 Hobgoblin™ Landglider [**A**]

One USA bag was issued

SM10 Spider-Man [**A**]

SM09 Spider-Man (under-three) [**A**]

Sportsball

New Zealand
January and April, 1992
Australia
January – February, 1992

SP02

SP04

SP03

SP01

A sports theme from New Zealand with four soft balls. Each Sportsball has the McDonald's "M" logo on the front. This is the only marking on the premiums. All premiums came in a clear polybag with insert cards. The insert cards are numbered one to four. One McDonaldland character sports-themed box was issued for all four premiums.

Insert cards marked: © 1993 McDonald's Australia Ltd. Contents made in China.

SP05 Front

Premiums

SP01   Cricket Ball   [**A**]

SP02   Basketball   [**A**]

SP03   Rugby Ball   [**A**]

SP04   Soccer Ball   [**A**]

New Zealand box

SP05   Generic

Sports Buddies

UK
June 12, 1992

S ports Buddies are made from semi-hard rubber and come with two accessories each, and are all interchangeable with each other. They each come with hair and with either shoes or a belt. This set is very much the same idea as McNugget Buddies from the USA in 1989. UK Premiums marked: © 1991 McDonald's China. In the earlier days you may have seen in some McDonald's restaurants a large poster-size plastic "Magnetic Message

Center Card" hanging up on which they could display the latest promotion, by using a magnetic display.

Sports Buddies also ran in Singapore and Japan in July 1992.

Premiums

SB01   Javelin Thrower   [**B**]

SB02   Hammer Thrower   [**B**]

SB03   Track   [**B**]

SB04   Weightlifter   [**B**]

Four UK boxes were issued (not shown)

SB05   Javelin Thrower   [**C**]

SB06   Hammer Thrower   [**C**]

SB07   Relay Runner   [**C**]

SB08   Weightlifter   [**C**]

Magnetic message center card

SB01   SB02   SB03   SB04

Storybook Muppet Babies

USA

October 28 – November 17, 1988

Three books released exclusively for McDonald's from the famous Muppet creator Jim Henson. Three colorful storybooks, each with 24 pages and a two-page coupon you could tear out for Muppet Babies merchandise. Each book measures 7 inches by 7 inches. Printed inside of each cover was Jim Henson's Muppet Babies™ © 1988 Henson Associates Inc. Printed in the United States of America. "Brought to you by McDonald's ® in cooperation with the American Library Association."

There were also three Muppet Babies plush toys issued, which followed on after the storybook as a regional holiday promotion. These were not premiums but a purchase sold around Christmas time in 1988, for $1.99 each. Some of the proceeds from these plush toys went to fund the Ronald McDonald House for children. *Baby Kermit* stands approximately 7 inches tall, and *Baby Fozzie* and *Baby Piggy* both stand about 10 inches high. All three toys came polybagged in clear bags. The same plush toys were issued in Canada as well. The packaging was in English and French and sold as a P.O.P. (Point of Purchase) for $2.69 each and *Baby Piggy* had no hair. The fabric label (the one sewn to the toys) reads: © 1987 Henson Associates Inc. There was also a cardboard gift tag attached to each toy, with To and From on it.

Germany issued identical soft toys, in January 1988, only available in Würzburg, as a Junior Tüte (Happy Meal).

Storybook Muppet Babies (books) were issued in Malaysia in 1994, packaging unknown.

MP26

MP27

MP28

MP32   MP34   MP33

Premiums

MP26   Just Kermit and Me [**A**]

MP27   The Legend of Gimme Gulch [**A**]

MP28   The Living Doll [**A**]

Three boxes were issued (not shown)

MP29   Library [**B**]

MP30   Nursery [**B**]

MP31   Picnic [**B**]

Three plush toys were issued

MP32   Fozzie [**C**]

MP33   Kermit [**C**]

MP34   Baby Piggy [**C**]

Superman Metallic Collectibles

Australia
June, 1996

SU03

SU04

SU01

SU02

Steel and Superman in two parts

Superman was created by Jerry Siegel and Joe Shuster and featured in DC Comics. He first appeared in his own comic in 1939 and the first time he got engaged to Lois Lane was in 1990, but alas he was killed off in 1992 by Dooms Day, then brought back a few months later by public demand. There have been spinoffs from Superman like Supergirl, Superdog, and even Superboy.

These four figures are made from a solid plastic and come attached to a triangular base which has the Superman "S" and the character's name embossed on it. *Lois Lane* and *Clark Kent* are one-piece figures, *Steel* and

Superman are both two-piece premiums. They each have a detachable cloak. Premiums stand between 3½ and 3¾ inches tall.

Each premium came in a clear polybag with details in black print: "S"™ Superman Metallic Collectibles. Superman and all related elements are the property of D.C. Comics™ and © 1996. All Rights Reserved. "M"™ © 1996 McDonald's Australia Ltd. Contents made in China by Creata Promotions.

Premiums marked on base: ™ and © 1996 D.C. Comics. All Rights Reserved. Made in China.

Premiums

SU01	Lois Lane™	[A]
SU02	Clark Kent™	[A]
SU03	Steel™	[A]
SU04	Superman™	[A]

One box was issued (not shown)

SU05	Superman	[A]

Polybag packaging

Super Mario 3 Bros Nintendo

UK

September 13 – October 10, 1991

USA • Canada

August 3 – 20, 1990

MO01

MO03

MO02

MO04

The concept for this promotion came from the popular video computer game called Super Mario Bros. and produced by Nintendo for the Nintendo computer. Then due to popularity this became a cartoon series on TV and in 1993 a film was released starring Bob Hoskins as Mario and John Leguizamo as Luigi. Mario and Luigi are both plumbers who go in search of a princess who was kidnapped and taken to a parallel dimension. All the premiums are made from a hard plastic except *Koopa's* pump action and *Mario's* and *Goomba's* suction pad. *Mario* is a spring-loaded toy, once pushed down he will jump up. *Luigi* is a pull-back-and-let-go toy and *Goomba* flips over when he is pressed down. *Koopa* is a pump action toy: press the pump and *Koopa* will jump. The UK premiums are identical to the American promotion except that the American set had an under-three, *Mario*, which was made of hollow rubber with no moving parts and was packed with the zebra stripes around the edge of the packaging. UK packaging marked 1991. © 1989 Nintendo of America Inc. China. It also ran in Japan in October 1990 and New Zealand in July 1993. Canada sold them at 59 cents each.

Premiums

MO01 Mario [**A**]

MO02 Luigi [**A**]

MO03 Little Goomba [**A**]

MO04 Koopa Paratroop [**A**]

MO09 Mario (under-three) USA only [**B**]

Four UK boxes were issued (not shown)

MO05 Desert Land [**C**]

MO06 Island World [**C**]

MO07 Pipe Land [**C**]

MO08 Sky Land [**C**]

Four USA boxes were issued

MO10 Desert Land [**C**]

MO11 Island World [**C**]

MO12 Pipe Land [**C**]

MO13 Sky Land [**C**]

MO09 (under-three)

213

MO10

MO11

MO12

MO13

Tale Spin

USA

November 2–29, 1990

TS02

TS03

TS01

TS04   TS06

TS05

This national promotion is from the Walt Disney cartoon series shown on Disney afternoon TV line-up, and was released in the fall of 1990 to coincide with the start of the series. *Rebecca* was the boss of the cargo company with *Baloo* the pilot and *King Louie* head barman of the local bar.

These are the first premiums in America to be die-cast, with each character, wheels, and propellers being able to turn or rotate. Two under-threes were issued made from soft-rubber, *Baloo's Seaplane* and *Wildcat's Flying Machine*. All premiums came in a printed polybag. © Disney China.

Premiums

TS01   Baloo's Seaplane [**A**]

TS02   Molly's Biplane [**A**]

TS03   Kit's Racing Plane [**A**]

TS04   Wildcat's Flying Machine [**A**]

Two under-threes were issued

TS05   Baloo's Seaplane [**B**]

TS06   Wildcat's Flying Machine [**B**]

Four boxes were issued

TS07   Higher for Hire [**C**]

TS08   Louies [**C**]

TS09   Pirate Island [**C**]

TS10   Sea Duck [**C**]

TS07

TS08

TS09

TS10

Tale Spin

UK
January 1, 1993

TS11

TS12

TS13

TS14

This Walt Disney animated cartoon series originated from the popular full-length animated movie *The Jungle Book* but with *Baloo* the bear and *King Louie* the orangutan playing totally different roles to the *The Jungle Book*. *Baloo* is an airplane pilot for a freight company and *King Louie* is his mischievous best friend; two new characters arrive on the scene, *Kit Cloudkicker* the daring co-pilot to *Baloo* and *Molly*, who is Rebecca's daughter.

Each character is made from a hard plastic. *Baloo* and *King Louie* are wind-up toys, *Baloo* spins around, and *King Louie*, if you wind up his arms, will flip head over heels. *Kit* and *Molly* are both push-down toys that shoot forward, once released. Each premium was polybagged with an insert card. Premiums marked: © Disney China. Germany also issued these toys, but only three of them. It was issued as a self-liquidator August 6–26, 1992 as a JT (Junior Tüte) and was called "Kapt'n Ballu." In Holland it was called "Super Baloo" and ran from September 24– November 1992.

Premiums

TS11   Baloo   [B]
TS12   Kit   [B]
TS13   King Louie   [B]
TS14   Molly   [B]

Four UK boxes issued (not shown)

TS15   Aeroplane Cockpit   [B]
TS16   Barn Hanger   [B]
TS17   Jungle Bar   [B]
TS18   Cliff Waterfall   [B]

Tale Spin

Australia
Summer, 1993

TS20

TS21

TS22

TS23

Disney's Tale Spin promotion had four solid plastic figures with *Baloo* and *Don Karnage* at 2½ inches high and *Molly* and *Kit* at 2 inches tall. *Baloo* is dancing and *Don Karnage* the sly fox is leaning on his sword. *Kit* is flying on his air board and *Molly* is standing with her arms outstretched.

All premiums came in a printed polybag marked: "M" logo, © 1993 McDonald's Australia Ltd. Contents made in China for Creata Promotions. Premiums have no McDonald's markings, only © Disney (not dated).

NOTE: These same figures have been released before in American cereal packets with the identification "© Disney Kellogg Co. 1991 China."

Premiums

TS20   Baloo   [A]
TS21   Don Karnage   [A]
TS22   Kit   [A]
TS23   Molly   [A]

Box/bag unknown

Teeny Beanie Babies

USA

April 11 – May 15, 1997

TBB03

TBB08

TBB05

TBB09

TBB01

Teeny *Beanie Babies* from McDonald's are smaller versions of "The Beanie Babies™ Collection" from a company called "© TY Inc." Oakbrook IL. USA. They are rapidly becoming very collectible with more American stores stocking these lovable toys every day. © TY Inc. expects annual sales of the "Beanie Babies" to exceed 100 million! There are more and more outlets opening up in the UK that sell the "Beanie Babies."

So what are "Beanie Babies?" They are colorful, plush, posable bean bag toys that have been filled with plastic (PVC) pellets. They are made of the highest quality material and each is approximately pocket-size. All "Beanie Babies" come with a heart-shaped red label, "TY Beanie original Baby" and inside the label you will find the character's name i.e. Chocolate™ and a poem with a date of birth. All "Beanie Babies" have names that would appeal to the children's imaginations. *Beanie Babies* are very collectible and the earlier ones a lot more difficult to find. This is when their prices start to increase.

Premiums marked: Teenie Beanie Babies™/MC, TY®, Animals name™/MC, Handmade in Korea, © year TY Inc, Oakbrook IL USA, surface washable all new material polyester fiber & PVC pellets. © 1996 McDonald's Corp. Made in China.

Premiums

TBB01   Patti Platypus™   **[C]**
TBB02   Pinky Flamingo™   **[D]**
TBB03   Chops Lamb™   **[C]**
TBB04   Chocolate Moose™   **[C]**
TBB05   Goldi Goldfish™   **[C]**
TBB06   Speedy Turtle™   **[D]**
TBB07   Seamore Seal™   **[C]**
TBB08   Snort Bull™   **[C]**
TBB09   Quacks Duck™   **[C]**
TBB10   Lizzy Lizzard™   **[C]**

Bags were issued (not shown)

TBB11   Beanie Babies

TBB02

TBB07

TBB10

TBB06

TBB04

The Rescuers Down Under

USA

November 30 – December 27, 1990

RU01

RU02

RU03

RU04

These premiums were released for the animated Walt Disney film *The Rescuers Down Under* on November 30, 1990. The setting for the film is Australia's Outback with the secret agent mice going to the aid of a young boy called Cody, who is trying to save a magnificent eagle from the trappers. Each premium is a translucent pocket viewer made from hard plastic with a handle on one side. When the handle is turned and you look into the eyeglass you can see mini-movies of the secret agent mice in action. There was an under-three issued; *Bernard* sat in a yellow cheese made from solid rubber. These premiums were made exclusively for McDonald's. © 1989 McDonald's Corp. China. © Disney.

Premiums

RU01 Bernard and Bianca [**C**]
RU02 Jake [**C**]
RU03 Cody [**C**]
RU04 Wilbur [**C**]
RU05 Bernard (under-three) [**B**]

Four boxes were issued (not shown)

RU06 Eagle – Bernard and Miss Bianca [**C**]
RU07 Fireflies – To Light the Night [**C**]
RU08 Lizard – Franc the Fill-Necked [**C**]
RU09 Rope – McLeach the Villain – Top Secret [**C**]

RU05

RU18

RU19

Purchases

RU18 Miss Bianca [**B**]
RU19 Bernard [**B**]

The Rescuers Down Under

USA

December, 1990

These purchases were released with The Rescuers Down Under USA viewers December 1990 over the Christmas period. Each character stands 3½ inches high and is made from a hollow plastic and their bodies are completely flocked. Packed in clear polybags inside a box. No McDonald's markings were on the toys. Toys marked: © Disney Made in China.

The Rescuers
Down Under

Germany
December, 1991

Four soft plush toys issued in Germany. Each stands about 4 inches high and was sold as a self-liquidator, no boxes (Junior Tüte). There are no markings on premiums. © Disney.

RU20   RU21   RU22   RU23

Premiums
RU20 Bernard [A]

RU21 Bianca [A]

RU22 Jake [A]

RU23 Wilbur [A]

The Rescuers
Down Under

UK
October 18 – November 14, 1991

This promotion was released to tie in with the release of the Walt Disney film *The Rescuers Down Under* in October 1991. This was the sequel to the film *The Rescuers* in 1990. Each figure is made from solid rubber and is bendy but only to a small degree, due to the size of the figures. © Disney China.

The Rescuers also ran in Belgium, Denmark, Finland, France, Greece, Italy, Holland, Norway, Portugal, Spain, Sweden, and Switzerland in November 28 – January 8, 1992.

Premiums
RU10 Bernard [B]

RU11 Wilbur (Albatros) [B]

RU12 Frank (Lizard) [B]

RU13 Miss Bianca [B]

Four boxes issued (not shown)
RU14 Bernard and Miss Bianca [C]

RU15 McLeach and Joanna [C]

RU16 Wilbur and Jake [C]

RU17 Cody and Marahute [C]

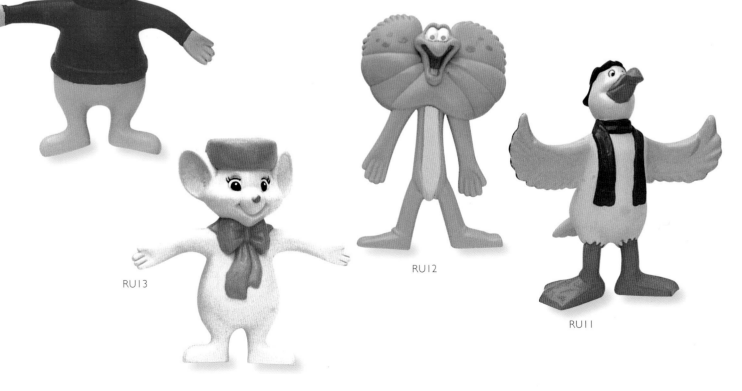

RU10

RU13

RU12

RU11

Tinosaurs

USA

September 12 – October 19, 1986

TI01

TI02

TI03

TI04

TI05

TI06

TI07

TI08

220

This promotion was based on a Saturday morning TV show called the "Wondrous Isle of Tiny." Each premium is made from solid rubber and has a Yellow "M" printed on it; they all came in a printed polybag. This was a regional promotion in St. Louis, Missouri, Nevada, Atlanta, Minnesota, Tennessee, and Arkansas in 1986. This promotion was also re-issued in August 1987 and January 1988.

Premiums marked: © 85 Aviva Enterprise Inc. Licensed by Prime Designs Licensing Ltd. Tinosaurs™, McDonalds®, Made in China.

Premiums

TI01   Bones – Merriest Tinosaur [**C**]

TI02   Dinah – Wisest Tinosaur [**C**]

TI03   Fern – Loveable Time Traveler [**C**]

TI04   Jad – Baby Dragon [**C**]

TI05   Kobby – the Kave Kolt [**C**]

TI06   Link – Acrobatic Elf [**C**]

TI07   Spell – Evil Gumpies Leader [**C**]

TI08   Tiny – A Not-so-tiny Tinosaur [**C**]

One box was issued

TI09   Tinosaurs (not shown)

Tiny Toon Adventures Flip Cars

USA

February 8 – March 7, 1991

TT01

TT02

TT03

TT04

TT07

TT08

Tiny Toon Adventures was an animated cartoon series from Warner Bros produced by Steven Spielberg for Saturday morning TV in America. The characters attend ACME Looniversity and they all reside in a place called Wackyland. Each of the premiums is two vehicles in one, you just flip from one character in a vehicle to another character in a different vehicle. Two of the wheels are related to the type of vehicle. Two under-threes were issued with this promotion, *Gogo Dodo* and *Plucky Duck*, both made from soft rubber.

Premiums marked: © 1990 Warner Bros. *Tiny Toon Flip Cars* also ran in Costa Rica and Mexico in January 1992 and Puerto Rico in February 1991.

TT09

TT10

TT05

TT06

Premiums

TT01   Babs Bunny and Plucky Duck   [**A**]
TT02   Buster Bunny and Elmyra Pig   [**A**]
TT03   Gogo Dodo and Montana Max   [**A**]
TT04   Dizzy Devil and Hampton Pig   [**A**]

Two under-threes were issued

TT05   Gogo Dodo in Bathtub [**B**]
TT06   Plucky Duck in Boat [**B**]

Four USA boxes were issued

TT07   Acme Acres   [**B**]
TT08   Acme Acres Forest   [**B**]
TT09   Acme Looniversity   [**B**]
TT10   Wackyland   [**B**]

Tiny Toon Adventures

USA • Canada
October 30 – November 26, 1992

TT11

TT12

TT13

TT14

TT15

TT16

Once again this was produced by Steven Spielberg for TV, an animated series from Warner Bros. Each premium is made from a hard plastic and all are push-along toys. Each character comes in a vehicle; they either have a roller-like wheel or a see-through dome attached to their vehicle. Inside the roller or dome is an item which will revolve when the vehicle is pushed along. The under-three premium is the same as *Sweetie* but in a zebra-striped packet and all premiums came in printed polybags. Each of the four boxes flattens out to create a drive-on road.

Premiums marked: ™ and © 1992 Warner China.

Premiums

TT11 Babs Bunny [**A**]
TT12 Buster Bunny [**A**]
TT13 Dizzy Devil [**A**]
TT14 Elmyra [**A**]
TT15 Gogo Dodo [**A**]
TT16 Mantana Max [**A**]
TT17 Plucky Duck [**A**]
TT18 Sweetie [**A**]
TT19 Sweetie (under-three)
        (not shown) [**A**]

Four boxes were issued

TT20 In The Arctic [**B**]
TT21 The Wackyland [**B**]
TT22 In The Redwood Forest [**B**]
TT23 In The Jungle [**B**]

TT17

TT18

TT20

TT21

TT22

TT23

Fisher-Price®
Toddler Toys

USA

September 20, 1996

In September 1996 the USA saw the start of the new under-three Fisher-Price Toddler Toys. These took over from the themed under-threes used in earlier promotions. "Aladdin and the King of Thieves" (issued in the USA August–September 1996), *Abu* being the last themed under-three to be issued. Fisher-Price in cooperation with McDonald's have designed 23 new toddler toys to be released a few at a time over a one-year period.

Starts September 20.
Distribute toys upon request with Happy Meal,
or if customer indicates child is under 3 years old.

Recommended for kids 1 and over.
©1996 Fisher-Price, Inc.
©1996 McDonald's Corporation, Oak Brook, IL 60521
FC# MCDY-934 Printed in the United States of America

Tonka

USA

December 2 – 29, 1994

TK08

TK09

TK10

TK11

TK12

Each premium is a vehicle, made to the usual tough *Tonka* standard. All vehicles have moving parts. Premiums marked: © 1994 Tonka Corp. China.

The under-three premium issued with this set is a hard plastic *Dump Truck*. Premium marked: © 1992 Tonka Corp. China/Chine. This under-three is identical to the *Dump Truck* issued in the 1992 set, except that China/Chine was on the base, and the packaging had green and black zebra stripes around the edging. The packaging was dated 1994.

This set was issued over the Christmas period, in a joint promotion with Cabbage Patch Kids for girls (USA December 1994). Premiums were in printed polybags.

Tonka was also issued in Puerto Rico and Canada.

Premiums

TK08 Loader [**A**]

TK09 Crane [**A**]

TK10 Grader [**A**]

TK11 Bulldozer [**A**]

One under-three was issued

TK12 Dump Truck [**B**]

One bag was issued

TK13 Tonka and Cabbage Patch [**A**]

TK13

TK01

TK06

Tonka

USA

November 27 – December 31, 1992

TK04

TK05

TK03

TK02

Each premium was a working vehicle, made to the usual tough *Tonka* standard. ® 1992 Tonka Corp. China. The under-three premium is a hard plastic *Dump Truck*. It was issued in a packet with black and white zebra stripes around the edge of the bag. This under-three was issued in the 1994 set, but with different color zebra stripes around the packing. All premiums were in printed polybags, with coupons from well-known toymakers: Hasbro, Playskool, Parker Bros, Kenner, and Milton Bradley.

This set was issued over the Christmas period. It was a dual promotion with Cabbage Patch Kids for girls (USA November 1992). One bag was issued with this dual promotion.

Tonka also ran in Canada in December 1993. This was Canada's first Happy Meal, dual language packaging, in French and English, with only four premiums issued (no Backhoe). Canada also issued two boxes.

New Zealand ran it on May 7 1993, Central America, Mexico, Puerto Rico (four toys, no Backhoe) in May 1994. The Philippines ran it (four toys only, no Backhoe) in October 1994. Singapore issued all five toys with one box in October 1994; Panama in 1993.

Premiums

TK01   Backhoe [**A**]

TK02   Loader [**A**]

TK03   Cement Mixer [**A**]

TK04   Dump Truck [**A**]

TK05   Fire Truck [**A**]

One under-three was issued

TK06   Dump Truck [**B**]

One bag was issued

TK07   Unscramble, Letters [**A**]

Totally Toy Holiday

USA
December 10 – January 6, 1994

TH03

TH04

TH02

TH01 Barbie Globe

TH05

TH07

TH06

Totally Toy Holiday was released to run over the Christmas period 1993/94. The first premium was the *Barbie Snowglobe* which is a green and red globe with a Barbie in a red dress. This premium only got to the display counter of each restaurant when it was recalled due to liquid leakage, so this is a very sought-after premium by collectors and fetches a high price. *Li'miss Candystripes* comes in a red and white striped dress that can detach itself from the front to reveal a short green polka dot dress. *The Magic Nursery Boy* and *Girl* were used as the under-threes. They came in a printed white polybag and you had no idea which one you would get. Both the *Magic Nursery Dolls* have a soft stuffed body and the head is hard hollow rubber. The Boy's body is a blue color and the Girl's body is a pink color with

hearts and green holly all over it. *Polly Pocket* is a case made from a hard plastic, with a red base and a green hinged lid. Inside is a *Polly Pocket* in a pink dress which moves around a Christmas tree inside her living room, by turning a knob underneath to make her move. A *Sally Secrets* (black) was released. This was produced for distribution in stores that requested it in ethnic areas. She has brown hair and eyes with a pink skirt and a green top and she has movable arms. *Sally Secrets* (white) also has the same outfit on but she has blond hair and blue eyes and

movable arms. Both *Sally Secrets* could press shapes out of paper (hearts and stars) by inserting paper between their shoe and sole, then pressing them down. The *Attack Pack Vehicle*, made from hard plastic, was a push-along toy that looks like a shark. When you press the towing hook at the back it reveals white teeth. The red *Key Force Car* was also used as an under-three in a printed polybag with zebra stripes around the edge of the packaging. The red *Key Force Car* is made from a hard plastic and is a push-along vehicle. When you turn the key the doors

TH08

TH10

TH09

TH11

TH12

spring open. The *Key Force Truck* is also a push-along vehicle and when you turn the key the back of the truck opens up to reveal the engine. *Mighty Max* premium is in the shape of a snow monster with yellow eyes and fangs when the case is shut. When the case is open it shows a yellow *Mighty Max* on a track circling a snow monster. There is a small knob on the base to move *Mighty Max*. The final premium is the *Tattoo Machine Car* which is made from die-cast and is green. It comes with transfers in the form of crocodiles that you have to stick on.

Polly Pocket/Mighty Max Made for McDonald's © 1993 Bluebird Toys China. *Key Force Car* and *Truck/Attack Pack/Tattoo Car Hot Wheels* ® © 1993 Mattel Inc. *Sally Secrets/Li'miss Candystripes/Magic Nursery.* Made for McDonald's © 1993 Mattel Inc.

Premiums

TH01   Holiday Barbie – Snowglobe [**E**]
TH02   Li'miss Candystripes [**A**]
TH03   Magic Nursery Boy [**A**]
TH04   Magic Nursery Girl [**A**]
TH05   Polly Pocket [**A**]
TH06   Sally Secrets (black) [**A**]
TH07   Sally Secrets (white) [**A**]
TH08   Attack Pack [**A**]
TH09   Key Force Car [**A**]
TH10   Key Force Truck [**A**]
TH11   Mighty Max [**A**]
TH12   Hot Wheels Tattoo [**A**]

Three under-threes were issued in zebra-striped packaging

TH13   Key Force Car [**B**]
TH03   Magic Nursery Boy [**B**]
TH04   Magic Nursery Girl [**B**]

One bag was issued

TH14   Totally Toy Holiday [**A**]

TH14

Totally Toy Holiday 2

USA • Canada
December 1, 1995 – January 5, 1996

TH25

TH26

TH21

TH18

228

TH20

TH19

Totally Toy Holiday promotion was run over the Christmas period, two per week, one for the girls and one for the boys. Each premium is made from a hard plastic, except the *Hot Wheels* red and green car (die-cast) and the two under-threes, *Magic Nursery Girl* and *Boy*. Week one was *Barbie* in a white sleigh and was a one-piece premium. She had real hair that could be styled. *Hot Wheels with Ramp* was a two-piece premium. There was a variation in this premium; the boxes of toys received by restaurant managers only had a very few of the *Green Tattoo cars* inside. The blue plastic ramp is approximately 6¼ inches long and stands about 2½ inches high. Week two was the *Polly Pocket* playset, a one-piece premium of a Swiss Chalet that opens up to reveal a layout of the house's interior. There is a floor track leading around the rooms. *Polly Pocket* is attached to this. Turn a white knob around, found on the base,

to move *Polly Pocket* through the different rooms. *Mighty Max* playset has a blue transparent lid in the shape of a skull. Inside is a game with a zig-zag slide. You control *Mighty Max* by a knob on the reverse side of the playset, to help him negotiate the slide and monsters. Monsters can swivel around and catch *Mighty Max* on his way down. Week three was the *Cabbage Patch Kids*, a one-piece hinged playset in the shape of a pony. Inside shows a *Cabbage Patch Kid* on a rocking horse in her bedroom. The rocking horse can be rocked by a lever on the reverse side of the playset. Also on the back is a red mill knob; when turned this will change the scene, seen through the window, from night to day. The *North Pole Explorer* is a one-piece toy that runs on wheels. The blue transparent top opens into two halves to reveal a small snow village with a track in which you can push a replica of

the *North Pole Explorer* vehicle. Week four was the *"Once Upon A Dream"* *princess* which is a one-piece premium with real hair for styling. She stands about 3¼ inches high. *"Great Adventures"* Knight figurine is a two-piece premium, *Knight and Dragon*. The only moving part is the sword arm to the Knight. Premiums came in a sealed printed polybag. Each polybag was numbered from one to eight and had three languages, English, French, and Spanish. The *Knight* was sealed in its own clear polybag within the main packaging. Week five was a combination of any toy that was issued in the 1993/94 Totally Toy Holiday promotion. Different premiums were issued in different states of America, even the restaurant managers did not know what to expect. One bag was issued and the three under-threes are the same premiums issued in the first Totally Toy promotion, but re-packaged.

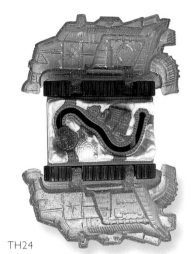

TH24

TH22

TH23

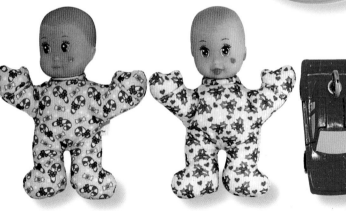

TH28   TH27   TH29

TH30

Premiums marked: *Barbie/Hot Wheels Ramp* © 1995 Mattel, Inc. China/Chine (Cars marked © 1993 China).
Polly Pocket/Mighty Max © 1995 Bluebird Toys Ltd. (UK) China/Chine.
Cabbage Patch © 1995 O.A.A., Inc. China/Chine.
Princess/Knight and Dragon © 1995 F–P Inc. China/Chine.

Premiums

TH18   Holiday Barbie® in White Sleigh [A]
TH19   Hot Wheels™ with Ramp (with red car) [A]
TH20   Hot Wheels™ with Ramp (with green car) (Car same as Totally Toy 1993/4) [A]
TH21   Polly Pocket™ Playset [A]
TH22   Mighty Max™ Playset [A]
TH23   Cabbage Patch™ Playset [A]
TH24   Hot Wheels® North Pole Explorer [A]
TH25   Fisher-Price® "Once Upon A Dream™" Princess Figurine [A]
TH26   Fisher-Price® "Great Adventures™" Knight Figurine [A]

Three under-threes were issued (Premiums the same as Totally Toy Holiday 1993/4)

TH27   Magic Nursery Girl (Holly Suit) [A] Purple/Yellow Zebra Stripe Packet
TH28   Magic Nursery Boy (Candy Cane Suit) [A] Purple/Yellow Zebra Stripe Packet
TH29   Key Force Car [A] Yellow/Green Zebra Stripe Packet

Toy Story

UK
March 29 – April 25, 1996

TY01   TY02   TY03   TY04   TY05

Disney's *Toy Story* was released in theaters on March 22. This promotion started a week later, so *Bo Peep* and *Woody* were issued in the same week and then one toy per week after that. *Toy Story* is the first full-length film to be made totally by computer. It is about toys belonging to Andy, that come to life when Andy is not there. Woody, Andy's favorite, is a talking cowboy. Birthdays arrive for Andy and he gets new presents, in this case Buzz Lightyear, space ranger, who thinks he is real and not a toy and who impresses all the other toys, except Woody, who becomes jealous. A fun

adventure film with intrigue, and a new friendship for Buzz and Woody. Five premiums were issued in this promotion, the second time in the UK (the first being *Pocahontas* in 1995). Each premium is a one-piece toy made from a hard plastic. Each one has moving parts, except *Hamm* who is used as a piggy bank. *Bo Peep*: press in the button on the base to see her spin. *Woody* has movable arms, waist, and head. These two toys are the tallest and stand 4¼ inches high. *Hamm* the pig is the shortest premium, standing just under 2¼ inches high. *Buzz Lightyear* is a wind-up toy and walks

forward. *Rex*'s head and tail will bob and swing to and fro with any vibration or surface movement. All premiums came in a polybag with an insert card showing all toys.

Premiums marked: *(Woody, Bo Peep, Buzz)*: © Disney made in China.

Premiums marked: *(Hamm, Rex)*: © Disney Made in Macau and Thailand.

Insert cards marked: © Disney. © 1996 McDonald's Corporation. Japan also issued Toy Story but only four premiums: *Hamm* was not issued. Packaging was in printed polybags with name of the premium on the front.

TY06   TY07   TY08

TY09   TY10

Premiums

TY01   Bo Peep   [A]

TY02   Woody   [A]

TY03   Hamm   [A]

TY04   Buzz Lightyear   [A]

TY05   Rex   [A]

Five boxes were issued

TY06   Rex, Potato Head, Woody and Hamm on window ledge   [B]

TY07   Buzz Lightyear on road with remote control vehicle   [B]

TY08   Potato Head on floor of bedroom   [B]

TY09   Green Alien Men   [B]

TY10   Woody standing on a bed   [B]

Transformers

USA • Canada
March 15 – April 11, 1996

This promotion came from a new Transformers series with new names and stories, originally created in comic form by Marvel Comics Ltd. back in 1984 called "The Transformers Comic." Soon after a TV animated series was produced with a full-length movie after that, followed by many toys. Two varieties of robots, the good called "Autobots" and the evil ones called "Decepticons," lived on a metal sphere, a mechanical world called "Cybertron." *Optimus Prime* was leader of the Autobots and *Megatron* was leader of the evil Decepticons in the original stories.

All premiums are made from a hard plastic and can transform into some form of animal. The *Manta Ray* and *Panther* are on the good side, and the *Beetle* and *Rhino* are both evil ones. On all premiums the animal's head flips back to reveal the robot's head and all their arms and legs can be moved. *Manta Ray* and *Rhino*'s legs can be extended. The premiums measure from just under 4 inches to 3 inches long. Premiums marked: © 1996 Hasbro © 1996 Takara China/Chine. The premiums came in a printed polybag with three languages, French, Spanish, and English, numbered five to eight. The under-three is a one-piece toy of a lion's head that opens up to show *Optimus Prime* in his new outfit, and came in a blue/white zebra stripe edging packet, packaging marked: © 1995 McDonald's Corporation.

Littlest Pet Store ran at the same time for girls (see *Littlest Pet Store USA 1996* page 128).

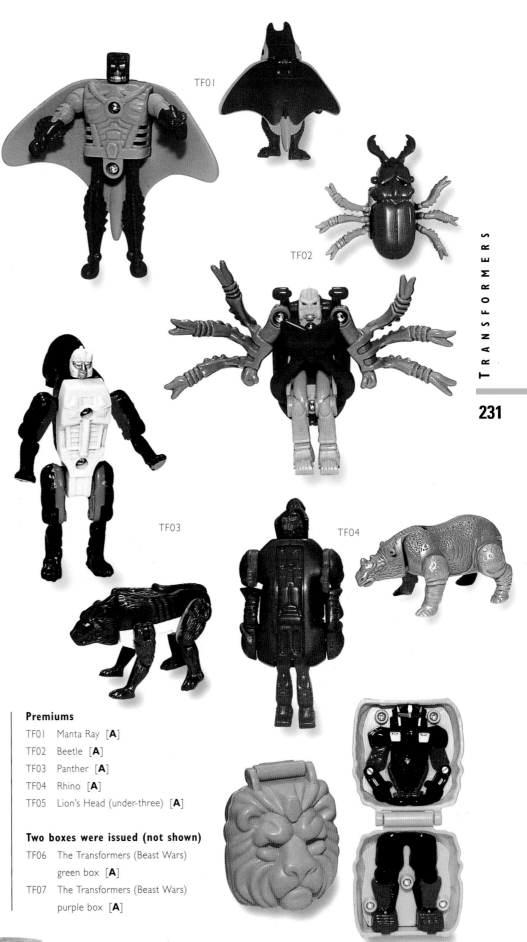

Premiums

TF01   Manta Ray [**A**]

TF02   Beetle [**A**]

TF03   Panther [**A**]

TF04   Rhino [**A**]

TF05   Lion's Head (under-three) [**A**]

Two boxes were issued (not shown)

TF06   The Transformers (Beast Wars) green box [**A**]

TF07   The Transformers (Beast Wars) purple box [**A**]

TF05 Open and Closed

Multi-language packaging shown in French, Spanish, and English.

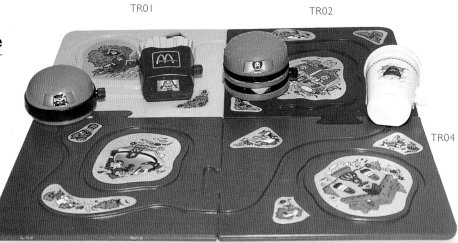

TR01

TR02

TR04

Tricky Trackers
New Year Parade

New Zealand
February, 1995

Japan
Tested January, 1994 – Ran October, 1994

Hong Kong
Test Market February, 1995

TR03

This promotion has been issued in three different countries and in each country the premiums had a slight variation. New Zealand and Hong Kong have almost identical premiums, i.e. *Birdie in Fries, Ronald in Big Mac, Hamburglar in Cheeseburger,* and *Grimace in Milkshake.* The only difference with these two countries' premiums is the stickers on a card you get to stick onto the vehicles and base mat. New Zealand stickers have houses to stick on the base mat, whereas Hong Kong stickers show a parade theme to celebrate the Chinese New Year.

The New Zealand and Japanese promotions both have the same stickers enclosed. The difference is, New Zealand has *Birdie in the Fries,* whereas Japan has *Birdie in an Aeroplane.* New Zealand has *Ronald in a Big Mac,* whereas Japan has *Ronald in a Shoe.* All three countries use

McDonaldland characters and the color bases are the same for each McDonaldland character. All premiums come with clear polybags and insert cards. Each premium has three parts: vehicle, base, and stickers. All premiums are made from a hard plastic and all vehicles are wind-up-and-go. They have a single track to go around on the base mat they came with, or you could join all four base mats together into a square so that all the vehicles can go around a larger track.

All Base Mats marked: © 1993 McDonald's Corp. China.

All vehicles marked (except *Birdie in Fries* and *Ronald in Big Mac*): © 1993 McDonald's Corp. China.

Argentina ran it in May 1994; Costa Rica, Panama, Venezuela, Chile in September 1994. Macau, China ran it as a self-liquidator in February 1995; Malaysia in 1994.

Premiums – New Zealand

TR01 Yellow Base with Birdie in Fries **[A]**

TR02 Red Base with Ronald in Big Mac **[A]**

TR03 Orange Base with Hamburglar in Cheese Burger **[A]**

TR04 Purple Base with Grimace in Milkshake **[A]**

Premiums – Japan

TR05 Yellow Base with Birdie in Aeroplane **[A]**

TR06 Red Base with Ronald in Shoe **[A]**

TR07 Orange Base with Hamburglar in Cheese Burger **[A]**

TR08 Purple Base with Grimace in Milkshake **[A]**

Purchases – Hong Kong (with New Year parade stickers) (not shown)

TR09 Yellow Base with Birdie in Fries **[A]** Golden Fortune Fries

TR10 Red Base with Ronald in Big Mac **[A]** Prosperous Big Mac

TR11 Orange Base with Hamburglar in Cheese Burger **[A]** Wealthy Bang Burger

TR12 Purple Base with Grimace in Milkshake **[A]** Lucky Lunar Shake

(Hong Kong self-liquidator, Test Market)

One box was issued, New Zealand

TR13 McDonaldland Characters

One bag was issued, Japan

TR14 Generic bag (see *Peanuts Japan 1995* page 183)

TR05 Aeroplane

TR13 Front

TR06 Shoe

Tricky Trackers

UK

February 19 – March 17, 1996

TR15   TR16

TR17   TR18

Tricky Trackers UK are identical in size and shape to the New Zealand and Hong Kong premiums but the UK version was issued with an aqua color base instead of the orange base. *Ronald* and *Grimace* had identical color bases and stickers that were issued in the New Zealand promotion, but *Hamburglar* and *Birdie* had different color bases and their stickers were swapped over in the UK version. All premiums came in a polybag with an insert card showing all four premiums. NOTE: the stickers that are displayed on the insert card for *Hamburglar* and

Birdie bases were issued the other way round inside the sealed packets. Each box can be made into a theme park backdrop.

All base mats marked: © 1993 McDonald's Corp. China. Vehicles for *Hamburglar* and *Grimace* marked: © 1993 Mcdonald's Corp. China. Vehicles for *Ronald* and *Birdie* marked: © 1995 McDonald's Corp. China.

Tricky Trackers were also issued in Europe in October 1995. In Germany they were called "Speed Macs" in August 1995.

Premiums

TR15   Red Base with Ronald in Big Mac [**A**]

TR16   Yellow Base with Hamburglar in Cheese Burger [**A**]

TR17   Purple Base with Birdie in Fries [**A**]

TR18   Aqua Base with Grimace in Milkshake [**A**]

UK boxes were issued

TR19   Roller Coaster [**A**]

TR20   Log Fume [**A**]

TR21   Swinging Chairs [**A**]

TR22   Ghost Train [**A**]

TR19   TR20   TR21   TR22

Turbo Macs

TB07

TB08

TB09

TB10

This Happy Meal promotion was first released in 1988, then again in 1989 as a regional promotion. All four premiums are made from a hard plastic, except their rear wheels, which has a rubber tire on the wheel. Each vehicle is about 2½ inches long and they are pull-back-and-let-go cars. The packaging was a polybag with insert cards, except the under-three packaging. The under-three is a one-piece premium and is made from soft rubber. One box was issued, *Ronald – Red Race Car*. *Birdie* has brown hair and drives a sports car, with a small yellow "M" on the front. *Grimace* drives an Indy-type car with a large yellow "M" on the front. *Hamburglar* drives a road racer with a medium red "M" on the front. *Ronald* drives another Indy-type car with a large yellow "M" on the front; *Ronald* has a teardrop mark under both eyes.

USA 1988 and 1989
Premiums (not shown)

TB01   Birdie [**B**]

TB02   Grimace [**B**]

TB03   Hamburglar [**B**]

TB04   Ronald [**B**]

TB05   Ronald (under-three) [**C**]

One box was issued

TB06   Ronald – Red Race Car [**B**]

USA 1990
Premiums

TB07   Birdie [**A**]

TB08   Grimace [**A**]

TB09   Hamburglar [**A**] (Box same as 1988)

TB10   Ronald [**A**] (under-three same as 1988) (except packaging)

There was a slight difference to these Turbo Macs from the earlier years. They are the same except that *Birdie* has red hair and a large yellow "M" on the front of her car. *Grimace* has a large red "M" on the front of his car. *Hamburglar* has a large red "M" on the front of his car. *Ronald* is identical to the earlier years, except that he has no teardrops under his eyes. Premiums are polybagged with insert cards. The vehicles have the ® trade mark plus the character's name on the bottom of their vehicle. *Birdie* has a ™ mark and her name printed on the underside of her vehicle. All premiums marked: McDonald's Corp. © 1988 China.

Identical cars (except the under-three) were issued in Germany as a Junior Tüte with one white bag with auto graphics, August 24 to September 16, 1990. Switzerland, Sweden, Spain, Norway, Holland, Italy, France, Finland, Denmark, and Belgium ran the promotion in March 1989.

TB05

TB13

TB14

TB15

TV16

TB13

L ike the two first Turbo Mac promotions in the USA, this Canadian set has a variation. *Birdie* has been replaced with *Officer Big Mac* in a blue police car with a large yellow "M" on it. All the Canadian premiums have a maple leaf under the "M" logo. The packaging is clear polybags with insert cards. Premiums marked: McDonald's Corp. © 1988 China. Insert cards marked: © 1988 McDonald's Restaurants of Canada Limited.

Premiums

TB13 Grimace [**A**]
TB14 Hamburglar [**A**]
TB15 Ronald [**A**]
TB16 Officer Big Mac [**A**]

Box same as USA 1988

Turbo Macs

UK
1990

TB17

TB18

TB19

TB20

T he UK premiums are identical to the Canadian premiums, except that the UK set do not have the maple leaf. The UK premiums are also different to all the other Turbo Macs issued in the USA and Canada. The UK toys were not given away as a Kids Happy Meal, but could be purchased. All premiums came polybagged with insert cards. One premium was issued per week.

Premiums marked: McDonald's Corp. © 1988 China. Insert card marked: © 1989 McDonald's Restaurants, Ltd.

Purchases • UK

August – September, 1989

TB17 Ronald [**A**]
TB18 Officer Big Mac [**A**]
TB19 Grimace [**A**]
TB20 Hamburglar [**A**]

No special food packaging was used

Twisting Sports

UK

September 10, 1993

Keep fit with the McDonaldland characters. These premiums are made from a hard plastic, except the top to *Ronald*'s trampoline, which is made from soft rubber. All the premiums can be connected together. Each toy has a small handle at the back of their platform; when turned it will work the toy or if all the toys are linked together any handle, when turned, will operate all the premiums at once. *Ronald* will move up and down on his trampoline and wave his arms up and down. *Birdie* will wave her hand with the tennis racket in it, and her head will turn from side to side. *Hamburglar* will raise his dumbbells up and down, and finally *Grimace*'s arms will move up and down and the football on his head will spin around. All the premiums came in polybags with insert cards.

Premiums marked: © 1993 McDonald's Corp. China.

Twisting Sports also ran in Puerto Rico, Argentina, and Venezuela. France was called "Sport Parade," Denmark was called "Twistende Sportsstjerner" 1993.

236

TW01 TW04 TW03 TW02

Premiums

TW01 Ronald [**A**]
TW02 Birdie [**A**]
TW03 Hamburglar [**A**]
TW04 Grimace [**A**]

Four UK boxes were issued

TW05 Arena [**A**]
TW06 Tennis Club [**A**]
TW07 Gym [**A**]
TW08 Football Pitch [**A**]

TW06 TW07 TW05 TW08

Under The Big Top

New Zealand
March, 1995
Malaysia
April – May, 1995

This is a nice promotion, featuring the McDonaldland characters in "Under the Big Top." Each premium is made from a hard plastic, except the *Fry Guys*. They all came with stickers except the *Fry Guys*. *Grimace* is a one-piece premium. When pushed along, he will balance on top of the drum. *Birdie* is a four-piece toy, the ladder comes in two parts. Place *Birdie* on the top rung of the ladder, let her go, and watch her go head over heels down the ladder. *Ronald* the ring master is a two-piece premium. He sits upon an elephant that is balancing on a platform, which will rock to and fro. The *Fry Guys* is a two-part premium. Strike the blue pump and the *Fry Guys* will be shot from the cannon. The Fry Guys did not pass the safety tests and was withdrawn before it reached the restaurants. McDonald's allowed collectors to write in and purchase only two of the *Fry Guys* premiums in New Zealand; so this premium is very difficult to obtain. Each premium came in polybags with insert cards, with instructions on the back.

Premiums marked: © 1995 McDonald's Corp. China.

Under the Big Top was also issued in Hong Kong and Singapore in 1994.

UT01

UT02

UT03

UT04

Premiums

UT01   Grimace   [**A**]
UT02   Birdie   [**A**]
UT03   Ronald   [**A**]
UT04   Fry Guys   [**A**]

One box was issued (generic)

UT05   McDonaldland Characters

UT05 Front   UT05 Back

United Airlines (Friendly Skies)

Friendly Skies 1991

USA

UA01

UA02

These premiums were only available on a United Airlines flight to and from Orlando, Florida, and you had to give six hours' notice before the flight was due to take off to get these toys. United Airlines ticket offices had a counter display on show, with the current premiums and box on offer. With a choice of food from the menu, you could have A) Cheese burger or fajita, carrot sticks, cookie, and milk. B) Sausage, cookie, fruit, and milk. C) (shorter flights – snacks) Jello and peanut butter sandwich with milk.

Friendly Skies Happy Meal was first advertised in October 1991, but the new Friendly Skies toys were not available at that time, so other premiums were used to start off with, and in the first part of 1992, the toys became available. There was a white four-engine plane, with either Ronald or Grimace waving from the top of the

plane. Both planes have UNITED in large letters on the side. The premiums are made from a hard plastic and are push-down-and-let-go toys. They measure 3 inches long. Premiums came in a printed polybag with the Friendly Skies wings logo and the McDonald's "M®." Two boxes were issued of different sizes. They were designed to fit on the serving trolleys. Both boxes had the same cover design; the only difference is that the smaller of the two boxes had the name of the toy in the box, on the yellow handle. A *Napkin Packet* came with each Happy Meal, and contained a napkin, straw, two color pencils, and a moist towelette wipe in a white sachet with the Friendly Skies logo.

Premiums marked: © 1991 McDonald's Corp. © 1991 United Airlines Inc. China.

Premiums

UA01   Ronald [**B**]

UA02   Grimace [**B**]

UA03   Napkin Packet (flat) size 9¾ inches long, 3½ inches wide [**A**]

UA04   Box (large) size 6½ inch square, 3¼ inches deep (not shown) [**B**]

UA05   Box (small) size 5¼ inches square, 2½ inches deep (not shown) [**B**]

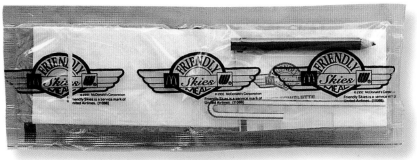

UA03

Friendly Skies 2
1993

UA06

UA08

UA07

A round 1993, United Airlines re-designed the color scheme of their planes, by painting them two-tone, gray on top and a blue under-carriage, hence two new premiums were issued in the new colors. The toys still have *Ronald* and *Grimace*, and are identical to the first issued toys, except the color, and United Airlines is printed on the side of premiums, instead of just UNITED. Premiums still came in a printed polybag with a red border and Friendly Skies wings logo. A new box was issued called "Windows to the World," just under 5½ inches square and 2¼ inches deep. With this Friendly Skies Happy Meal box, we received the *Napkin Packet* and also a box of McDonaldland Cookies with *Birdie* on them. Also available are cookies with *Fry Guys* on them.

Premiums marked: © 1991 McDonald's Corp. © 1991 United Airlines Inc. China.

Premiums

UA06   Ronald [**C**]

UA07   Grimace [**C**]

One box was issued

UA08   Windows to the World [**A**]

UA03   Napkin Packet [**A**]

Friendly Skies 3
1995

UA09

I n early 1995 the premiums changed to a two-piece toy. The plane is a lot smaller than earlier premiums, approximately 2 inches long and 2 inches wide, and is a push-along on wheels. Lift a flap on top of the plane to reveal *Ronald*. The plane came with a *Hangar* with a large "M" on the yellow door, size about 3 x 2 inches. The plane was sealed in a clear polybag inside the *Hangar*, and the *Hangar* came in a printed polybag with blue borders and the Friendly Skies wings logo. The premium also came with stickers, one for each end of the *Hangar*, *Birdie* and *Grimace* on one, and the *Fry Friends* on the other. A new box was issued, the same size as the last promotion, called *"Look-Out Point."*

Premiums and *Hangar* marked: © 1994 McDonald's Corp. © 1994 United Airlines Inc. China.

Premiums

UA09   Ronald and Hangar [**B**]

One box was issued

UA10   Look-Out Point (not shown) [**A**]

UA03   Napkin Packet [**B**]

Village Houses

New Zealand
January, 1994

VH01

VH02

VH03

VH04

Each premium comes in three pieces: 1) House, 2) Vehicle, 3) Stickers. All houses and vehicles are made from a hard plastic. The vehicles are sealed in their own, clear polybag, within the main packaging. The main packaging is a clear polybag with insert cards. The houses measure approximately 3 inches long by 2¾ inches high, and each one has a hinged door on the side, so the houses can be used as garages. All vehicles are push-along and measure 2–2¼ inches long. *Ronald* is in a red shoe, *Grimace* is in a green train, *Birdie* is in a blue truck with apples in the back, and the *Fry*

Guys are in a red fire engine. All premiums marked: © 1993 McDonald's Corp. China.

NOTE: The countries listed below may have issued any one of the two sets mentioned. *Village Houses* also ran in Venezuela and Canada (regional in Quebec, the box had French and English writing on it). The under-three was either cancelled or withdrawn in January 1994. Chile ran it in June 1994; Japan in July 1994; Argentina on October 8, 1994. Macau and China ran it as a self-liquidator in December 1993; Israel in January 1994.

Premiums

VH01 Ronald and McDonald's Restaurant
(red, yellow, blue house) [**A**]

VH02 Grimace and Toy Store
(yellow, pink, green house) [**A**]

VH03 Birdie and Grocer Store
(blue, yellow, red house) [**A**]

VH04 Fry Guys and Fire Station
(green, red, yellow house) [**A**]

Bags and boxes are not shown

VH05 Generic Box (New Zealand)

VH06 Generic Box (Canada)

VH07 Generic Bag, Spanish Design
(Chile, Argentina, Venezuela)

Village Houses

Hong Kong
Early 1995

VH08

VH10   VH09   VH11

In this promotion from Hong Kong the houses, vehicles, and stickers are almost identical to the New Zealand premiums, except that there is a color variation on some of the vehicles and houses. The only premium that is the same in all promotions is *Birdie* in a blue truck with a blue, yellow, and red house. *Ronald* this time is in a light blue, yellow, and mauve house. *Grimace* is in a pink, light green, and yellow house; he is also in a bright orange train this time. *Fry Guys* are in a mauve, orange, light green house and their fire engine is the same color as other promotions, except that the green *Fry*

Guy is a lighter green in this set, and they both have a yellow "M" on their helmets. Once again the premiums are packed in the same way, in clear polybags with insert cards. There was one generic bag issued.

Premiums marked: © 1993 McDonald's Corp. China.

NOTE: Village Houses in Hong Kong was the very first Test Market Happy Meal issued in this country. Previous premiums were either Test Markets, or point of purchase (P.O.P.).

Premiums

VH08   Ronald and McDonald's Restaurant [**A**]
VH09   Grimace and Toy Store [**A**]
VH10   Birdie and Grocer Store [**A**]
VH11   Fry Guys and Fire Station [**A**]

VH12   Generic Bag (not shown)

Water Fun
(Animal Water Squirters)

UK
August 11 – September 7, 1995

This summertime promotion featured Water Fun, with four animal water squirters made from a hard plastic. Each premium has a hole in the top, used for filling up with water, and a trigger underneath. Premiums measure between 4¼ and 5¼ inches long. One bag was issued with McDonaldland characters on it. McDonald's only issue one bag per year on a promotion. The previous year's was "World Cup USA 94." Premiums came in polybags with insert cards. There was also a competition to win a Bubble Extinguisher play kit for three to five year olds, plus two Wildlife Discovery books and an animal story book for the six to seven year old winner. Just answer two questions, color the picture, and fill in the tie-breaker. No purchase was necessary to enter the competition.

Premiums marked: © 1995 McDonald's Corp. Macau. Water Fun was also issued in Europe, the Middle East, and North Africa in July 1995.

WA01

WA02

WA03

WA04

Plastic poster for window display

WA05

Premiums

WA01 Toucan [**A**]

WA02 Hippopotamus [**A**]

WA03 Whale [**A**]

WA04 Shark [**A**]

One bag was issued

WA05 Beach Scene [**A**]

Wild Friends

USA

February 7 – March 6, 1992

GORILLAS   WI03

CROCODILES   WI02

ELEPHANTS   WI01

GIANT PANDAS   WI04

WI05

This promotion was aimed at the endangered animals, and was a regional in the Los Angeles and Indianapolis areas, in what is known as an Open Window. This is where the restaurant managers have a choice of ordering optional premiums, to be used for the Happy Meal at certain times of the year. Each figure is made from hard plastic, and sits on a plastic base, which measures 1¾ x 2¾ inches in size, and underneath the base was a

16-page booklet with information about the animal. The point of purchase (P.O.P.) and food bag was entitled "Wild Friends." All premiums came polybagged with an insert card. The under-three was a one-piece soft rubber toy, with no booklet. Each premium had a moving part. Premiums marked: © 1992 SM China. Inside the book cover: © 1991 McDonald's Corporation. © 1991 Simon Marketing, Inc.

Premiums

WI01   Elephant [**B**]
WI02   Crocodile [**B**]
WI03   Gorilla [**B**]
WI04   Giant Panda [**B**]

One under-three was issued

WI05   Giant Panda [**B**]

One bag was issued

WI06   Wild Friends (not shown) [**C**]

Winnie The Pooh

Australia

May 5 – June 1, 1995

The first short story from Winnie the Pooh was released by Disney in 1966. Three more short stories followed in 1977, "Winnie the Pooh and the Honey Tree," "Winnie the Pooh and the Blustery Day," and finally "Winnie the Pooh and Tigger Too." These three short stories were combined to make a full-length animated movie called, "The Many Adventures of Winnie the Pooh." In 1983 "Winnie the Pooh and a Day for Eeyore" was released.

This promotion coincided with the release of the Walt Disney video in Australia. The cups are a three-piece premium made from hard plastic: cup, lid, and straw. Each cup showed illustrations from the Walt Disney home video with the same name. Each

WP01   WP03   WP02   WP04

cup stands 7¼ inches high with lid (with no straw) and all the lids have "M"s going around the outside. The lids' colors as shown in the photograph are yellow, orange, mauve, and blue. One box was issued showing all the characters.

Premiums marked: "The Collectibles ®" Made in Toronto Canada (on the base of the cup). © Disney © 1995 McDonald's Australia Limited (on the side of the cup).

Premiums

WP01   Winnie the Pooh and the Honey Tree [**A**]
WP02   Winnie the Pooh on a Blustery Day [**A**]
WP03   Winnie the Pooh and Tigger Too [**A**]
WP04   Winnie the Pooh and a Day for Eeyore [**A**]

One box was issued

WP05   Winnie the Pooh Story Book [**A**]

Winter Sports

UK
February 25 – March 24, 1994

WS04

WS01

WS03

WS02

McDonaldland characters with a Winter Sports theme to this promotion. Each premium is made from a hard plastic and measures 3 inches long and 3½ inches tall. All premiums came in a polybag with an insert card. *Ronald* and *Grimace* are wind-up toys. Winding *Ronald* up will send him forward with his body rocking from side to side. *Grimace* will move forward and his snow plow will rock very slightly from side to side. *Birdie* is a two-piece premium, with her black pull-through plastic launcher. This will send her spinning. *Hamburglar* is a two-piece premium that is attached by a piece of string to his snow trailer. *Hamburglar* is actually a pull-back-and-go vehicle.

Premiums marked: © 1994 McDonald's Corp China. *Winter Sports* was also released in Japan as a Test Market in November 1994; Germany in January 1995 as a Junior Tüte. No boxes were issued. France and Belgium (maybe other parts of Europe as well) ran it in November 1994.

Premiums

WS01 Ronald on Skis **[A]**

WS02 Grimace on Snow Plow **[A]**

WS03 Birdie Ice Skating **[A]**

WS04 Hamburglar on Snowmobile **[A]**

Four UK boxes issued (not shown)

WS05 Slalom Run – Ronald **[A]**

WS06 Chair Lift – Grimace **[A]**

WS07 Village – Birdie **[A]**

WS08 Mountain Cabin – Hamburglar **[A]**

Winter Worlds

USA
November 28, 1983 – February 5, 1984

A set of five 4-inch high, flat McDonaldland characters, each made from a vinyl plastic, which came with a string cord for hanging from a Christmas tree. This was an optional promotion over the Christmas period of 1983. Each premium had the character name printed on the reverse, with: © 1983 McDonald's Corp. "Safety tested for children three and older."

These very same premiums were re-issued in 1984 as free give-aways, but had © McDonald's 1984 (safety tested etc.), and the character's name printed on the reverse instead. The promotion also ran in Taiwan.

WW05　　　　WW04　　　　　WW01　　　　WW03

Premiums

WW01 Birdie © 1983 **[B]**

WW02 Grimace © 1983 (not shown) **[B]**

WW03 Hamburglar © 1983 **[B]**

WW04 Mayor McCheese © 1983 **[B]**

WW05 Ronald © 1983 **[B]**

Boxes (not shown)

WW06 Birds from the Ice and Snow **[E]**

WW07 Lands of Ice and Snow

WW08 Land of Midnight Sun

WW09 Mammals from the Ice Shores

WW10 People from the Frosty Frontier

World Cup USA 94

WORLD CUP FUN

UK
June 3, 1994

WF04

WF02

WF01

WF03

WF09

As the title suggests, this was to commemorate the start of the World Cup 1994. The *Noise Rattle* is made from a hard plastic and has two hinged flaps, which cause noise when the rattle is waved. The *Drinks Bottle* is also made from a hard plastic and comes with a plastic straw. It is approximately 3½ inches in diameter and on the packaging is a warning, "Wash thoroughly before use." The *Wristband* is made from a nylon type material on the outside and a flannel soft fabric for the inside. Velcro is used to fasten it around your wrist. The *Inflatable Ball* is made from a soft plastic and measures approximately 7 inches in diameter when inflated. This was the only premium to be double-bagged. All premiums came in polybags with an insert card.

Premiums marked: © 1991 ISL World Cup USA94 ™ (*Ball, Bottle, Wristband*). Premiums marked: © 1992

ISL World Cup USA94 ™ (*Rattle*). Insert card marked: © 1994 McDonald's Corporation. Made in China Simon Marketing International GmbH D-63268 Dreieich.

One bag was issued with the premiums showing all the different countries' flags that took part in World Cup USA 94 (flags were printed on the side of the bag). But it was soon withdrawn because one of the flags out of the 24 countries that took part was found to be offensive to Muslims. The bag was withdrawn on June 7 1994 and replaced with a Generic Bag (brown bag). World Cup USA 94 also ran in Europe, Costa Rica, Panama, Venezuela, and Argentina. Germany (did not issue the inflatable ball, nor boxes), June 1994. Israel ran it in June 1994. Kuwait and Saudi (box, Arabic graphics).

Premiums
WF01 Striker Noise Rattle [**A**]
WF02 Water Bottle [**A**]
WF03 Wrist Purse [**A**]
WF04 Inflatable Football [**A**]

Purchases
WF07 T-shirt [**B**]
WF08 Soft Leather Ball [**B**]

WF09 One small paper cup and two different types of cartons issued with meal

Two bags were issued
WF05 World Cup USA 94 (withdrawn)
WF06 World Cup USA 94 (brown)

WF05

WF08

WF06

WF07

Purchases

A soft *Leather Ball* and a white *T-shirt* both at £1.49 each. No food purchase was necessary. Both had the McDonald's "M" logo, followed by: © 1991 ISL, World Cup USA 1994 logo, with a SQUAD 1994 logo. Both came polybagged with a WARNING about suffocation: "keep away from small children." The Leather Ball polybag was tied at one end and the T-shirt polybag was sealed with Sellotape.

The *Leather Ball* is about 4½ inches in diameter and had all the American states that took part printed on it.

The *Leather Ball* marked: Simon Marketing Int Ltd. London 5LJ © 1993 McDonald's Corporation. Made in Pakistan. The *T-shirt* label reads: "American Style T-shirts XL."

WF12   WF13   WF11   WF10

Shoot-Out scratch cards were given out as a free give-away with each visit. Win a trip to see the World Cup in the USA. Scratch off the footballs. To win find three matching symbols and win that prize. If you reveal two or more fouls, you lose.

Shoot-Out Scratch Cards

WF10   American Airlines   [**B**]

WF11   Stadium   [**B**]

WF12   Hollywood   [**B**]

WF13   World Cup Trophy   [**B**]

WF14   Badge (worn by McDonald's crew members)

WF14

World of Dinosaurs

UK
October 22, 1993
Germany
March, 1994

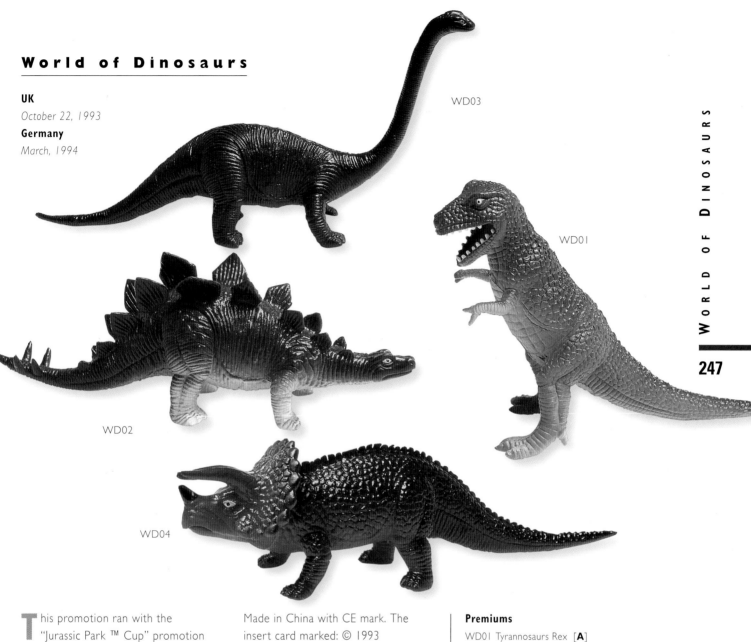

WD03

WD01

WD02

WD04

This promotion ran with the "Jurassic Park ™ Cup" promotion in 1993, both to coincide with the Steven Spielberg film "Jurassic Park." Each premium was a hollow mold made from PVC plastic and measured 8 inches long. All premiums came in a clear polybag with a color insert showing all four premiums. Premiums marked: with the dinosaur's name plus

Made in China with CE mark. The insert card marked: © 1993 McDonald's Corporation. Contents made in China.

Germany issued the "World of Dinosaurs" in March 1994, but repacked with a different insert card, written in German, as a Junior Tüte (Happy Meal). No boxes were issued.

Premiums

WD01 Tyrannosaurs Rex [A]
WD02 Stegosaurus [A]
WD03 Diplodocus [A]
WD04 Triceratops [B]

Four UK boxes were issued

WD05 Tyrannosaurs Rex [B]
WD06 Stegosaurus
WD07 Diplodocus
WD08 Triceratops

WD06

WD07

WD05

WD08

Year of the Dog

(FIVE LUCKY STARS) – TEST MARKET
Singapore
February, 1994
CHINESE NEW YEAR/FORTUNE DOGGIES
Hong Kong
1994

YD05   YD04   YD01

Associated with the Chinese Horoscopes, with the Dog being the eleventh in the animal cycle. (Also see Year of the Rooster – 1993 page 249.) Each premium is made from a hollow PVC plastic and measures between 2¾ and 3½ inches high. *Precious* is not shown. This premium is a white dog with brown patches and is standing on a red sledge. Premiums marked: © 1994 McDonald's Corp. China.

This promotion was a self-liquidator (Test Market) and *not* a Happy Meal.

See photographs to "Year of the Dog" (All of the seven dogs pictured) plus two other dogs that are not shown were issued as a self-liquidator and not Happy Meals. Their names are different than the ones issued in Singapore and they had no special packaging. We do not know which

YD02

name goes with which dog, except that Daffy Dalmatian is the black and white dalmatian. Premiums marked: © 1994 McDonald's Corp. China.

Chinese New Year/Fortune Doggies were also issued in Macau and China.

Purchases

YD01   Bucks **[B]**
YD02   Happy **[B]**
YD03   Precious (not shown) **[B]**
YD04   Richie **[B]**
YD05   Lucky **[B]**

One bag was issued

YD06   Brown with five star graphics
          (not shown)

Purchases

YD07   Bouncy Bernie **[B]**
YD08   Groovie Griff **[B]**
YD09   Brisky Bull **[B]**
YD10   Pert Peke **[B]**
YD11   Cheeky Chow Chow **[B]**
YD12   Chubby Yorkie **[B]**
YD13   Shaggy Shep **[B]**
YD14   Daffy Dalmatian **[B]**
YD15   Bounty Bassey **[B]**

Year of the Rooster

Hong Kong • Singapore
1993
TEST MARKET
Repeated 1995

YR13

YR12

YR14

This very nice promotion from Singapore has four one-piece premiums, all made from a solid rubber and very colorful. The trayliner which advertised this promotion read, "Usher in the New Year with good luck and prosperity." Collect all four, for just 80 cents with a Muffin or Burger purchase.

Larry is wearing a blue coat, *Willy* a green top, *Henry* purple trousers, and *Harry* violet trousers. Each figure stands approximately 2¾ inches high and they all have a large "M" on their backs. Premiums came in just a clear sealed cellophane packet, with no printing or insert cards with packets. Each premium was marked on the bases: © 1993 McDonald's Corp. Made in China.

This promotion was a self-liquidator (Test Market) and *not* a Happy Meal.

Purchases

YR12   Lucky Larry   [**B**]
YR13   Wealthy Willy   [**B**]
YR14   Healthy Henry   [**B**]
YR15   Happy Harry   [**B**]

One generic bag was issued

YR15

Young Astronauts II

USA
March 6 – April 2, 1992
Germany
July – August, 1994

YA02

YA01

YA03

YA04

YA05

F our premiums are available in this set. Each one is made from a sturdy printed cardboard, with one black plastic connector with each premium. Each toy comes in several pieces which slot together. The *Command Module* has 13 cardboard pieces. *Lunar Rover* has 13 cardboard pieces. *Satellite Dish* has 8 cardboard pieces and the *Space Shuttle* is a 10-piece premium. One under-three was issued, *Ronald in a Lunar Rover*, a one-piece made from a soft rubber. Each premium came in a clear polybag with an insert card, with instructions on how to assemble and with an address for the Young Astronaut Council in Washington for more information on science, space exploration, and discovery.

Premiums marked: © 1991 McDonald's Corporation Young Astronaut Council ™ Toy made in China.

Germany: Premiums were used as a clean-up in July–August 1994 and repacked for the German market.

Premiums

YA01   Command Module   **[A]**

YA02   Lunar Rover   **[A]**

YA03   Satellite Dish   **[A]**

YA04   Space Shuttle   **[A]**

One USA under-three was issued

YA05   Ronald Luner Rover   **[B]**

One USA bag was issued

YA06   Astronauts

YA06

Zoo-Face

SET 1 • Germany
January – February, 1989

This promotion was identical to the 1988 USA Zoo-Faces, except of course that these were re-packaged for the German market. No boxes were issued with this Junior Tüte. (Happy Meal.) (Premiums are not shown.)

SET 2
January – February, 1991

The Monkey and Tiger Zoo-Faces were re-issued in Set 2, from the first German promotion, and two new masks were added, the *Dinosaur* and *Duck*. Once again they were packaged for the German market and each had the three air holes underneath. No boxes were issued with this Junior Tüte. (Premiums are not shown.)

Set 1 Premiums

ZF16	Toucan	[A]
ZF17	Monkey	[A]
ZF18	Tiger	[A]
ZF19	Alligator	[A]

Set 2 Premiums

ZF20	Dinosaur	[A]
ZF21	Duck	[A]
ZF22	Monkey	[A]
ZF23	Tiger	[A]

Zoomballs

Australia
1995

This Australian promotion has a sports theme. Each premium is made from a hard plastic and is approximately 3 to 3½ inches in diameter. The football is about 4 inches long. Each premium is a game in itself which can be played in a group or with just two of you. Each premium has a built-in timer and distance scale. The timer is activated by turning the top half of each ball around. As you turn the timer, a distance scale will be revealed in the small cut-out window, where it reads "Too Slow" on the photograph. Each premium came in a clear polybag with insert cards, with instructions on the back.

Instructions as follows: RED distance meter measures the ball thrown over 15 meters. BLACK distance meter measures the ball thrown over 25 meters. The idea is as follows: 1) Stand either 15 or 25 meters apart. 2) Wind the ball to the start position. 3) Throw the ball – this will start the timer. 4) Your teammate catches the ball to stop the timer. 5) Read the speed thrown on the scale, before releasing the timer.

Your teammates or mate then have their go. If played in a group, the two fastest throwers can play off against each other, likewise the two slowest players can do the same. Each ball has an "M" above the "Too Slow" window and marked: McDonald's © 1995 Made in China US and Foreign Patents Pending. Insert cards marked: © Copyright 1995 McDonald's Australia Limited. WARNING "Safety tested for children age four and over. Caution may contain small parts. Toy not intended for children under four."

Premiums

ZM01	Soccer Ball	[A]
ZM02	Football (Aussie Rules)	[A]
ZM03	Netball	[A]
ZM04	Basketball	[A]

ZM02

ZM04

ZM01

ZM03

PARTY TIME

Ronald McDonald you funny clown.
Your laughing mouth and nose so round.
I like to see you dance and sing,
It makes my heart go ding-a-ling,
Come along and dance with me
Before I have my cup of tea.

Grimace your friend, a funny fellow,
Why is he purple and not yellow?
With his big feet and flipper hands,
He could build you castles in the sand.

It's party time, here comes Mayor McCheese.
He is so happy and very pleased,
Proud to be Mayor of McDonaldland,
Come on now, get out that noisy band.

Watch out, that Hamburglar is about,
He likes to steal the burgers, but he's getting naught.
The McDonaldland gang is watching him,
If he is not careful, he will be put in the bin.

Birdie my dear, sweet little gal,
Come and help out your old pal.
Fly us home in your Helicopter,
Be very careful, or we may need the doctor.

Index